*D*ear Friends of MAGNIFICAT,

We will bask in the graces of the risen Lord all month long. And isn't it beautiful that May, Mary's month, is completely within the Easter season this year? I think that's a wonderful thing to have in mind and to inspire our prayer over the coming weeks—the link between Mary and the Resurrection.

When we think about Mary, we do not have to think of her only as an exceptional case, someone that is far removed from what we could ever hope for, with our sins, our brokenness, and the many centuries that separate us from the earthly life of Jesus. In fact, the way she is now—already enjoying the glory of heaven, body and soul—is "a singular participation in her Son's Resurrection and an anticipation of the resurrection of other Christians" (CCC 966).

Mary is God's declaration, his "proof," of what is possible for you and me, too: eternal life, with our glorified bodies, seeing the Lord face to face.

Have a blessed month!

In Jesus and Mary,

Fr. Sebastian

Rev. Sebastian White, O.P.

2

Table of Contents

EDITORIAL

Father Sebastian White, O.P.

FOR THE FIRST FOUR YEARS OF MY PRIESTHOOD, while serving as chaplain at the Catholic Center at New York University, my daily commute was a quick jaunt across Washington Square Park, which, along with its arch, is probably the best-known feature of Greenwich Village. Several months ago, however, when I made the jump to MAGNIFICAT, my commute jumped with me.

Our offices are located north of New York City, along the Hudson River, in a city called Yonkers. But I live in a Dominican priory on Manhattan's Upper East Side. So most days I have an hour-long commute: a twenty-five minute walk down Park Avenue to Grand Central Station (unless the weather turns ugly, bullying me into taking the subway), followed by a thirty-five minute train ride north along the Hudson.

Very few people I know enjoy commuting. It feels like lost time, there are often delays, and if you forget something at home or the office, you're stuck. But I've come to see my commute as a blessing.

For one, while on the train I have an opportunity to do some light reading (often literary essays in the hope that I'll hail a writer's muse before sitting down at the desk). Also, being a reverse commute, the train is fairly quiet…a nice time to think and pray.

More importantly, however, built right in to each day is a golden opportunity to pray the rosary while I walk each morning and afternoon. Usually, I'll offer one for a specific intention: the deceased members of the Order of Preachers, for example; or our benefactors; or family, friends, and others who have asked for my prayers; or even all the people I might pass on any given day, many of whom may be in great need of prayer. On the other leg, I offer a rosary for all the readers of Magnificat—that an abundance of graces from the Word of God and a closer kinship with the saints may be yours. That's basically the Magnificat mission, and I pray it is as effective as possible in each of our lives.

The month of Mary

Why am I saying all this? First, because being at Magnificat is so much more than a job. In fact, I consider my daily commute to be something of a miniature pilgrimage: In the office, I have the great honor of coming to the venue where a beautiful aid to Catholic prayer is put together, and where it's a daily duty to discover the wisdom of the great spiritual authors of the Catholic Faith. Then, when I arrive home, I hang my hat in a holy place that has nourished the Catholic faithful for a century and a half.

Second, because in this month of May we are invited to renew our devotion to the one who first sang the Magnificat, the Woman whom all generations call blessed—our Lady, our Queen, our Mother.

It is not entirely clear why the month of May became so tightly associated with Mary—the Annunciation has already passed, and the Assumption is yet to come. Is it simply that the earth's natural fecundity in this season reminds us of the supernatural life given to us through Mary's Child? Because spring's red roses bespeak the "rose e'er blooming"? Whatever the case—and why quibble over the details—let's throw ourselves wholeheartedly under the patronage of the Queen of heaven and earth this month.

In a way, every time we utter the Hail Mary we recognize that life itself is a commute: *For here we have no lasting city, but we seek the one that is to come* (Heb 13:14). When we ask our Lady to *pray for us sinners, now and at the hour of our death*, we are calling upon an intercessor who sticks with us. If at any time we are in the midst of a terrible trial, even unbeknownst to anyone else in the entire world, we may rest assured that Mary prays for us *now*. And even if we are completely forgotten and alone at the end of our lives or suffering beyond words, Mary is there, keeping a close eye on *the hour of our death*.

A priest I know and respect greatly once pointed out a simple and arresting fact: At some point in our lives, those two moments—now, and the hour of our death—will be the same. I am so grateful to know that Jesus meant what he said from the cross: *Behold, your mother*. Mary sees. Mary knows. Mary loves.

"Ad Jesum per Mariam"

Saint Louis de Montfort's memorable motto should be ours, too. And as with words, so it is with phrases—pronunciation matters. I like to think of it this way: Ad *Jesum* per Mariam; to *Jesus* through Mary. It's like saying: "Where else would Mary lead us if not to Jesus?!" We need never fear that going to Mary will lead us astray, or constitute a detour from being close to Jesus.

Mary's one desire is that each of us be just like Jesus—and according to de Montfort, our own devotion to Mary is a tell-tale sign that we are on the path to being just that.

Mary, Mother of the Savior and our Mother, pray for us sinners, now and at the hour of our death. As we ourselves sing your Magnificat, make us more like your Son. ■

Blessings

May Blessing for Marian Graces _____

"Happy, indeed sublimely happy, is the person to whom the Holy Spirit reveals the secret of Mary, thus imparting to him true knowledge of her. Happy the person to whom the Holy Spirit gives access to this sealed fountain where he can draw water and drink deep draughts of the living water of grace."

Saint Louis Marie Grignion de Montfort

"I invite you once again to contemplate Mary's love…"

Pope Francis

Word of God

Sunday

Mary said, "Behold, I am the handmaid of the Lord. May it be done to me according to your word." Lk 1:38

Monday

And Mary said: "My soul proclaims the greatness of the Lord;/ my spirit rejoices in God my savior." Lk 1:46-47

Tuesday

So [the shepherds] went in haste and found Mary and Joseph, and the infant lying in the manger…. And Mary kept all these things, reflecting on them in her heart.

Lk 2:16, 19

Wednesday

Simeon blessed them and said to Mary his mother,… "(You yourself a sword will pierce) so that the thoughts of many hearts may be revealed." Lk 2:34a, 35

Thursday

[Jesus'] mother said to the servers, "Do whatever he tells you." Jn 2:5

Friday

[Jesus] said to the disciple, "Behold, your mother." And from that hour the disciple took [Mary] into his home. Jn 19:27

Saturday

They went to the upper room where they were staying.... All these devoted themselves with one accord to prayer, together with some women, and Mary the mother of Jesus. Acts 1:13a, 14

Litany based on
True Devotion to the Blessed Virgin

℟   *Mary, may you lead us ever closer to Jesus.*

God deigned to perfect his greatest designs through the most Blessed Virgin, ℟

Through Mary alone God gave his Only Begotten Son to the world, ℟

The Father gave his Son to Mary so that the world would receive him through her, ℟

God communicated to Mary his own fecundity so that she might bring forth the members of his mystical Body, ℟

God-made-Man found his freedom in being shut within Mary's womb, ℟

The more the Holy Spirit finds Mary in a soul, the more powerfully he works to produce Jesus Christ in that soul, ℟

God made a gathering of all graces and called it Mary, ℟

It is through Mary that Jesus applies his merits, communicates his virtues, and distributes his graces, ℟

Mary is the mysterious channel by which Christ pours forth his mercies, ℟

God has designed that we should have all things in Mary, ℟

God the Son desires to be formed and incarnated daily through his Mother, ℟

It is Mary alone who has found grace before God without the aid of another mere creature, ℟

Whoever finds Mary shall find Jesus Christ, the Way, the Truth, and the Life, ℟

Mary's purpose is to unite us with Jesus Christ, her Son, ℟

It is the wish of her Son that we should come to him through his Blessed Mother, ℟

Seeing Mary, we see our own human nature, ℟

We come to Mary as to the way which leads directly to Jesus, ℟

The truly devout live by the faith of Jesus and Mary, and not by natural emotions and feelings, ℟

We do not love the Blessed Virgin because of what we obtain; we love her because she is worthy of our love, ℟

The more we are consecrated to Mary, the more perfectly are we united with Jesus Christ, ℟

Seeing that we are unworthy, God gives graces to Mary so that through her we may receive all that he wishes to give us, ℟

Through Mary's mediation our Lord receives the glory and the gratitude that we owe him, ℟

Mary purifies all our good works from every stain of self-love and false attachment, ℟

We will never bear heavy crosses joyfully and with perseverance unless we have a tender devotion to the Blessed Virgin, ℟

Devotion to the Blessed Virgin is the perfect way to reach Jesus Christ and to unite ourselves with him, ℟

No one is filled with the living thought of God except through Mary, ℟

The frequent thought and loving invocation of Mary is a sure indication that a soul is not estranged from God, ℟

We trust in Mary's fidelity, we lean on her strength, we build upon her mercy and charity in order that she may preserve and increase our virtues, ℟

The Mother of fair love removes from our hearts all scruples and every taint of slavish and disordered fear, ℟

Mary opens our heart and makes it big and generous, ℟

The Blessed Virgin will fill us with great confidence in God and in herself, ℟

Mary is the mold designed to form and shape God-like creatures, ℟

The Hail Mary devoutly said causes the Word of God to germinate in our souls, ℟

To be led by the spirit of Mary, we must renounce our own spirit, ℟

Let us cast ourselves down with a profound sense of our own nothingness in the presence of Jesus living in Mary, ℟

Whoever desires to have the fruit of life, Jesus Christ, must have the tree of life, which is Mary, ℟

Closing Prayer

Heavenly Father, thank you for blessing us with the love, care, and protection of the Mother of your Son. We fasten ourselves faithfully and entirely to her, as to a firm anchor. May our devotion to her bring us to a deeper love of Jesus, who lives and reigns with you in the unity of the Holy Spirit, now and for ever.

Blessings for the Table

GRACE BEFORE THE MEAL:

Loving Father,
you bless us in every way,
especially with the love of the Mother of your Son.
United in a special way with the Blessed Virgin Mary,
our souls magnify you.
We thank you for all good things,
especially this meal,
through Christ our Lord.
℟ Amen.

GRACE AFTER THE MEAL:

Our spirits rejoice in God our Savior,
for he has filled the hungry with good things.
Bless those who have provided for us in any way,
and fill all those who live in want.
Through Christ our Lord.
℟ Amen.

Hymn of the Month

Imperatrix reginarum

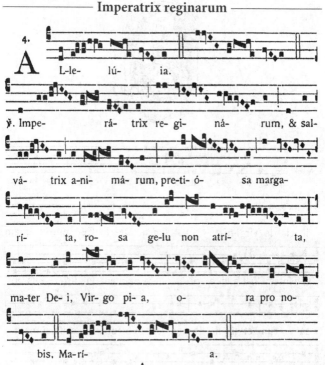

Alleluia.
Verse: Empress of queens,
and rescuer of souls,
pearl of great price,
rose unruined by the cold [of death],
Mother of God, holy Virgin,
pray for us, O Mary.

Translated by James Monti

Marian Antiphon

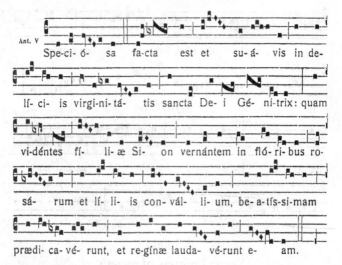

Ant. V

Spe-ci- ó- sa fa-cta est et su-á- vis in de-
lí-ci- is virgi-ni-tá- tis sancta De- i Gé- ni-trix: quam
vi-déntes fí- li-æ Si- on vernántem in fló-ri-bus ro-
sá- rum et lí-li-is con-vál- li-um, be-a-tís-si-mam
præ-di-ca-vé-runt, et re-gínæ lauda- vé-runt e- am.

In the raiment of virginity, the holy Mother of God
has been made beautiful and gracious,
whom the daughters of Zion seeing,
flourishing in rose blossoms and lilies of the valley,
pronounced most blessed; queens also praised her.

Translated by James Monti

Regina Caeli

Regina caeli, laetare, alleluia,
quia quem meruisti portare, alleluia,
resurrexit sicut dixit, alleluia;
ora pro nobis Deum, alleluia.

℣ *Gaude et laetare, Virgo Maria, alleluia.*
℟ *Quia surrexit Dominus vere, alleluia.*

Queen of heaven, rejoice, alleluia.
The Son whom you merited to bear, alleluia,
has risen as he said, alleluia.
Pray for us to God, alleluia.

℣ Rejoice and be glad, O Virgin Mary,
   alleluia!
℟ For the Lord has truly risen, alleluia!

Prayer at Night

Options for May 2019

Prayer at Night is traditionally a short prayer, with fewer variations than the Prayers for Morning and Evening, so that, if desired, it can be memorized. People have most often prayed it alone immediately before retiring for the night. Families or other groups might also want to pray it together.

Two options are suggested for this month.

[Option 1]

God, come to my assistance.
Lord, make haste to help me.

Glory to the Father, and to the Son,
and to the Holy Spirit, as it was in the beginning,
is now, and will be for ever. Amen. Alleluia!

Examination of Conscience/Penitential Act (optional)

Reflect in silence on the past day or week. In what ways have you blessed God in prayer and in deeds of charity toward others as you seek to renew your baptismal commitment in this Easter season? In what ways have you refused God your blessing?

If several people are praying together, a penitential act may be used:

I confess to almighty God
and to you, my brothers and sisters,
that I have greatly sinned,
in my thoughts and in my words,
in what I have done and in what I have failed to do,
through my fault, through my fault,
through my most grievous fault;

therefore I ask blessed Mary ever-Virgin,
all the Angels and Saints,
and you, my brothers and sisters,
to pray for me to the Lord our God.

May almighty God have mercy on us,/ forgive us our
sins,/ and bring us to everlasting life. Amen.

HYMN   Meter: CM
This hymn can be sung to the tune used for
We Walk by Faith

Now that the daylight dies away,
By all thy grace and love,
Thee, Maker of the world, we pray
To watch our bed above.

Let dreams depart and phantoms fly,
The offspring of the night,
Keep us, like shrines, beneath thine eye,
Pure in our foe's despite.

This grace on thy redeemed confer,
Father, coequal Son,
And Holy Ghost, the Comforter,
Eternal Three in One.

PSALM 134

I will bless the LORD who gives me counsel,/ who even at night di-
rects my heart. (Ps 16:7)

We bless God at the end of the day for all the good he has enabled
us to do, all the love he has enabled us to show, and all the failures
he has forgiven us. We bless him especially for the peace we find in
Christ, God's living temple, at day's end.

O come, bless the Lord,
all you who serve the Lord,
who stand in the house of the Lord,
in the courts of the house of our God.

Lift up your hands to the holy place
and bless the Lord through the night.
May the Lord bless you from Zion,
he who made both heaven and earth.

Glory to the Father….

Word of God   Colossians 3:15, 17

L ET THE PEACE of Christ control your hearts, the peace
into which you were also called in one body. And be
thankful. Whatever you do, in word or in deed, do everything in the name of the Lord Jesus, giving thanks to
God the Father through him.

*Into your hands I commend my spirit./ It is you
who will redeem me, LORD. (Ps 31:6)*

CANTICLE OF SIMEON   (Text, back cover D)
Protect us, Lord, as we stay awake; watch over us as we sleep, that
awake, we may keep watch with Christ, and asleep, rest in his peace,
alleluia.

PRAYER

Blessed are you, Lord our God, maker of the day and
the night. You have given us the daily round of work
and rest, labor and prayer in which to make real the
new life of Easter. Waking or sleeping, may we praise
your name by our self-surrender in faith and love,
through Christ our Lord. Amen.

BLESSING

*May the Lord grant a peaceful night and a perfect end to
us and to all our absent sisters and brothers. Amen.*

MARIAN ANTIPHON   (page 12 or 13)

[Option 2]

God, come to my assistance.
Lord, make haste to help me.

Glory to the Father, and to the Son,
and to the Holy Spirit, as it was in the beginning,
is now, and will be for ever. Amen. Alleluia!

Examination of Conscience/Penitential Act (optional)

What have you loved? What have you sought? How has Easter transformed your seeking?

If several people are praying together, a penitential act may be used:

Lord, you are the one we seek.
Lord, have mercy.

All: Lord, have mercy.

Christ, you are the one we love.
Christ have mercy.

All: Christ, have mercy.

Lord, you are the one in whom we put our faith.
Lord, have mercy.

All: Lord, have mercy.

May almighty God have mercy on us,/ forgive us our sins,/ and bring us to everlasting life. Amen.

HYMN   Meter: SM
This hymn can be sung to the tune used for
Rise Up, O Men of God

Firm through the endless years,
Your kingdom stands secure,

And your dominion evermore,
Through ages shall endure.

For, from the Paraclete,
O Word, you came to earth
And, Christ our God, you humbly stooped
To share our lowly birth.

You came as Light from Light
Within our world to shine
And brought into the darkest heart
The hope of light divine.

O Savior, God most high,
Incarnate Word of Light,
Be merciful and save us all
From sin's eternal night.

PSALM 4

In the light of the Lord's countenance is life. (cf. Prv 16:15)

The risen Christ is the light that outlasts all darkness. In his love, we rest secure.

When I call, answer me, O God of justice;
from anguish you released me; have mercy and hear me!

O men, how long will your hearts be closed,
will you love what is futile and seek what is false?

It is the Lord who grants favors to those whom he loves;
the Lord hears me whenever I call him.

Fear him; do not sin: ponder on your bed and be still.
Make justice your sacrifice and trust in the Lord.

"What can bring us happiness?" many say.
Let the light of your face shine on us, O Lord.

You have put into my heart a greater joy
than they have from abundance of corn and new wine.

I will lie down in peace and sleep comes at once
for you alone, Lord, make me dwell in safety.

Glory to the Father....

Word of God   1 Chronicles 16:10-11

G LORY IN HIS HOLY NAME;/
rejoice, O hearts that seek
the LORD!/ Look to the LORD in his strength;/ seek to
serve him constantly.

> *Into your hands I commend my spirit./ It is you*
> *who will redeem me, LORD.*
> *(Ps 31:6)*

CANTICLE OF SIMEON   (Text, back cover D)

Protect us, Lord, as we stay awake; watch over us as we sleep, that
awake, we may keep watch with Christ, and asleep, rest in his peace,
alleluia.

PRAYER

O God, we seek you because you have found us and
redeemed us in the Death and Resurrection of Jesus
Christ our Lord. Keep us through this night and guide
us, when the day returns, to seek you in all we do,
through the same Christ our Lord. Amen.

BLESSING

May the Lord grant a peaceful night and a perfect end to
us and to all our absent sisters and brothers. Amen.

MARIAN ANTIPHON   (page 12 or 13)

❧❧❧

WEDNESDAY, MAY 1
Saint Joseph the Worker

Prayer for the Morning

The LORD our God renews the face of the earth:
let us praise him. Alleluia! (cf. Ps 104:30)

Glory to the Father.... Alleluia!

HYMN   Meter: 10 10 11 11

O worship the King, all glorious above,
O gratefully sing his power and his love;
Our Shield and Defender, the Ancient of Days,
Pavilioned in splendor, and girded with praise.

O tell of his might, O sing of his grace,
Whose robe is the light, whose canopy space,
His chariots of wrath the deep thunderclouds form,
And dark is his path on the wings of the storm.

The earth with its store of wonders untold,
Almighty, your power has founded of old,
Established it fast by a changeless decree,
And round it has cast, like a mantle, the sea.

Frail children of dust, and feeble as frail,
In you do we trust, nor find you to fail;
Your mercies how tender, how firm to the end,
Our Maker, Defender, Redeemer, and Friend.

PSALM 104   1-6, 10-14, 24, 31

Just as you know not how the breath of life/ fashions the human frame in the mother's womb,/ So you know not the work of God/ which he is accomplishing in the universe. (Eccl 11:5)

Throughout the Easter season, we catch glimpses of the hidden work of the Spirit, the breath of life bestowed in baptism and confirmation, coming in wind and fire to complete God's work of recreating humanity and the whole cosmos in Christ.

Bless the Lord, my soul!
Lord God, how great you are,
clothed in majesty and glory,
wrapped in light as in a robe!

You stretch out the heavens like a tent.
Above the rains you build your dwelling.
You make the clouds your chariot,
you walk on the wings of the wind;
you make the winds your messengers
and flashing fire your servants.

You founded the earth on its base,
to stand firm from age to age.
You wrapped it with the ocean like a cloak:
the waters stood higher than the mountains.

You make springs gush forth in the valleys:
they flow in between the hills.
They give drink to all the beasts of the field;
the wild-asses quench their thirst.
On their banks dwell the birds of heaven;
from the branches they sing their song.

From your dwelling you water the hills;
earth drinks its fill of your gift.
You make the grass grow for the cattle
and the plants to serve man's needs.

How many are your works, O Lord!
In wisdom you have made them all.
The earth is full of your riches.

May the glory of the Lord last for ever!
May the Lord rejoice in his works!

Glory to the Father....

Word of God

Isaiah 32:15-17

[**W**HEN] THE SPIRIT from on high/ is poured out on us./ Then will the desert become an orchard/ and the orchard be regarded as a forest.

Right will dwell in the desert/ and justice abide in the orchard./ Justice will bring about peace;/ right will produce calm and security.

Send forth your Spirit, O Lord! (cf. Ps 104:30)

CANTICLE OF ZECHARIAH

(Text, back cover B)

The wind blows where it wills, and you can hear the sound it makes, but you do not know where it comes from or where it goes; so it is with everyone who is born of the Spirit. (Jn 3:8)

INTERCESSIONS

The Spirit of God is ever at work in the world. Let us pray:

℟ O God, make all things new!

Lord Jesus Christ, the Spirit drove you into the desert to face the tempter:
– send forth the Spirit to strengthen us against all that would undo your Easter work. ℟

Lord Jesus Christ, the Spirit descended on you in the form of a dove at your baptism:
– inspire all the baptized to live the Gospel with fervor. ℟

Lord Jesus Christ, the Spirit comes to renew the face of the earth:
– make us worthy stewards of the earth you have given us for our home. ℟

Personal intentions

Our Father....

O Lord our God, between Easter and Pentecost, you speak to us of the Spirit at work in your Church. Send your renewing fire into the hearts of all your people during this holy season, that we may live with enthusiasm the life of your Son, our Lord Jesus Christ, who lives and reigns with you in the unity of the Holy Spirit, one God, for ever and ever. Amen.

MASS

Wednesday of the Second Week of Easter

ENTRANCE ANTIPHON   Cf. Ps 18 (17):50; 22 (21):23

I will praise you, Lord, among the nations;/ I will tell of your name to my kin, alleluia.

COLLECT

As we recall year by year the mysteries
by which, through the restoration of its original dignity,
human nature has received the hope of rising again,
we earnestly beseech your mercy, Lord,
that what we celebrate in faith
we may possess in unending love.
Through our Lord Jesus Christ, your Son,
who lives and reigns with you in the unity
    of the Holy Spirit,
one God, for ever and ever.

● *The men whom you put in prison are in the temple area and are teaching the people.* ●

A reading from
the Acts of the Apostles   5:17-26

T HE HIGH PRIEST rose up and all his companions, that is, the party of the Sadducees, and, filled with jealousy, laid hands upon the Apostles and put them in the public jail. But during the night, the angel of the Lord opened the

doors of the prison, led them out, and said, "Go and take your place in the temple area, and tell the people everything about this life." When they heard this, they went to the temple early in the morning and taught. When the high priest and his companions arrived, they convened the Sanhedrin, the full senate of the children of Israel, and sent to the jail to have them brought in. But the court officers who went did not find them in the prison, so they came back and reported, "We found the jail securely locked and the guards stationed outside the doors, but when we opened them, we found no one inside." When the captain of the temple guard and the chief priests heard this report, they were at a loss about them, as to what this would come to. Then someone came in and reported to them, "The men whom you put in prison are in the temple area and are teaching the people." Then the captain and the court officers went and brought them, but without force, because they were afraid of being stoned by the people.

The word of the Lord.

—• PSALM 34 •—

℟ (7a) **The Lord hears the cry of the poor.**

Or: **Alleluia.**

I will bless the LORD at all times;
   his praise shall be ever in my mouth.
Let my soul glory in the LORD;
   the lowly will hear me and be glad. ℟

Glorify the LORD with me,
   let us together extol his name.
I sought the LORD, and he answered me
   and delivered me from all my fears. ℟

Look to him that you may be radiant with joy,
    and your faces may not blush with shame.
When the poor one called out, the LORD heard,
    and from all his distress he saved him. ℟

The angel of the LORD encamps
    around those who fear him, and delivers them.
Taste and see how good the LORD is;
    blessed the man who takes refuge in him. ℟

Alleluia, alleluia. God so loved the world that he gave
his only-begotten Son,/ so that everyone who believes in
him might have eternal life. Alleluia, alleluia.

> • *God sent his Son that the world might be saved
> through him.* •

A reading from
the holy Gospel according to John   3:16-21

G OD SO LOVED the world that
he gave his only-begotten
Son, so that everyone who believes in him might not
perish but might have eternal life. For God did not
send his Son into the world to condemn the world, but
that the world might be saved through him. Whoever
believes in him will not be condemned, but whoever
does not believe has already been condemned, because
he has not believed in the name of the only-begotten
Son of God. And this is the verdict, that the light came
into the world, but people preferred darkness to light,
because their works were evil. For everyone who does
wicked things hates the light and does not come toward
the light, so that his works might not be exposed. But
whoever lives the truth comes to the light, so that his
works may be clearly seen as done in God.
The Gospel of the Lord.

Prayer over the Offerings

O God, who by the wonderful exchange effected in
this sacrifice
have made us partakers of the one supreme Godhead,
grant, we pray,
that, as we have come to know your truth,
we may make it ours by a worthy way of life.
Through Christ our Lord.

Preface I-V of Easter ———————— pages 218 to 219

Communion Antiphon   Cf. Jn 15:16, 19

I have chosen you from the world, says the Lord,/ and have
appointed you to go and bear fruit,/ fruit that will last,
alleluia.

Prayer after Communion

Graciously be present to your people, we pray, O Lord,
and lead those you have imbued with heavenly mysteries
to pass from former ways to newness of life.
Through Christ our Lord.

Saint Joseph the Worker   *Optional memorial*

• *Saint Joseph loved Jesus and Mary and lived for
them. They were the center of his life and activity:
he found the stable where Mary gave birth, and
sheltered the Holy Family during its sojourn in Egypt;
he provided for Mary and Jesus through his work as
a carpenter; the legal father of Jesus, he trained him
in the trade of carpentry and educated him in the
Law. Therefore, as Pope Pius XII declared on this day
in 1955, "Saint Joseph is also always the guardian of
you and your families." May we always pray: "All
for Jesus, all through Mary, all after your example,
O Patriarch, Saint Joseph. Such shall be my motto in
life and in death. Amen."* •

Readings: Gn 1:26–2:3 or Col 3:14-15, 17, 23-24/ Mt 13:54-58

ENTRANCE ANTIPHON   Ps 128 (127):1-2

Blessed are all who fear the Lord and walk in his ways!/ By
the labor of your hands you shall eat;/ blessed are you, and
blessed will you be, alleluia.

COLLECT

O God, Creator of all things,
who laid down for the human race the law of work,
graciously grant
that by the example of Saint Joseph
    and under his patronage
we may complete the works you set us to do
and attain the rewards you promise.
Through our Lord Jesus Christ, your Son,
who lives and reigns with you
    in the unity of the Holy Spirit,
one God, for ever and ever.

PRAYER OVER THE OFFERINGS

O God, fount of all mercy,
look upon our offerings,
which we bring before your majesty
in commemoration of Saint Joseph,
and mercifully grant that the gifts we offer
may become the means of protection for those
    who call upon you.
Through Christ our Lord.

PREFACE: THE MISSION OF SAINT JOSEPH

It is truly right and just, our duty and our salvation,
always and everywhere to give you thanks,
Lord, holy Father, almighty and eternal God,
and on the commemoration of Saint Joseph
to give you fitting praise,
to glorify you and bless you.

For this just man was given by you
as spouse to the Virgin Mother of God
and set as a wise and faithful servant
in charge of your household

to watch like a father over your Only Begotten Son,
who was conceived by the overshadowing
   of the Holy Spirit,
our Lord Jesus Christ.

Through him the Angels praise your majesty,
Dominions adore and Powers tremble before you.
Heaven and the Virtues of heaven
   and the blessed Seraphim
worship together with exultation.
May our voices, we pray, join with theirs
in humble praise, as we acclaim: Holy....

COMMUNION ANTIPHON   Cf. Col 3:17
Whatever you do in word or deed,/ do everything in the name
of the Lord, giving thanks to God through him, alleluia.

PRAYER AFTER COMMUNION
Having fed upon heavenly delights,
we humbly ask you, O Lord,
that, by Saint Joseph's example,
cherishing in our hearts the signs of your love,
we may ever enjoy the fruit of perpetual peace.
Through Christ our Lord.

MEDITATION OF THE DAY

He Gave His Only Son a Father

It is the same hand that forms the hearts of men
one by one who placed a father's heart in Joseph and
a son's heart in Jesus. This is why Jesus obeyed, and
why Joseph did not fear to command him. Whence the
boldness to command his Creator? The true Father of
Jesus Christ, the God who begot him in eternity, chose
holy Joseph to serve as the father for his Only Begotten
Son in time and caused his veins to flow with a certain
ray or spark of his infinite love for his Son. He changed
his heart; he gave him a father's love. And Joseph, who

sensed in himself a paternal heart, formed by the very hand of God, also sensed that God had ordained him to employ paternal authority; and thus, he dared to command the one whom he recognized as his master.

And after all of this, need I explain Joseph's fidelity in guarding this sacred trust? Could he have been wanting in fidelity toward the one whom he recognized as his only Son?…

For here we learn, by the continual journeys that were required of Saint Joseph once Jesus Christ was placed under his protection, that this trust cannot be preserved without effort, and that, to be faithful to grace, one must be prepared to suffer. Yes, certainly, when Jesus came into a place, he brought his cross, he carried with him all of his spines, and he shared them with those he loved. Joseph and Mary were poor, but they did not yet lack a home. They had a roof over their heads. As soon as this Child came into the world, there was no more home for them, and their shelter was a stable….

They lived together in their home, in poverty but with sweetness, overcoming their poverty by their patience and hard work…. Picture for yourselves a poor artisan. His hands are his only inheritance. He has no wealth beyond his workshop, no income beyond what his labor provides. He is forced to go to Egypt and to suffer a troublesome exile, and why? Because he has Jesus Christ with him. Does he complain about this difficult Child, who tears him away from his homeland and brings torment upon him? On the contrary, he counts himself happy to suffer in his company; all that troubles him is the peril of the divine Infant, more dear to him than his own life.

BISHOP JACQUES-BÉNIGNE BOSSUET

Jacques-Bénigne Bossuet († 1704), known as the "Eagle of Meaux," was a French bishop, theologian, and renowned orator.

Prayer for the Evening

Let us always praise God's name! Alleluia!

Glory to the Father.... Alleluia!

HYMN Meter: LM

This hymn can be sung to the tune used for
Praise God from Whom All Blessings Flow

Fear not! I am the first and last,
I am the Lord, the living one;
As I lay down my life, alone,
I'll take it up when death's undone.

Was Christ not bound to suffer so
Before his glory was revealed?
His chastisement has made us whole
And by his scourging we are healed.

God's will it was that Christ be bruised,
His life a sacrifice unstained.
May he who bears such glorious wounds
Guard and preserve us as he reigns.

Baptized into this death of his,
We also hope to live in him.
If we endure, his reign is ours;
Upon his cross is nailed our sin.

Christ yesterday and Christ today!
All things' beginning and their end!
The Alpha and Omega now,
Toward whom the course of ages tends.

PSALM 61

In the shadow of your wings I take refuge/ till the storms of destruction pass by. (Ps 57:2b)

Christ was raised upon the cross, and we are raised up through his Death on the cross. He is the shelter in whom we dwell secure while we complete the work of our baptism and our ongoing conversion to the fullness of Gospel life.

O God, hear my cry!
Listen to my prayer!
From the end of the earth I call:
my heart is faint.

On the rock too high for me to reach
set me on high,
O you who have been my refuge,
my tower against the foe.

Let me dwell in your tent for ever
and hide in the shelter of your wings.
For you, O God, hear my prayer,
grant me the heritage of those who fear you.

May you lengthen the life of the king:
may his years cover many generations.
May he ever sit enthroned before God:
bid love and truth be his protection.

So I will always praise your name
and day after day fulfill my vows.

Glory to the Father....

Word of God   Hebrews 12:1b-4

LET US RID OURSELVES of every burden and sin that clings to us and persevere in running the race that lies before us while keeping our eyes fixed on Jesus, the leader and perfecter of faith. For the sake of the joy that lay before him he endured the cross, despising its shame, and has taken his seat at the right of the throne of God. Consider how he endured such opposition from sinners, in order that you may not grow weary and lose heart. In your struggle against sin you have not yet resisted to the point of shedding blood.

They that hope in the LORD will renew their strength,/ they will soar as with eagles' wings;/ They will run and not grow weary,/ walk and not grow faint. (Is 40:31)

CANTICLE OF MARY   (Text, back cover A)

My God, the sons of men/ find refuge in the shelter of your wings. (Ps 36:8)

INTERCESSIONS

Jesus Christ has won for us the power to live the vows of baptism. In trust, let us pray:

℟   Hide us in the shelter of your wings!

In baptism the Church is ever confirmed in faith:
– make strong in faith all those whom you have made your own. ℟

In baptism the Church refuses sin:
– make firm in virtue all those who bear your name. ℟

In baptism the Church embraces the Gospel to the full:
– make deep the evangelical life of all those marked with the sign of the cross. ℟

Personal intentions

Our Father....

May we receive a full reward from the LORD, the God of Israel, under whose wings we have come for refuge. Amen. (cf. Ru 2:12)

MARIAN ANTIPHON   (page 12 or 13)

SAINT WHO?

Saints Who Were Visionaries

The Church has never required that we accept private visions, dreams, or prophecies; we know that Christ's words and deeds in the Scriptures are sufficient for salvation. And yet, the lives of the saints are filled with extraordinary mystical occurrences. They hear voices and receive intimations of the future. They see heaven and hell, Mary and Jesus. The devil appears to assault them, or the saints to console them. What are we to make of such occurrences?

We might be tempted to draw back from such stories. After all, we are ordinary sinners, and they are saints. We struggle to discover God in our everyday circumstances, while the saints receive supernatural insight.

But this is to miss the point of our *communion*. Saint Thérèse of Lisieux is our great teacher in this regard. Except for the mysterious smile that appeared on a statue of the Virgin when she was a girl, Thérèse had no mystical experiences to report. But this did not stop her from drawing upon all the graces given to the saints. Whatever belonged to the saints, she knew, already belonged to her as well. Like a little child raiding her parents' larder, Thérèse soaked up the consolations of the saints with abandon. Let us do likewise. Let us receive from the saints every sign of help and hope as a sign for ourselves.

Father of all, I am your little child, full of need. But all that you have given is more than sufficient for me. Today, I want to receive everything you offer me. I throw myself into your arms!

THURSDAY, MAY 2
Saint Athanasius

Prayer for the Morning

*The word of the Lord is faithful, and all his works
to be trusted: come, let us adore, alleluia!*

Glory to the Father.... Alleluia!

HYMN
Meter: CM
This hymn can be sung to the tune used for
Where Charity and Love Prevail

Christ is the likeness that reveals
God, whom no eye has seen.
In him creation came to be,
God's firstborn, Lord of all.

On him creation still depends,
Heav'n, earth, things seen, unseen,
Thrones, dominations, princedoms, powers,
All through him, for him, made.

He is before all else that is,
All is in him made whole.
He is the head who rules the Church,
One Body with its Lord.

He is the First, as firstborn Son
Who rose the first from death,
Who as creation's sovereign Lord
All primacy now owns.

In him God's fullness chose to dwell,
By him to make all one,
Through death to bring in peace to him
All things of heav'n and earth.

CANTICLE   Colossians 1:12-17

In the beginning was the Word,/ and the Word was with God,/ and the Word was God. (Jn 1:1)

Saint Athanasius championed with ardor the Church's belief that Jesus Christ, the Word of God made flesh, is both true God and true man. The saint suffered intensely at the hands of the politically powerful in the long struggle for the truth. Is our faith in Christ worth that much to us?

Let us give thanks to the Father
for having made you worthy
to share the lot of the saints
in light.

He rescued us
from the power of darkness
and brought us
into the kingdom of his beloved Son.
Through him we have redemption,
the forgiveness of our sins.

He is the image of the invisible God,
the first-born of all creatures.
In him everything in heaven and on earth was created,
things visible and invisible.

All were created through him;
all were created for him.
He is before all else that is.
In him everything continues in being.

Word of God   1 John 1:1-2

WHAT WAS FROM the beginning,/ what we have heard,/ what we have seen with our eyes,/ what we looked upon/ and touched with our hands/ concerns the Word of life—/ for the life was made visible;/ we have seen it and testify to it/ and proclaim to you the eternal life/ that was with the Father and was made visible to us.

Splendor and majesty go before him;/
praise and joy are in his holy place. (1 Chr 16:27)

CANTICLE OF ZECHARIAH (Text, back cover B)

The Word became flesh/ and made his dwelling among us,/ and we saw his glory,/ the glory as of the Father's only Son,/ full of grace and truth. (Jn 1:14)

INTERCESSIONS

Through the intercession of Saint Athanasius, let us pray for the gift of ardent faith for all who believe in Christ:

℟ We trust in you, O Lord!

For all the Church:
– that we may hold our belief in you as the center of our lives. ℟

For all Church leaders:
– that they may be courageous champions of Gospel faith. ℟

For all preachers and teachers:
– that they may always seek and find their inspiration in the Word of God. ℟

Personal intentions

Our Father....

O God and Father, you brought life to the whole world by the power of your Word spoken into the darkness of the primal chaos; you brought new life by the power of your Word made flesh, crucified and raised for our salvation. Keep us firm in the faith which Saint Athanasius taught and for which he suffered, through the same Christ our Lord. Amen.

Mass

Thursday of the Second Week of Easter

Saint Athanasius   *Memorial*

● *One of the four great Doctors of the Eastern Church,*
Athanasius defended the orthodox Faith against the
Arian heresy. A devoted bishop in Alexandria, Egypt,
for forty-six years, Athanasius was repeatedly exiled
for his defense of the creed of the Council of Nicea.
While in exile, Athanasius discovered a deep kinship
with the great ascetic Anthony of the Desert. After
Anthony's death, Athanasius recorded the hermit's
story in The Life of Anthony. *It proved to be one of*
the fundamental texts for monasticism in both the East
and the West. Athanasius died in 373 and was one of
the first non-martyrs, or confessors, to be venerated as
a saint. ●

Entrance Antiphon   Cf. Sir 15:5

In the midst of the Church he opened his mouth,/ and the
Lord filled him with the spirit of wisdom and understanding/
and clothed him in a robe of glory, alleluia.

Collect

Almighty ever-living God,
who raised up the Bishop Saint Athanasius
as an outstanding champion of your Son's divinity,
mercifully grant,
that, rejoicing in his teaching and his protection,
we may never cease to grow in knowledge
    and love of you.
Through our Lord Jesus Christ, your Son,
who lives and reigns with you in the unity
    of the Holy Spirit,
one God, for ever and ever.

● *We are witnesses of these words, as is the Holy*
Spirit. ●

A reading from
the Acts of the Apostles   5:27-33

WHEN THE COURT officers had brought the Apostles in and made them stand before the Sanhedrin, the high priest questioned them, "We gave you strict orders, did we not, to stop teaching in that name. Yet you have filled Jerusalem with your teaching and want to bring this man's blood upon us." But Peter and the Apostles said in reply, "We must obey God rather than men. The God of our ancestors raised Jesus, though you had him killed by hanging him on a tree. God exalted him at his right hand as leader and savior to grant Israel repentance and forgiveness of sins. We are witnesses of these things, as is the Holy Spirit whom God has given to those who obey him."

When they heard this, they became infuriated and wanted to put them to death.

The word of the Lord.

——— • PSALM 34 • ———

℟ (7a) The Lord hears the cry of the poor.

Or: Alleluia.

I will bless the LORD at all times;
   his praise shall be ever in my mouth.
Taste and see how good the LORD is;
   blessed the man who takes refuge in him. ℟

The LORD confronts the evildoers,
   to destroy remembrance of them from the earth.
When the just cry out, the LORD hears them,
   and from all their distress he rescues them. ℟

The LORD is close to the brokenhearted;
  and those who are crushed in spirit he saves.
Many are the troubles of the just man,
  but out of them all the LORD delivers him. ℟

Alleluia, alleluia. You believe in me, Thomas, because
you have seen me, says the Lord;/ blessed are those who
have not seen, but still believe! Alleluia, alleluia.

> ● *The Father loves the Son and has given everything
> over to him.* ●

A reading from
the holy Gospel according to John   3:31-36

THE ONE WHO comes from above is above all. The one
who is of the earth is earthly and speaks of earthly
things. But the one who comes from heaven is above
all. He testifies to what he has seen and heard, but no
one accepts his testimony. Whoever does accept his testimony certifies that God is trustworthy. For the one
whom God sent speaks the words of God. He does not
ration his gift of the Spirit. The Father loves the Son
and has given everything over to him. Whoever believes in the Son has eternal life, but whoever disobeys
the Son will not see life, but the wrath of God remains
upon him.
The Gospel of the Lord.

PRAYER OVER THE OFFERINGS
  Look, O Lord, upon the offerings we present to you
  in commemoration of Saint Athanasius,
  and may witnessing to your truth
  bring salvation to those
  who profess, as he did, an unblemished faith.
  Through Christ our Lord.

Preface I-V of Easter ———————— pages 218 to 219

Communion Antiphon   1 Cor 3:11
No one can lay a foundation other than the one that is there,/
namely, Jesus Christ, alleluia.

Prayer after Communion
> Grant us, we pray, almighty God,
> that the true divinity of your Only Begotten Son,
> which we firmly profess with Saint Athanasius,
> may, through this Sacrament, ever give us life
>   and protection.
> Through Christ our Lord.

MEDITATION OF THE DAY

The Father Has Given Him Everything

The Son of God must, as such, have been begotten of the Father from all eternity....

It is surely not impossible to believe that God has a Son, begotten of his own nature. And when we call this Person his Son, and his Offspring, we do not intend to imply that there is a division in the Godhead; but this we believe—that the Son is the true and Only Begotten Son of God....

Thus there remains no doubt that this Son is that Wisdom and Word of the Father, in and by which he creates and makes all things. This is he, I say, whose Brightness illuminates all things, and who reveals himself to whomever he will. This is that express Image of his Person, in which he is discerned and contemplated.... In a word, this is that Christ, by whom we all have been redeemed, and who has made us *a new creation* (2 Cor 5:17).

Saint Athanasius

Saint Athanasius († 373) was Bishop of Alexandria and the champion of the Council of Nicea.

Prayer for the Evening

He has rescued us from the power of darkness!
Let us give thanks and praise, alleluia!

Glory to the Father.... Alleluia!

HYMN
Meter: LM
This hymn can be sung to the tune used for
Jesu Dulcis Memoria

This gentle prelate let us praise
And to his courage tribute pay,
For he both conquered and dispelled
The raging tempests of his day.

The mysteries the Scriptures hold
He loved to fathom and explain,
He taught with flowing eloquence
The truth and doctrine they contain.

PSALM 97

What came to be through him was life,/ and this life was the light of the human race;/ the light shines in the darkness,/ and the darkness has not overcome it. (Jn 1:3-5)

By the light of Christ, the Word incarnate, Saint Athanasius lived and taught; by the light of Christ crucified, he chose suffering over infidelity to his faith; by the light of Christ Risen, he found his joy.

The Lord is king, let earth rejoice,
let all the coastlands be glad.
Cloud and darkness are his raiment;
his throne, justice and right.

A fire prepares his path;
it burns up his foes on every side.
His lightnings light up the world,
the earth trembles at the sight.

The mountains melt like wax
before the Lord of all the earth.
The skies proclaim his justice;
all peoples see his glory.

Let those who serve idols be ashamed,
those who boast of their worthless gods.
All you spirits, worship him.

Zion hears and is glad;
the people of Judah rejoice
because of your judgments, O Lord.

For you indeed are the Lord
most high above all the earth
exalted far above all spirits.

The Lord loves those who hate evil:
he guards the souls of his saints;
he sets them free from the wicked.

Light shines forth for the just
and joy for the upright of heart.
Rejoice, you just, in the Lord;
give glory to his holy name.

Glory to the Father....

Word of God   Hebrews 1:1-4

IN TIMES PAST, God spoke in partial and various ways to
our ancestors through the prophets; in these last days,
he spoke to us through a son, whom he made heir of all
things and through whom he created the universe,
    who is the refulgence of his glory, the very imprint
of his being,/ and who sustains all things by his mighty
word./ When he had accomplished purification from
sins,/ he took his seat at the right hand of the Majesty

on high,/ as far superior to the angels/ as the name he
has inherited is more excellent than theirs.

> *From his fullness we have all received,*
> *grace in place of grace. (Jn 1:16)*

CANTICLE OF MARY   (Text, back cover A)

Those God foreknew he also predestined to be conformed to the
image of his Son, so that he might be the firstborn among many
brothers. (cf. Rom 8:29)

INTERCESSIONS

O Lord, you have guided your Church through the minds
and hearts of your holy Doctors. With them, we now pray:

℟   Make known your ways; teach us your paths.

O Lord, you filled Saint Athanasius with the spirit of
wisdom and understanding:
– pour out your Spirit on all those you have called to
leadership. ℟

O Lord, you sent Saint Athanasius to teach the wisdom
he had learned through prayer and study:
– send us wise teachers in our day. ℟

O Lord, you brought Saint Athanasius at last to
contemplate you in your glory at the right hand of the
Father:
– gather into your presence all our dead. ℟

Personal intentions

Our Father....

May the Lord strengthen our hearts, to be blameless in
holiness before our God and Father at the coming of our
Lord Jesus with all his holy ones. Amen. (cf. 1 Thes 3:13)

MARIAN ANTIPHON   (page 12 or 13)

Saint Who?

Saints Who Were Visionaries

Saint Thérèse Couderc

Foundress († 1885)   Feast: September 26

Thérèse was born in Le Mas, France, to hardworking landowners. Her youthful sense of mission was confirmed when she met Father Stephen Terme. He received her into his fledgling community of sisters and sent her to the shrine of Saint John Francis Regis in Lalouvesc to minister to female pilgrims. Seeing a great need, Thérèse opened a house of prayer for women. Father Terme had the inspiration to center the pilgrims' devotion on the Ignatian retreat. In 1826, Thérèse and Father Terme founded the congregation that would come to be known as the Congregation of Our Lady of the Retreat (the Cenacle Sisters) to further the work.

Thérèse led the growing congregation until 1838, when one of her nuns misled Father Terme's successor concerning the community's finances. Thérèse immediately took responsibility and resigned. The bishop appointed a wealthy widow who had only recently joined the order as "Foundress Superior," and Thérèse was relegated to menial tasks. The next superior was no kinder to Thérèse.

Thérèse patiently persevered through the mistreatment, giving the sisters discreet help only when asked. Even after she was reinstated as foundress in 1854, she continued to remain in the background. In 1864, Thérèse received a vision of Christ's blood poured out on all the altars of the world. For the next twenty years she accepted interior darkness and increasing infirmity. She was canonized in 1970. Her incorrupt body lies today at Lalouvesc.

Father in heaven, through the intercession of Saint Thérèse Couderc, help me to surrender myself to your purpose for me.

FRIDAY, MAY 3
Saints Philip and James; First Friday of the Month

Prayer for the Morning

Christ shows his followers the path of life,/
the fullness of joy in his presence:
come, let us adore, alleluia! (cf. Ps 16:11)

Glory to the Father, and to the Son,
and to the Holy Spirit, as it was in the beginning,
is now, and will be for ever. Amen. Alleluia!

HYMN   Meter: 76 76 D
This hymn can be sung to the tune used for
All Glory, Laud, and Honor

By all your saints still striving,
For all your saints at rest,
Your holy name, O Jesus,
For evermore be blessed.
You rose, our King victorious,
That they might wear the crown
And ever shine in splendor
Reflected from your throne.

We praise you, Lord, for Philip,
Blest guide to Greek and Jew,
And for young James the faithful,
Who heard and followed you.
O grant us grace to know you,
The victor in the strife,
That we with all your servants
May wear the crown of life.

PSALM 66   1-6a, 16-17
The Gospel must be preached to all nations. (cf. Mk 13:10)

After the profound pain of Jesus' suffering and death, and of their own failure, the Apostles were impelled by the joy of Easter to proclaim with exuberant conviction the amazing news: Jesus lives! Death has died!

Cry out with joy to God all the earth,
O sing to the glory of his name.
O render him glorious praise.
Say to God: "How tremendous your deeds!

Because of the greatness of your strength
your enemies cringe before you.
Before you all the earth shall bow;
shall sing to you, sing to your name!"

Come and see the works of God,
tremendous his deeds among men.
He turned the sea into dry land,
they passed through the river dry-shod.

Come and hear, all who fear God.
I will tell what he did for my soul:
to him I cried aloud,
with high praise ready on my tongue.

Glory to the Father....

Word of God   1 Corinthians 15:3-7

I HANDED ON TO YOU as of first importance what I also received: that Christ died for our sins in accordance with the scriptures; that he was buried; that he was raised on the third day in accordance with the scriptures; that he appeared to Cephas, then to the Twelve. After that, he appeared to more than five hundred brothers at once, most of whom are still living, though some have fallen asleep. After that he appeared to James, then to all the apostles.

Praised be Jesus Christ!

CANTICLE OF ZECHARIAH   (Text, back cover B)

Go, therefore, and make disciples of all nations, baptizing them in the name of the Father, and of the Son, and of the holy Spirit. (Mt 28:19)

INTERCESSIONS

God has granted us a rich inheritance of faith from the Apostles. With gratitude let us pray:

℟   O God, we praise you!

Blessed be God for the holy Church
– built upon the foundation of the Apostles' witness to the Death and Resurrection of Jesus: ℟

Blessed be God for the good news of our salvation
– handed on from generation to generation from the Apostles: ℟

Blessed be God for the Sacraments of Baptism and Penance
– through which we receive the new life of the risen Christ proclaimed by the Apostles: ℟

Blessed be God for the Eucharist
– in which we participate in the mystery of the cross witnessed by the Apostles: ℟

Personal intentions

Our Father....

O Lord our God, you chose to build your Church upon the faith of ordinary people made extraordinary by the companionship of your Son and the power of the Holy

Spirit. Keep us faithful to the gift which they received with such joy and handed on at such cost, through Christ our Lord. Amen.

Mass

Feast of Saints Philip and James

This feast commemorates the Apostles Philip and James. Their relics are believed to have been housed, in ancient times, in what is now the Church of the Twelve Apostles in Rome. Philip, a fisherman from Bethsaida, makes the moving request of Jesus, "Master, show us the Father and that will be enough for us." In reply, Jesus reveals, "Believe me that I am in the Father and the Father is in me." James is James "the Lesser," who is identified with James, the "brother," or cousin, of the Lord. Tradition considers him the first Bishop of Jerusalem. Both were martyred in the 1st century.

Entrance Antiphon
These are the holy men/ whom the Lord chose in his own perfect love;/ to them he gave eternal glory, alleluia.

Gloria ———————————————————— page 212

Collect
O God, who gladden us each year
with the feast day of the Apostles Philip and James,
grant us, through their prayers,
a share in the Passion and Resurrection
of your Only Begotten Son,
so that we may merit to behold you for eternity.
Through our Lord Jesus Christ, your Son,
who lives and reigns with you in the unity
of the Holy Spirit,
one God, for ever and ever.

● *After that he appeared to James, then to all the Apostles.* ●

A reading from
the first Letter of Saint Paul to the Corinthians   15:1-8

I AM REMINDING YOU, brothers and sisters, of the Gospel I preached to you, which you indeed received and in which you also stand. Through it you are also being saved, if you hold fast to the word I preached to you, unless you believed in vain. For I handed on to you as of first importance what I also received: that Christ died for our sins in accordance with the Scriptures; that he was buried; that he was raised on the third day in accordance with the Scriptures; that he appeared to Cephas, then to the Twelve. After that, he appeared to more than five hundred brothers and sisters at once, most of whom are still living, though some have fallen asleep. After that he appeared to James, then to all the Apostles. Last of all, as to one born abnormally, he appeared to me.

The word of the Lord.

⎯⎯ • PSALM 19 • ⎯⎯

℟ (5) **Their message goes out through all the earth.**

Or: **Alleluia.**

The heavens declare the glory of God;
    and the firmament proclaims his handiwork.
Day pours out the word to day;
    and night to night imparts knowledge. ℟

Not a word nor a discourse
    whose voice is not heard;
Through all the earth their voice resounds,
    and to the ends of the world, their message. ℟

Alleluia, alleluia. I am the way, the truth, and the life, says the Lord;/ Philip, whoever has seen me has seen the Father. Alleluia, alleluia.

● *Have I been with you so long and you still do not know me?* ●

A reading from
the holy Gospel according to John   14:6-14

JESUS SAID TO THOMAS, "I am the way and the truth and the life. No one comes to the Father except through me. If you know me, then you will also know my Father. From now on you do know him and have seen him." Philip said to him, "Master, show us the Father, and that will be enough for us." Jesus said to him, "Have I been with you for so long a time and you still do not know me, Philip? Whoever has seen me has seen the Father. How can you say, 'Show us the Father'? Do you not believe that I am in the Father and the Father is in me? The words that I speak to you I do not speak on my own. The Father who dwells in me is doing his works. Believe me that I am in the Father and the Father is in me, or else, believe because of the works themselves. Amen, amen, I say to you, whoever believes in me will do the works that I do, and will do greater ones than these, because I am going to the Father. And whatever you ask in my name, I will do, so that the Father may be glorified in the Son. If you ask anything of me in my name, I will do it."
The Gospel of the Lord.

PRAYER OVER THE OFFERINGS
    Receive, O Lord, the offerings we bring
    for the feast day of the Apostles Philip and James
    and bestow on us religion pure and undefiled.
    Through Christ our Lord.

PREFACE I OF THE APOSTLES: THE APOSTLES,
SHEPHERDS OF GOD'S PEOPLE

> It is truly right and just, our duty and our salvation,
> always and everywhere to give you thanks,
> Lord, holy Father, almighty and eternal God.
>
> For you, eternal Shepherd, do not desert your flock,
> but through the blessed Apostles
> watch over it and protect it always,
> so that it may be governed
> by those you have appointed shepherds
> to lead it in the name of your Son.
>
> And so, with Angels and Archangels,
> with Thrones and Dominions,
> and with all the hosts and Powers of heaven,
> we sing the hymn of your glory,
> as without end we acclaim: Holy....

Or:

PREFACE II OF THE APOSTLES: THE APOSTOLIC
FOUNDATION AND WITNESS

> It is truly right and just, our duty and our salvation,
> always and everywhere to give you thanks,
> Lord, holy Father, almighty and eternal God,
> through Christ our Lord.
>
> For you have built your Church
> to stand firm on apostolic foundations,
> to be a lasting sign of your holiness on earth
> and offer all humanity your heavenly teaching.
>
> Therefore, now and for ages unending,
> with all the host of Angels,
> we sing to you with all our hearts,
> crying out as we acclaim: Holy....

COMMUNION ANTIPHON   Cf. Jn 14:8-9
Lord, show us the Father, and that will be enough for us./
Whoever has seen me, Philip, has seen the Father also,
alleluia.

Prayer after Communion

Purify our minds, we pray, O Lord,
by these holy gifts we have received,
so that, contemplating you in your Son
together with the Apostles Philip and James,
we may be worthy to possess eternal life.
Through Christ our Lord.

Solemn Blessing: The Apostles (optional)

May God, who has granted you
to stand firm on apostolic foundations,
graciously bless you through the glorious merits
of the holy Apostles Philip and James.
℟ Amen.

And may he, who endowed you
with the teaching and example of the Apostles,
make you, under their protection,
witnesses to the truth before all.
℟ Amen.

So that through the intercession of the Apostles,
you may inherit the eternal homeland,
for by their teaching you possess firmness of faith.
℟ Amen.

And may the blessing of almighty God,
the Father, and the Son, ✠ and the Holy Spirit,
come down on you and remain with you for ever.
℟ Amen.

MEDITATION OF THE DAY

"Whatever you ask in my name"

I begged the Lord to grant me the grace of never consciously and deliberately offending him by even the smallest sin or imperfection.

Jesus, I trust in you! Jesus, I love you with all my heart....

For love of you, O Jesus, I die completely to myself today and begin to live for the greater glory of your Holy Name…. It is for love of you, O Most Holy Trinity, that I offer myself to you as an oblation of praise…. I desire the exaltation of your name, O Lord….

Jesus…I beg you for the triumph of the Church, [and] for blessings on the Holy Father…and on all the clergy; for the grace of conversion for impenitent sinners. And I ask you for a special blessing and for light, O Jesus, for the priests before whom I will make my confessions throughout my lifetime….

I beg your blessings on our Congregation, and may it be filled with great zeal…. Bless my dearest parents. Bestow your grace, O Jesus, on our wards; strengthen them so powerfully by your grace so that those who leave our houses will no longer offend you by any sin. Jesus, I beg you for my homeland; protect it against the assaults of its enemies.

Jesus, I plead with you for the souls that are most in need of prayer. I plead for the dying; be merciful to them. I also beg you, Jesus, to free all souls from purgatory….

Jesus…you can do everything for those for whom I am pleading. For myself I ask, Lord, transform me completely into yourself, maintain in me a holy zeal for your glory, give me the grace and spiritual strength to do your holy will in all things. (*Diary*, 240)

SAINT MARIA FAUSTINA KOWALSKA

From Divine Mercy in My Soul, Diary of Saint Maria Faustina Kowalska *(† 1938), a Polish Sister of Our Lady of Mercy. She was canonized in 2000.*

Prayer for the Evening

How great is the glory of the Lord!
Come, let us adore, alleluia!

Glory to the Father, and to the Son,
and to the Holy Spirit, as it was in the beginning,
is now, and will be for ever. Amen. Alleluia!

Hymn

Meter: LM
This hymn can be sung to the tune used for
Creator of the Stars of Night

Th'eternal gifts of Christ the King,
The Apostles' glorious deeds, we sing;
And while due hymns of praise we pay,
Our thankful hearts cast grief away.

The Church in these her princes boasts,
These victor chiefs of warrior hosts;
The soldiers of the heavenly hall,
The lights that rose on earth for all.

'Twas thus the yearning faith of saints,
Th'unconquered hope that never faints,
The love of Christ that knows not shame,
The prince of this world overcame.

Redeemer, hear us of your love,
That, with this glorious band above,
Hereafter, of your endless grace,
Your servants also may have place.

Psalm 138

1-5, 7b-8

Behold, I am with you always, until the end of the age. (Mt 28:20b)

The grateful fidelity of the Apostles is built upon the rock of the unshakable fidelity of God.

I thank you, Lord, with all my heart,
you have heard the words of my mouth.
In the presence of the angels I will bless you.
I will adore before your holy temple.

I thank you for your faithfulness and love
which excel all we ever knew of you.
On the day I called, you answered;
you increased the strength of my soul.

All earth's kings shall thank you
when they hear the words of your mouth.
They shall sing of the Lord's ways:
"How great is the glory of the Lord!"

You stretch out your hand and save me,
your hand will do all things for me.
Your love, O Lord, is eternal,
discard not the work of your hands.

Glory to the Father....

Word of God   James 1:1-4

J AMES, A SLAVE of God and of
the Lord Jesus Christ, to the
twelve tribes in the dispersion, greetings.
Consider it all joy, my brothers, when you encounter various trials, for you know that the testing of your faith produces perseverance. And let perseverance be perfect, so that you may be perfect and complete, lacking in nothing.

Be patient until the coming of the Lord!
(cf. Jas 5:7)

CANTICLE OF MARY   (Text, back cover A)
Jesus found Philip and said to him: Follow me! (cf. Jn 1:43)

INTERCESSIONS

The Apostles followed their Lord through the darkness of death into the glorious light of life. Through their intercession, let us pray:

℟   Lord, hear your people's plea.

You are faithful when your people fail in faithfulness:
– raise up those who have fallen from the promises they have made. ℟

You are faithful when your chosen witnesses fail in courage:
– strengthen those who have compromised the Gospel message out of fear. ℟

You are faithful when your disciples fail in love:
– restore the faith of those who have taken offense at our lack of compassion. ℟

You are faithful through death:
– raise up all those who have died. ℟

Personal intentions

Our Father....

May the God of endurance and encouragement grant us the grace to think in harmony with one another, in keeping with Christ Jesus. Amen. (cf. Rom 15:5)

MARIAN ANTIPHON   (page 12 or 13)

❧ ❧ ❧

CREDIBLE WITNESSES

"What the world is in particular need of today is the credible witness of people…capable of opening the hearts and minds of many to the desire for God and for true life."–*Porta Fidei* 15

Father Suitbert Mollinger

————————— Heather King —————————

Father Suitbert Mollinger (1828–1892), a Pittsburgh priest, established the Saint Anthony Chapel, site of the largest number of Catholic relics anywhere outside the Vatican.

Born in Belgium to a family of Dutch nobility, Mollinger was the youngest of eight. His mother, a devout Catholic, saw to it that her children were similarly instructed.

He completed undergraduate studies in Amsterdam, studied medicine in Italy, and attended seminary in Ghent. There, he met an American bishop who was seeking missionary volunteers to the Americas.

Mollinger set sail for New York, arriving in 1854. From there he went first to Latrobe, Pennsylvania, then to Ohio. Ordained a priest in 1857, he served for several years as a missionary throughout southwestern Pennsylvania.

He came to Pittsburgh in 1865, founded several mission parishes, and on July 4, 1868, was installed as pastor of Most Holy Name of Jesus parish in what is today the working-class Troy Hill neighborhood.

Of noble bearing and striking appearance, he was said to possess a "large and powerful frame, and the voice of Boanerges." In 1877, he presided over the construction of a grand rectory. The walls of the dining room are still hung with trophies from his hunting expeditions.

Though Father Mollinger was rumored to have been fabulously wealthy, many said he spent almost all his fortune over the ensuing decades quietly amassing an extraordinary collection of relics. The collection would eventually be housed in the chapel he also paid for from his own funds. When he took a trip to Europe in 1880, he would only make a large donation to any monastery whose effects had caught his eye, and then ask the abbot, "Have you, perhaps, a relic or two to spare for my chapel in America?"

Meanwhile, members of the faithful began streaming to Troy Hill for Father Mollinger's miraculous cures. The feast day of Saint Anthony of Padua falls on June 13, and the flow of supplicants increased during the summer. Some whispered that his miracle cures were faked. No matter: by 1890, his healing Masses, attended by as many as ten to fifteen thousand pilgrims from around the world, had attracted international attention.

Father Mollinger died on June 15, 1892, two days after Saint Anthony's feast day, from a gastric disorder reputedly exacerbated by overwork. His tombstone towers over all others in the Most Holy Name cemetery.

Perhaps humility was not his strong suit.

But there are many rooms in my Father's mansion.

The chapel was sold after he died for $30,000, almost torn down, and in the 1970s lovingly restored. It has never drawn the crowds Father Mollinger did in his prime. Still, schoolchildren, pilgrims, and the curious continue to trickle into the reliquary chapel he left in order to deepen the world's devotion to Christ.

On display are over five thousand pieces: a scrap from the Virgin Mary's veil, twenty-two splinters of the True Cross, bone fragments from all twelve Apostles…

His own love for relics served Father Mollinger well. He died with a crucifix in his hand.

(*Heather King* is a contemplative laywoman and author of several books. She blogs at www.heather-king.com.

SATURDAY, MAY 4
First Saturday of the Month

Prayer for the Morning

*Let us give thanks to the Lord
and acclaim his name! Alleluia!*

Glory to the Father.... Alleluia!

HYMN
Meter: LM
This hymn can be sung to the tune used for
I Know that My Redeemer Lives

Lord, let me love you more and more,
My love for you a flowing tide;
You did not love with grudging heart,
But loved us all with arms spread wide.

Let me not measure love's return
But love you, Lord, with all my soul;
Let my small love be lost in you,
And found once more as love made whole.

Teach me to love as Mary loved,
The Virgin-Mother of her Lord;
You shared with her your agony,
Two hearts made one by sorrow's sword.

She is your Bride, the sinless Eve,
Who now in glory gazes down
On us, the children of her pain:
Lead us, we pray, to share her crown.

CANTICLE OF ISAIAH
12:2-6

Sing and rejoice, O daughter Zion! See, I am coming to dwell among you, says the LORD. (cf. Zec 2:14)

Throughout her life, Mary emptied herself of every shred of even sinless self-interest. Filled instead with the presence of God, the water of life from the fountain of salvation, she was free to offer her Son to the Father on the cross and to sing with joy in his Resurrection.

God indeed is my savior;
I am confident and unafraid.
My strength and my courage is the Lord,
and he has been my savior.

With joy you will draw water
at the fountain of salvation, and say on that day:
Give thanks to the Lord, acclaim his name;
among the nations make known his deeds,
proclaim how exalted is his name.

Sing praise to the Lord for his glorious achievement;
let this be known throughout all the earth.

Shout with exultation, O city of Zion,
for great in your midst
is the Holy One of Israel!

Glory to the Father….

Word of God Isaiah 62:11

S EE, THE LORD proclaims/ to the ends of the earth:/ Say to daughter Zion,/ your savior comes!/ Here is his reward with him,/ his recompense before him.

You have brought them abundant joy! (Is 9:2)

CANTICLE OF ZECHARIAH (Text, back cover B)

I shall offer within the LORD's tent/ a sacrifice of joy./ I will sing and make music for the LORD. (cf. Ps 27:6)

Intercessions

Mary's joy overflowed into a canticle of praise. Let us pray with her to God, the source of all joy:

℟   My soul rejoices in God my savior!

You sent your only Son to take on our flesh for our redemption: ℟

You raised the crucified Lord to everlasting life for our salvation: ℟

You poured forth your Spirit for our transformation: ℟

You promised life in abundance: ℟

Personal intentions

Our Father….

God of power and might, through the intercession of the Blessed Virgin Mary, empty us of all that is self-centered, fill us with your Spirit, and center our lives on your Son, our Lord Jesus Christ, who lives and reigns with you in the unity of the Holy Spirit, one God, for ever and ever. Amen.

Mass

Saturday of the Second Week of Easter

In the midst of their fear and anxiety on the storm-tossed sea, the disciples do not recognize Jesus. They can't imagine he would be close to them in such awful circumstances. Christ's authoritative word—"It is I. Do not be afraid"—overcomes their weakness. Confident in Jesus, we say with the Psalmist, "we place our trust in you." The Twelve appoint seven deacons so that they themselves can be free to offer the presence of Jesus to others who contend with their own storms.

Entrance Antiphon   Cf. 1 Pt 2:9
O chosen people, proclaim the mighty works of him/ who called you out of darkness into his wonderful light, alleluia.

COLLECT

Set aside, O Lord,
the bond of sentence written for us by the law of sin,
which in the Paschal Mystery you canceled
through the Resurrection of Christ your Son.
Who lives and reigns with you in the unity
    of the Holy Spirit,
one God, for ever and ever.

Or:

O God, who willed that through the paschal mysteries
the gates of mercy should stand open for your faithful,
look upon us and have mercy,
that as we follow, by your gift, the way you desire for us,
so may we never stray from the paths of life.
Through our Lord Jesus Christ, your Son,
who lives and reigns with you in the unity
    of the Holy Spirit,
one God, for ever and ever.

● *They chose seven men filled with the Holy Spirit.* ●

A reading from
the Acts of the Apostles   6:1-7

As the number of disci-
ples continued to grow, the
Hellenists complained against the Hebrews because
their widows were being neglected in the daily distribution. So the Twelve called together the community of
the disciples and said, "It is not right for us to neglect
the word of God to serve at table. Brothers, select from
among you seven reputable men, filled with the Spirit
and wisdom, whom we shall appoint to this task, where-
as we shall devote ourselves to prayer and to the ministry of the word." The proposal was acceptable to the
whole community, so they chose Stephen, a man filled
with faith and the Holy Spirit, also Philip, Prochorus,
Nicanor, Timon, Parmenas, and Nicholas of Antioch,

a convert to Judaism. They presented these men to the Apostles who prayed and laid hands on them. The word of God continued to spread, and the number of the disciples in Jerusalem increased greatly; even a large group of priests were becoming obedient to the faith.

The word of the Lord.

—— • PSALM 33 • ——

℟ (22) **Lord, let your mercy be on us, as we place our trust in you.**

Or: **Alleluia.**

Exult, you just, in the LORD;
  praise from the upright is fitting.
Give thanks to the LORD on the harp;
  with the ten-stringed lyre chant his praises. ℟

Upright is the word of the LORD,
  and all his works are trustworthy.
He loves justice and right;
  of the kindness of the LORD the earth is full. ℟

See, the eyes of the LORD are upon those who fear him,
  upon those who hope for his kindness,
To deliver them from death
  and preserve them in spite of famine. ℟

Alleluia, alleluia. Christ is risen, who made all things;/
he has shown mercy on all people. Alleluia, alleluia.

  • *They saw Jesus, walking on the sea.* •

A reading from
the holy Gospel according to John   6:16-21

WHEN IT WAS evening, the
disciples of Jesus went

down to the sea, embarked in a boat, and went across the sea to Capernaum. It had already grown dark, and Jesus had not yet come to them. The sea was stirred up because a strong wind was blowing. When they had rowed about three or four miles, they saw Jesus walking on the sea and coming near the boat, and they began to be afraid. But he said to them, "It is I. Do not be afraid." They wanted to take him into the boat, but the boat immediately arrived at the shore to which they were heading. The Gospel of the Lord.

Prayer over the Offerings
> Sanctify graciously these gifts, O Lord, we pray,
> and, accepting the oblation of this spiritual sacrifice,
> make of us an eternal offering to you.
> Through Christ our Lord.

Preface I-V of Easter ——————— pages 218 to 219

Communion Antiphon   Jn 17:24
Father, I wish that, where I am,/ those you gave me may also be with me,/ that they may see the glory that you gave me, alleluia.

Prayer after Communion
> We have partaken of the gifts of this sacred mystery,
> humbly imploring, O Lord,
> that what your Son commanded us to do
> in memory of him
> may bring us growth in charity.
> Through Christ our Lord.

MEDITATION OF THE DAY

Walking on Waves

The feet of God in darkness tread
the surface of the waves
just as His Spirit streamed Its breath
before the earth was made.

His lightning robe can strike our souls
much more than squalls at sea
that crash and cast our hapless craft
another farther league.

"It is I!" His thunderous cry
startles more than storm.
His call for courage cracks the sky.
We're drenched to be reborn.

Our Lord is the Master of the depths
Whom wind and waves obey.
With storm and step He steers our wreck
and lets the waters rage.

RITA A. SIMMONDS

Rita Simmonds is an award-winning poet, and author of three books of poetry: Souls and the City, Bitterness and Sweet Love *and* Greeting the Seasons.

Prayer for the Evening

Vigil of the Third Sunday of Easter

Let us rejoice in the name of the Lord, alleluia!

Glory to the Father.... Alleluia!

HYMN Meter: CM
This hymn can be sung to the tune used for
O God, Our Help in Ages Past

How sweet the Name of Jesus sounds
In a believer's ear!
It soothes our sorrows, heals our wounds,
And drives away our fear.

It makes the wounded spirit whole,
And calms the troubled breast;
'Tis manna to the hungry soul,
And to the weary rest.

Dear Name, the rock on which I build,
My shield and hiding-place,
My never-failing treasury, filled
With boundless stores of grace.

Psalm 9   1-5, 10-15

So they left the presence of the Sanhedrin, rejoicing that they had
been found worthy to suffer dishonor for the sake of the name.
(Acts 5:41)

In the midst of Easter, we remember the cross. We who have been
baptized in the name of the Father, Son, and Holy Spirit, bear willing testimony to the One whose name we bear with honor and with
gratitude, even if the price is persecution. When we say we love the
"name" of the Lord, we are saying in biblical language that we love
the person of the Lord.

I will praise you, Lord, with all my heart;
I will recount all your wonders.
I will rejoice in you and be glad,
and sing psalms to your name, O Most High.

See how my enemies turn back,
how they stumble and perish before you.
You upheld the justice of my cause;
you sat enthroned, judging with justice.

For the oppressed let the Lord be a stronghold,
a stronghold in times of distress.
Those who know your name will trust you:
you will never forsake those who seek you.

Sing psalms to the Lord who dwells in Zion.
Proclaim his mighty works among the peoples;
for the Avenger of blood has remembered them,
has not forgotten the cry of the poor.

Have pity on me, Lord, see my sufferings,
you who save me from the gates of death;
that I may recount all your praise

at the gates of the city of Zion
and rejoice in your saving help.

Glory to the Father....

Word of God
Jeremiah 14:9b

Y<small>OU ARE IN OUR MIDST,</small>
O L<small>ORD</small>,/ your name we
bear:/ do not forsake us!

> *Those who know your name will trust you:/ you will
> never forsake those who seek you. (Ps 9:11)*

CANTICLE OF MARY
(Text, back cover A)

Let me sing to the Lord for his goodness to me,/ singing psalms to
the name of the Lord, the Most High. (Ps 13:7)

INTERCESSIONS

With trust in our risen Lord, let us pray in his name:

℟   Hear us, O Lord!

We dare to invoke your name, O Lord:
– may we never dishonor you in word or deed. ℟

We bear your name, O Lord:
– may we also bear your likeness. ℟

We love your name, O Lord:
– may we also love the cross we take up in your name. ℟

Personal intentions

Our Father....

*May the Lord rescue us from every evil threat and bring
us safe to his heavenly kingdom. (cf. 2 Tm 4:18)*

MARIAN ANTIPHON
(page 12 or 13)

SAINT WHO?

Saints Who Were Visionaries

Saint Brendan of Birr
Abbot († 573)   Feast: November 29

Brendan of Birr is sometimes confused with the better known Saint Brendan the Navigator; both studied at the monastery of Clonard in Ireland. This group of students grew to be holy men and were known as the Twelve Apostles of Erin (Ireland). Our Brendan eventually became abbot at Birr and was esteemed for his mystical gifts.

It is said that Saint Columba, the great Irish saint and missionary, was excommunicated for a time by his brother bishops for an unjust reason. While attending a synod of bishops in Teltown, County Meath, Brendan saw Columba approaching from afar. He immediately rose and ran to him, welcoming him with a reverential kiss. The other bishops were shocked at Brendan's behavior and asked how he could treat Columba that way. In reply, Brendan told them that he had beheld a luminous pillar traveling before Columba, and angels at his sides. "I do not treat with contempt," Brendan concluded, "him whom I see ordained by God as a guide of nations unto life." The other bishops lifted the excommunication straightaway and accepted Columba back into the unity of the Church.

A warm friendship arose between Columba and Brendan. When Brendan died, Columba was across the sea in Iona. In a vision he beheld Brendan's soul being received into the heavens by angels. The ancient *Martyrology of Oengus* hails Brendan as "a fair and noble diadem—the white chief of all Erin's prophets!"

Father of mercies, through the intercession of Saint Brendan of Birr, help me to treasure the virtues of my friends.

A LIGHT UNTO MY PATH
Third Sunday of Easter

——————— Bishop Robert Barron ———————

The account of the appearance of the risen Jesus by the shore of the Sea of Galilee is one of the most beautiful and theologically textured narratives in the Gospel of John. Every detail is worthy of contemplation.

I would draw attention, for our purposes, to a few fascinating features. We hear that Peter and six other Apostles were in a boat on the sea. Now whenever a Gospel writer speaks of Peter and the disciples in a boat, we are meant to think of the Church, and the peculiar number of seven—evocative of completion or fulfillment—is meant to make us consider the eschatological Church, the community of Jesus approaching the end of its journey through space and time. On the shore (though they don't clearly recognize him at first) is the Lord Jesus. At his command, they lower their nets and bring in an extraordinary catch. Well, this is the work of the Church until the end of the age: to gather in souls and to bring them to Christ at the end of time.

When they empty their nets before Jesus, they discover 153 large fish. Numbers are never accidental in the Gospel of John, and many theories as to the meaning of this figure have been proposed. My favorite is the one put forward by Saint Augustine. According to the science of that time, Augustine argued, there were 153 species of fish in the sea, and therefore, this extraordinary number is meant to signal the universality of the Church's salvific mission.

Suggested Prayer of the Faithful

(Each local community should compose its own Universal Prayer, but may find inspiration in the texts proposed here.)

God the Father sent his only Son into the world so that we might have life through him. We beg him now for the fullness of life as we pray:

> That those who were baptized at Easter may grow ever stronger in their faith and be powerful witnesses of the Gospel.

> That God will grant our civil leaders wisdom, courage, and a firm commitment to true goodness.

> For Christian families: that they will sanctify Christ as Lord in their hearts and homes.

> That the Church in Africa, through the commitment of its members, may be the seed of unity among her peoples and a sign of hope for this continent. *(Holy Father's Prayer Intention)*

> For the poor, the sick, the unemployed, the homeless, those facing financial distress, and those enslaved by addiction: that the power of Christ's Resurrection will touch their lives.

> For the grace this week to keep Christ's commandments and to be perfected in his love.

Most merciful Father, reveal to us your saving power and preserve us always in your grace, for we trust in you. Through Christ our Lord. Amen. ■

SUNDAY, MAY 5
Third Sunday of Easter

Prayer for the Morning

Jesus Christ is our life:
come, let us adore him, alleluia!

Glory to the Father.... Alleluia!

HYMN

Meter: LM
This hymn can be sung to the tune used for
Praise God from Whom All Blessings Flow

The waters of our mother earth,
Her rivers, oceans, lakes and springs,
Are mirrors to the depths of God—
The freshness at the heart of things.

Our sister water, wondrous gift,
Can cleanse and cool, destroy and drown
The mistress of both life and death,
Through her all living things are bound.

Her currents held the Lord of life,
Abyss of death, baptismal tomb.
With blood she came forth from his side
As breaking waters from the womb.

O Christ in whom we are baptized,
Washed clean, refreshed, and sanctified:
Be praised for this our sister fair
By whom we live, in whom we died.

PSALM 90   1-2, 14-17

I saw water flowing out from beneath the threshold of the temple
toward the east. (Ez 47:1)

The great catch of fish signals the fulfillment of God's promise of
salvation, carried through the centuries by the people of the Old
Testament. The water from the side of Christ, the new Temple,

spreads out into the life-giving river in which all things live, and the catch is plentiful for the new "fishers of people."

O Lord, you have been our refuge
from one generation to the next.
Before the mountains were born
or the earth or the world brought forth,
you are God, without beginning or end.

In the morning, fill us with your love;
we shall exult and rejoice all our days.
Give us joy to balance our affliction
for the years when we knew misfortune.

Show forth your work to your servants;
let your glory shine on their children.
Let the favor of the Lord be upon us:
give success to the work of our hands,
give success to the work of our hands.

Glory to the Father….

Word of God Ezekiel 47:9-10

WHEREVER the river flows, every sort of living creature that can multiply shall live, and there shall be abundant fish, for wherever this water comes the sea shall be made fresh. Fishermen shall be standing along it from En-gedi to En-eglaim, spreading their nets there. Its kinds of fish shall be like those of the Great Sea, very numerous.

God said, "Let the water teem with an abundance of living creatures." (Gn 1:20)

CANTICLE OF ZECHARIAH (Text, back cover B)

Jesus said to them, "Come after me, and I will make you fishers of men." (cf. Mt 4:19)

INTERCESSIONS

In joy we pray:

℟   You are our life and our salvation!

You sent your disciples to fish the seas of the world for new believers:
– may our lives of faith draw many to put their trust in you. ℟

You pour forth the life-giving waters of the Spirit on all parts of the world:
– may many find fullness of life in you. ℟

You call for new laborers in the work of the Gospel:
– may the Church be blessed with eager and faithful workers. ℟

Personal intentions

Our Father….

O God, your gift of life is abundant beyond all understanding. May we whom you have called to life in Christ be willing servants of the Gospel so that we may share with others all that you have given to us in your goodness. Through Jesus Christ our Lord. Amen.

MASS
Third Sunday of Easter

In the face of Peter's triple denial of him, Jesus asks Peter three times, "Do you love me?" In other words, Jesus enables Peter to make reparation; Jesus uses Peter's own failure and contrition to give him a deeper love. The "honor and glory and blessing" that the slain Lamb is worthy to receive is this confidence in his love when all we see in ourselves is misery and betrayal. Like Peter, "We must obey God rather than men"—which means that we remain confident in Christ's love even when our own weak humanity tempts us to give up.

ENTRANCE ANTIPHON   Cf. Ps 66 (65):1-2
Cry out with joy to God, all the earth;/ O sing to the glory of
his name./ O render him glorious praise, alleluia.

GLORIA ————————————————— page 212

COLLECT

May your people exult for ever, O God,
in renewed youthfulness of spirit,
so that, rejoicing now in the restored glory of our
    adoption,
we may look forward in confident hope
to the rejoicing of the day of resurrection.
Through our Lord Jesus Christ, your Son,
who lives and reigns with you in the unity
    of the Holy Spirit,
one God, for ever and ever.

● *We are witnesses of these words as is the Holy
Spirit.* ●

A reading from
the Acts of the Apostles   5:27-32, 40b-41

WHEN THE CAPTAIN and the court officers had
brought the apostles in and made them stand before the
Sanhedrin, the high priest questioned them, "We gave
you strict orders, did we not, to stop teaching in that
name? Yet you have filled Jerusalem with your teaching
and want to bring this man's blood upon us." But Peter
and the apostles said in reply, "We must obey God rather than men. The God of our ancestors raised Jesus,
though you had him killed by hanging him on a tree.
God exalted him at his right hand as leader and savior
to grant Israel repentance and forgiveness of sins. We
are witnesses of these things, as is the Holy Spirit whom
God has given to those who obey him."

The Sanhedrin ordered the apostles to stop speaking in the name of Jesus, and dismissed them. So they left the presence of the Sanhedrin, rejoicing that they had been found worthy to suffer dishonor for the sake of the name. The word of the Lord.

—— • PSALM 30 • ——

℟ (2a) I will praise you, Lord, for you have rescued me.

Or: Alleluia.

I will extol you, O LORD, for you drew me clear
   and did not let my enemies rejoice over me.
O LORD, you brought me up from the netherworld;
   you preserved me from among those going down
      into the pit. ℟

Sing praise to the LORD, you his faithful ones,
   and give thanks to his holy name.
For his anger lasts but a moment;
   a lifetime, his good will.
At nightfall, weeping enters in,
   but with the dawn, rejoicing. ℟

Hear, O LORD, and have pity on me;
   O LORD, be my helper.
You changed my mourning into dancing;
   O LORD, my God, forever will I give you thanks. ℟

   • *Worthy is the Lamb that was slain to receive power and riches.* •

**A reading from
the Book of Revelation**   5:11-14

I, JOHN, LOOKED and heard
the voices of many angels

who surrounded the throne and the living creatures and the elders. They were countless in number, and they cried out in a loud voice:

"Worthy is the Lamb that was slain/ to receive power and riches, wisdom and strength,/ honor and glory and blessing."

Then I heard every creature in heaven and on earth and under the earth and in the sea, everything in the universe, cry out:

"To the one who sits on the throne and to the Lamb/ be blessing and honor, glory and might,/ forever and ever."

The four living creatures answered, "Amen," and the elders fell down and worshiped.

The word of the Lord.

Alleluia, alleluia. Christ is risen, creator of all;/ he has shown pity on all people. Alleluia, alleluia.

● *Jesus came and took the bread and gave it to them and in like manner the fish.* ●

A reading from
the holy Gospel according to John   21:1-19

[For the shorter form (21:1-14), omit the text in brackets.]

A T THAT TIME, Jesus revealed himself again to his disciples at the Sea of Tiberias. He revealed himself in this way. Together were Simon Peter, Thomas called Didymus, Nathanael from Cana in Galilee, Zebedee's sons, and two others of his disciples. Simon Peter said to them, "I am going fishing." They said to him, "We also will come with you." So they went out and got into the boat, but that night they caught nothing. When it was already dawn, Jesus was standing on the shore; but

was pleased to confer on you
the gift of redemption and of adoption,
give you gladness by his blessing.
℟ **Amen.**

May he, by whose redeeming work
you have received the gift of everlasting freedom,
make you heirs to an eternal inheritance.
℟ **Amen.**

And may you, who have already risen with Christ
in Baptism through faith,
by living in a right manner on this earth,
be united with him in the homeland of heaven.
℟ **Amen.**

And may the blessing of almighty God,
the Father, and the Son, ✠ and the Holy Spirit,
come down on you and remain with you for ever.
℟ **Amen.**

MEDITATION OF THE DAY

"Do you love me?"

Here is the Lord, again appearing to the disciples after the Resurrection, and questioning the Apostle Peter; and he obliges him three times to confess his love, because three times he had denied him through fear. Christ rose again in the flesh, and Peter in the spirit; because when Christ died in his Passion, Peter died by his denial. Christ the Lord was raised from the dead; out of his love he raised Peter. He questioned him about the love he was confessing, and entrusted him with his sheep. After all, what benefit could Peter confer on Christ, by the mere fact of his loving Christ? If Christ loves you, it's to your advantage, not Christ's; and if you love Christ, it's to your advantage, not Christ's. And yet Christ the Lord wanted to indicate in what way people ought to indicate that they love Christ, and he made it plain enough by entrusting him with his sheep. *Do you love me? I do. Feed my sheep* (Jn 21:15-17). All this once, all this a second time, all this a third time. Peter made no other reply than that he loved him; the Lord asked no other question but whether he loved him; when he answered, he did nothing else but entrust his sheep to him....

So let us love him, let there be nothing dearer to us than he. So do you imagine that the Lord is not questioning us? Was Peter the only one who qualified to be questioned, and didn't we? When that reading is read, every single Christian is being questioned in his heart. So when you hear the Lord saying, *Peter, do you love me?* think of it as a mirror, and observe yourself there. I mean, what else was Peter doing but standing for the Church? So when the Lord was questioning Peter, he was questioning us, he was questioning the Church.

SAINT AUGUSTINE OF HIPPO

Saint Augustine (✝ 430) is called the Doctor of Grace.

Prayer for the Evening

Jesus Christ is the Lamb who was slain:
come, let us sing his praise, alleluia!

Glory to the Father.... Alleluia!

HYMN

Meter: 87 87 77
This hymn can be sung to the tune used for
Once in Royal David's City

Prophet of the Lord, beside us,
Now upon the watch-tower stand;
Let us see the light-clad angel
Earthward come at God's command,
Telling of his power to save,
Who has risen from the grave.

He was born of Virgin Mother,
Lamb of God on whom we feed;

Free from every spot, and blameless,
Yea, a Passover indeed:
Very God his wondrous claim,
And perfection is his name.

As a yearling lamb he suffered,
He, our blessed, saving crown;
That he might from vileness cleanse us,
Freely was his life laid down;
Now, with beauty in our eyes,
See the glorious Sun arise.

As the ark was borne in triumph,
David leaped with gladness then;
Now before the Type's fulfillment
We should joy as holier men;
For, omnipotent to save,
Christ has left the dismal grave.

CANTICLE   Revelation 4:11; 5:9-12

You made him for a little while lower than the angels;/ you crowned
him with glory and honor. (Hb 2:7)

The One who told Peter to feed his lambs and sheep is himself the
Shepherd of Israel and the victorious Lamb of God to whom all
praise is due!

O Lord, our God, you are worthy
to receive glory and honor and power.

For you have created all things;
by your will they came to be and were made.

Worthy are you, O Lord,
to receive the scroll and break open its seals.

For you were slain,
with your blood you purchased for God
men of every race and tongue,
of every people and nation.

You made of them a kingdom,
and priests to serve our God,
and they shall reign on the earth.

Worthy is the Lamb that was slain
to receive power and riches,
wisdom and strength,
honor and glory and praise.

Word of God   Revelation 7:17

FOR THE LAMB who is in the center of the throne will shepherd them/ and lead them to springs of life-giving water,/ and God will wipe away every tear from their eyes.

Give to the LORD, you families of nations,/
give to the LORD glory and praise. (1 Chr 16:28)

CANTICLE OF MARY   (Text, back cover A)

Let them give glory to the LORD,/ and utter his praise in the coastlands. (Is 42:12)

INTERCESSIONS

Let us join our voices with the voices of all creation singing praise to Jesus Christ our life:

℟   We praise you, O Lord!

For your Death and Resurrection from the dead: ℟

For your ascension to God's right hand: ℟

For your eternal glory: ℟

Personal intentions

Our Father....

May God keep us firm to the end, irreproachable on the day of our Lord Jesus Christ. Amen. (cf. 1 Cor 1:8)

MARIAN ANTIPHON   (page 12 or 13)

MONDAY, MAY 6

Prayer for the Morning

Arise, bless the LORD, your God,/
from eternity to eternity, alleluia! (cf. Neh 9:5)

Glory to the Father, and to the Son,
and to the Holy Spirit, as it was in the beginning,
is now, and will be for ever. Amen. Alleluia!

HYMN
Meter: LM
This hymn can be sung to the tune used for
Creator of the Stars of Night

O Christ, our King, Creator, Lord,
Savior of all who trust thy Word,
To them who seek thee ever near,
Now to our praises bend thine ear.

In thy dear cross a grace is found,
It flows from every streaming wound,
Whose power our inbred sin controls,
Breaks the firm bond, and frees our souls.

Thou didst create the stars of night,
Yet thou hast veiled in flesh thy light,
Hast deigned a mortal form to wear,
A mortal's painful lot to bear.

When thou didst hang upon the tree,
The quaking earth acknowledged thee,
When thou didst there yield up thy breath
The world grew dark as shades of death.

Now in the Father's glory high
Great Conqueror, never more to die,

Us by thy mighty power defend,
And reign through ages without end.

PSALM 24 1-6

Blessed are the clean of heart,/ for they will see God. (Mt 5:8)

To be a disciple means to follow the Master. He ascended the hill of the cross and transformed it into the seat of glory, a holy place. Risen, he invites us to leave behind all worthless desires and seek him in holiness, that is, in love, not for the signs and wonders he can do but for the life he gives.

The Lord's is the earth and its fullness,
the world and all its peoples.
It is he who set it on the seas;
on the waters he made it firm.

Who shall climb the mountain of the Lord?
Who shall stand in his holy place?
The man with clean hands and pure heart,
who desires not worthless things,
who has not sworn so as to deceive his neighbor.

He shall receive blessings from the Lord
and reward from the God who saves him.
Such are the men who seek him,
seek the face of the God of Jacob.

Glory to the Father....

Word of God Exodus 15:11-13

WHO IS LIKE to you among the gods, O LORD?/ Who is like to you, magnificent in holiness?/ O terrible in renown, worker of wonders,/ when you stretched out your right hand, the earth swallowed them!/ In your mercy you led the people you redeemed;/ in your strength you guided them to your holy dwelling.

> *I will sing to the LORD,*
> *for he is gloriously triumphant.*
> *(Ex 15:1)*

CANTICLE OF ZECHARIAH   (Text, back cover B)

May the LORD, who is good, grant pardon to everyone who has resolved to seek God, the LORD, the God of his fathers, though he be not clean as holiness requires. (2 Chr 30:18-19)

INTERCESSIONS

As disciples of the risen Lord, we pray:

℞   Light our way, O Lord!

For those appointed to tasks of leadership,
– may they lead your people in the way of holiness: ℞

For those who lead the way with joy to the mountain of the Lord,
– may they be richly blessed: ℞

For those who have passed through the gates of death,
– may they rejoice for all eternity: ℞

Personal intentions

Our Father....

O God and giver of all good gifts, you cleanse us from stain of sin and make us pure of heart through the Death and Resurrection of Jesus Christ. Lead us to dwell with you in holiness in our everyday lives through constant growth in love for you and for all those whose lives we touch, through the same Christ our Lord. Amen.

MASS

Monday of the Third Week of Easter

The Lord Jesus knows the persistent longing of our hearts: "You are looking for me." In order to satisfy that longing, Jesus tells us, "Work for the food that endures for eternal life." But that work is not simply a matter of human effort—when asked, "What can we do…?" Jesus instructs us to believe in him. "The wisdom and Spirit with which Stephen spoke" come from Jesus.

ENTRANCE ANTIPHON
The Good Shepherd has risen,/ who laid down his life for his sheep/ and willingly died for his flock, alleluia.

COLLECT
Grant, we pray, almighty God,
that, putting off our old self with all its ways,
we may live as Christ did,
for through the healing paschal remedies
you have conformed us to his nature.
Who lives and reigns with you in the unity
of the Holy Spirit,
one God, for ever and ever.

• *They could not withstand the wisdom and the Spirit with which he spoke.* •

A reading from
the Acts of the Apostles   6:8-15

STEPHEN, FILLED with grace and power, was working great wonders and signs among the people. Certain members of the so-called Synagogue of Freedmen, Cyreneans, and Alexandrians, and people from Cilicia and Asia, came forward and debated with Stephen, but they could not withstand the wisdom and the Spirit with which he spoke. Then they instigated some men to say, "We have heard him speaking blasphemous words

against Moses and God." They stirred up the people,
the elders, and the scribes, accosted him, seized him,
and brought him before the Sanhedrin. They presented false witnesses who testified, "This man never stops
saying things against this holy place and the law. For we
have heard him claim that this Jesus the Nazorean will
destroy this place and change the customs that Moses
handed down to us." All those who sat in the Sanhedrin
looked intently at him and saw that his face was like the
face of an angel.
The word of the Lord.

──• Psalm 119 •──

℟ (1ab) **Blessed are they who follow the law of the
Lord!**

Or: **Alleluia.**

Though princes meet and talk against me,
　your servant meditates on your statutes.
Yes, your decrees are my delight;
　they are my counselors. ℟

I declared my ways, and you answered me;
　teach me your statutes.
Make me understand the way of your precepts,
　and I will meditate on your wondrous deeds. ℟

Remove from me the way of falsehood,
　and favor me with your law.
The way of truth I have chosen;
　I have set your ordinances before me. ℟

Alleluia, alleluia. One does not live on bread alone/ but
on every word that comes forth from the mouth of God.
Alleluia, alleluia.

● *Do not work for food that perishes but for food that endures for eternal life.* ●

A reading from
the holy Gospel according to John
6:22-29

[After Jesus had fed the five thousand men, his disciples saw him walking on the sea.] The next day, the crowd that remained across the sea saw that there had been only one boat there, and that Jesus had not gone along with his disciples in the boat, but only his disciples had left. Other boats came from Tiberias near the place where they had eaten the bread when the Lord gave thanks. When the crowd saw that neither Jesus nor his disciples were there, they themselves got into boats and came to Capernaum looking for Jesus. And when they found him across the sea they said to him, "Rabbi, when did you get here?" Jesus answered them and said, "Amen, amen, I say to you, you are looking for me not because you saw signs but because you ate the loaves and were filled. Do not work for food that perishes but for the food that endures for eternal life, which the Son of Man will give you. For on him the Father, God, has set his seal." So they said to him, "What can we do to accomplish the works of God?" Jesus answered and said to them, "This is the work of God, that you believe in the one he sent."

The Gospel of the Lord.

Prayer over the Offerings
May our prayers rise up to you, O Lord,
together with the sacrificial offerings,
so that, purified by your graciousness,
we may be conformed to the mysteries of your
mighty love.
Through Christ our Lord.

PREFACE I-V OF EASTER ———————— pages 218 to 219

COMMUNION ANTIPHON   Jn 14:27
Peace I leave with you; my peace I give to you./ Not as the
world gives do I give it to you, says the Lord, alleluia.

PRAYER AFTER COMMUNION
    Almighty ever-living God,
    who restore us to eternal life
    in the Resurrection of Christ,
    increase in us, we pray, the fruits of this paschal
      Sacrament
    and pour into our hearts the strength of this saving food.
    Through Christ our Lord.

MEDITATION OF THE DAY

Working for the Food that Endures for Eternal Life

I have consecrated my life to God; I have given myself to him with my whole heart; I have prayed fervently for those whom I love, for [my husband] whom I love more than all others. Now I want to be no longer useless; I have seen my greatest obligations clearly, and I want to fulfill them. To do each day all the good that can be done humbly, so that only God may see it; always to seek out all the misery and grief surrounding me in order to relieve it, to cultivate a lively affection for everyone; and to do all this for God alone—that is the goal of all human life. My own life, which until now has often been so empty, will be transformed, I hope, by the strength of close union with God.

There are around me many that I love deeply, and I have a task to fulfill in relationship to them. Many of them do not know God or know him only imperfectly. It is not in arguing or lecturing that I can make them know who God is for us. But in struggling with myself, in becoming with his help more Christian and more courageous, I will witness to him whose disciple I am.

By the serenity and strength that I intend to acquire I will show that Christian life is great and beautiful and full of joy. By cultivating the best qualities of my mind I will proclaim that God is the highest intelligence, and that those who serve him can draw without end from that blessed source of intellectual and moral light. In order to give, one must receive; to serve my brothers and sisters before God for one day, or for even a small part of one, I must first purify and strengthen myself for many days.

Servant of God Elisabeth Leseur

Elisabeth Leseur († 1914) was a French married laywoman whose cause for canonization is underway.

Prayer for the Evening

The Lord's love reaches to heaven:
let us give thanks and praise, alleluia!

Glory to the Father.... Alleluia!

Hymn
Meter: CM
This hymn can be sung to the tune used for
Amazing Grace

The King of heav'n his table spreads,
And blessings crown the board;
Not paradise, with all its joys,
Could such delight afford.

Pardon and peace to dying men,
And endless life are giv'n,
Through the rich blood that Jesus shed
To raise our souls to heav'n.

Millions of souls, in glory now,
Were fed and feasted here;

And millions more, still on the way,
Around the board appear.

All things are ready, come away,
Nor weak excuses frame;
Come to your places at the feast,
And bless the Founder's Name.

PSALM 36   6-10

I will now rain down bread from heaven for you. (Ex 16:4)

During this season especially we are invited to feast on the
Eucharistic Body and Blood of Jesus Christ, God's Only Begotten
Son, the riches of God's house. The Spirit poured out upon the
world through his Death and Resurrection is the stream of God's
delight and the source of life. These gifts of God's love are the origin
of all holiness.

Your love, Lord, reaches to heaven;
your truth to the skies.
Your justice is like God's mountain,
your judgments like the deep.

To both man and beast you give protection.
O Lord, how precious is your love.
My God, the sons of men
find refuge in the shelter of your wings.

They feast on the riches of your house;
they drink from the stream of your delight.
In you is the source of life
and in your light we see light.

Glory to the Father....

Word of God   Isaiah 55:2-3

WHY SPEND your money
for what is not bread;/
your wages for what fails to satisfy?/ Heed me, and you
shall eat well,/ you shall delight in rich fare./ Come

to me heedfully,/ listen, that you may have life./ I will renew with you the everlasting covenant,/ the benefits assured to David.

Do not work for food that perishes but for the food that endures for eternal life, which the Son of Man will give you. For on him the Father, God, has set his seal.
(Jn 6:27)

Canticle of Mary　　　　　　(Text, back cover A)
He rained down manna for their food,/ and gave them bread from heaven. (Ps 78:24)

Intercessions

With trust in our Father, who gives his children bread, we pray:

℟　O Lord, how precious is your love!

You fed your people in the desert:
– feed the hungry with the fruits of the earth and the work of human hands. ℟

You fed the crowds in a deserted place:
– feed the hungry of soul in the solitude of prayer. ℟

You fed your disciples by the Sea of Galilee:
– feed all whom you call to serve you with bread to strengthen the heart. ℟

You feed all who come to you with the bread of life:
– bring all our beloved dead to the banquet of life everlasting. ℟

Personal intentions

Our Father....

May the Lord our God accept our offering of prayer and praise. Amen. (cf. 2 Sm 24:23)

Marian Antiphon　　　　　　(page 12 or 13)

SAINT WHO?

Saints Who Were Visionaries

Saint Jean de Brébeuf
Martyr († 1649)   Feast: October 19

A native of Condé-sur-Vire in Normandy, France, Jean was ordained at thirty, and two years later went to the Jesuit mission among the Huron natives in the New World. Though the natives, ravaged by the smallpox virus unwittingly brought by the French, were generally closed to the missionaries, Jean was able to live among them for some time. He mastered their language.

In 1629, political circumstances forced the Jesuits back to France. Jean focused his prayers on Christ's Passion, and an intense desire for martyrdom filled his soul. He returned to the Huron in 1633. A few years later he wrote to other would-be missionaries, urging them to look upon the natives "as ransomed by the blood of the Son of God, and as our brethren, with whom we are to pass the rest of our lives."

In 1640, Jean received a vision of a great cross stretched over the territory of the Iroquois, the native enemies of the Huron. The cross was big enough, he told his superior, for all of the men on the mission. In the end, eight were to give their lives. Jean was captured by the Iroquois with fellow Jesuit Gabriel Lalemant in 1649. He was presented with a "necklace" of red-hot hatchet blades that seared his flesh and then "baptized" with boiling water. In the end, his head was split open, and his heart ripped out. Throughout, he remained silent.

Merciful Father, through the intercession of Saint Jean de Brébeuf, help me to see my pain not as a punishment but as the possibility of union with the saving Passion of your Son.

TUESDAY, MAY 7

Prayer for the Morning

Jesus Christ is the king of martyrs:
come, let us adore him, alleluia!

Glory to the Father, and to the Son,
and to the Holy Spirit, as it was in the beginning,
is now, and will be for ever. Amen. Alleluia!

HYMN   Meter: LM
This hymn can be sung to the tune used for
The Glory of These Forty Days

The martyr Stephen met his death
Forgiveness in his final breath.
He interceded for them all
Whose cloaks lay at the feet of Saul.

The Father, hearing Stephen's prayer,
Gave gifts for all the Church to share
When grace and mercy overflowed
In light upon Damascus Road.

Then bless the Lord of heart and mind
Who gives new vision to the blind,
Whose reign throughout the world extends,
Whose loving-kindness never ends.

CANTICLE   Wisdom 3:1-6

You will be hated by all because of my name, but whoever endures
to the end will be saved. (Mt 10:22)

Lest the Easter season, with its emphasis on life, tempt us to euphoria, the Church today sets before us the example of Stephen, first
of martyrs, icon of the Crucified. The tomb remains the prelude to

the glory until the end of time. Life in Christ is always costly, and always worth the cost.

The souls of the just are in the hand of God,
and no torment shall touch them.

They seemed, in the view of the foolish, to be dead;
and their passing away was thought an affliction
and their going forth from us, utter destruction.
But they are in peace.

For if before men, indeed, they be punished,
yet is their hope full of immortality;
chastised a little, they shall be greatly blessed,
because God tried them
and found them worthy of himself.

As gold in the furnace, he proved them,
and as sacrificial offerings he took them to himself.

Glory to the Father....

Word of God
Hebrews 13:6-8

We may say with confidence:/ "The Lord is my helper,/ [and] I will not be afraid./ What can anyone do to me?"/ Remember your leaders who spoke the word of God to you. Consider the outcome of their way of life and imitate their faith. Jesus Christ is the same yesterday, today, and forever.

Stephen, filled with the holy Spirit,
looked up intently to heaven and saw the glory of God
and Jesus standing at the right hand of God. (cf. Acts 7:55)

CANTICLE OF ZECHARIAH
(Text, back cover B)

When they hand you over, do not worry about how you are to speak or what you are to say. You will be given at that moment what you are to say. (Mt 10:19)

INTERCESSIONS

Through the intercession of Saint Stephen, who prayed for his murderers as he died, let us offer our petitions to our merciful Father:

℟   Christ our Light, light our way.

Saint Stephen preached the word of God without fear:
– fill all your people with his fidelity and zeal for the Gospel. ℟

Saint Stephen prayed that his tormentors might be forgiven:
– inspire us with the true spirit of forgiveness in this season of joy. ℟

Saint Stephen lived the mystery of Christ to the end:
– lead all your people through death to life. ℟

Personal intentions

Our Father....

God our Father, you inspired in Saint Stephen a love for Christ that shaped his life according to the pattern set by his Master. Grant us that same love, fidelity, and true discipleship as we too seek to live the mystery of Easter, through the same Christ our Lord. Amen.

MASS

Tuesday of the Third Week of Easter

How often are we tempted to say to Jesus, "What sign can you do, that we may see and believe in you?"—that is, "How am I supposed to believe in you, Lord, if you don't do what I say and make all my difficulties go away?" The Lord responds that the Father provides true bread from heaven—Jesus, who is himself "the bread of life." Thus, even in the midst of Stephen's persecution and death, Jesus has not abandoned him, for "the heavens

*opened." May we have Stephen's confidence in Jesus today, even if
the only thing we can say is "Lord Jesus, receive my spirit."*

ENTRANCE ANTIPHON   Rv 19:5; 12:10

Sing praise to our God,/ all you who fear God, both small and
great,/ for now salvation and strength have come,/ and the
power of his Christ, alleluia.

COLLECT

O God, who open wide the gates of the heavenly
    Kingdom
to those reborn of water and the Holy Spirit,
pour out on your servants
an increase of the grace you have bestowed,
that, having been purged of all sins,
they may lack nothing
that in your kindness you have promised.
Through our Lord Jesus Christ, your Son,
who lives and reigns with you in the unity
    of the Holy Spirit,
one God, for ever and ever.

● *Lord Jesus, receive my spirit.* ●

A reading from
the Acts of the Apostles   7:51–8:1a

STEPHEN SAID TO the people,
the elders, and the scribes:
"You stiff-necked people, uncircumcised in heart and
ears, you always oppose the Holy Spirit; you are just like
your ancestors. Which of the prophets did your ancestors not persecute? They put to death those who fore-
told the coming of the righteous one, whose betrayers
and murderers you have now become. You received the
law as transmitted by angels, but you did not observe it."
    When they heard this, they were infuriated, and they
ground their teeth at him. But Stephen, filled with
the Holy Spirit, looked up intently to heaven and saw

the glory of God and Jesus standing at the right hand of God, and Stephen said, "Behold, I see the heavens opened and the Son of Man standing at the right hand of God." But they cried out in a loud voice, covered their ears, and rushed upon him together. They threw him out of the city, and began to stone him. The witnesses laid down their cloaks at the feet of a young man named Saul. As they were stoning Stephen, he called out, "Lord Jesus, receive my spirit." Then he fell to his knees and cried out in a loud voice, "Lord, do not hold this sin against them"; and when he said this, he fell asleep.

Now Saul was consenting to his execution.

The word of the Lord.

———• Psalm 31 •———

℟ (6a) Into your hands, O Lord, I commend my spirit.

Or: Alleluia.

Be my rock of refuge,
    a stronghold to give me safety.
You are my rock and my fortress;
    for your name's sake you will lead and guide me. ℟

Into your hands I commend my spirit;
    you will redeem me, O Lord, O faithful God.
My trust is in the Lord;
    I will rejoice and be glad of your mercy. ℟

Let your face shine upon your servant;
    save me in your kindness.
You hide them in the shelter of your presence
    from the plottings of men. ℟

Alleluia, alleluia. I am the bread of life, says the Lord;/ whoever comes to me will never hunger. Alleluia, alleluia.

• *It was not Moses, but my Father who gives you the true bread from heaven.* •

A reading from
the holy Gospel according to John   6:30-35

T HE CROWD SAID to Jesus: "What sign can you do, that we may see and believe in you? What can you do? Our ancestors ate manna in the desert, as it is written:

He gave them bread from heaven to eat."
So Jesus said to them, "Amen, amen, I say to you, it was not Moses who gave the bread from heaven; my Father gives you the true bread from heaven. For the bread of God is that which comes down from heaven and gives life to the world."

So they said to Jesus, "Sir, give us this bread always." Jesus said to them, "I am the bread of life; whoever comes to me will never hunger, and whoever believes in me will never thirst."
The Gospel of the Lord.

PRAYER OVER THE OFFERINGS
   Receive, O Lord, we pray,
   these offerings of your exultant Church,
   and, as you have given her cause for such great
      gladness,
   grant also that the gifts we bring
   may bear fruit in perpetual happiness.
   Through Christ our Lord.

PREFACE I-V OF EASTER ——————— pages 218 to 219

COMMUNION ANTIPHON   Rom 6:8
If we have died with Christ,/ we believe that we shall also live with Christ, alleluia.

PRAYER AFTER COMMUNION
Look with kindness upon your people, O Lord,
and grant, we pray,
that those you were pleased to renew by eternal mysteries
may attain in their flesh
the incorruptible glory of the resurrection.
Through Christ our Lord.

MEDITATION OF THE DAY

Fed by the Bread of Life

Oh, wonderful condescension of your affection toward us, that you, the Lord God, Creator and Giver of life to all, should see fit to come to a poor soul and to appease its hunger with all your divinity and humanity! O happy mind and blessed soul which deserves to receive you, the Lord God, and in receiving you, is filled with spiritual joy!

How great a Master [the soul] entertains, what a beloved guest it receives, how sweet a companion it welcomes, how true a friend it gains, how beautiful and noble is the spouse it embraces, beloved and desired above all things that can be loved and desired! Let heaven and earth and all their treasures stand silent before your face, most sweetly beloved, for whatever glory and beauty they have is of your condescending bounty, and they cannot approach the beauty of your name, whose wisdom is untold.

VENERABLE THOMAS À KEMPIS

Thomas à Kempis (†1471) was a German priest and monk who wrote many spiritual works.

Prayer for the Evening

God, our gracious Father, cares for us always:
come, let us adore, alleluia!

Glory to the Father, and to the Son,
and to the Holy Spirit, as it was in the beginning,
is now, and will be for ever. Amen. Alleluia!

HYMN

Meter: 76 76 D
This hymn can be sung to the tune used for
The Church's One Foundation

O living bread from heaven,
How well you fed your guest!
The gifts that you have given
Have filled my heart with rest.
O wondrous food of blessing,
O cup that heals our woes,
My heart, this gift possessing,
With praises overflows!

You gave me all I wanted,
This food can death destroy;
And you have freely granted
The cup of endless joy.
O Lord, I do not merit
The favor you have shown,
And all my soul and spirit
Bow down before your throne.

Lord, grant me that, thus strengthened
With heav'nly food, while here
My course on earth is lengthened,
I serve with holy fear,
And when you call my spirit
To leave this world below,

I enter, through your merit,
Where joys unmingled flow.

Psalm 68   5-11

God destined us for adoption to himself through Jesus Christ, in
accord with the favor of his will. (cf. Eph 1:5)

In God the Father's care to feed all his children on the bread of life
through Jesus Christ, we see the mark of one who truly gives and
sustains life.

O sing to the Lord, make music to his name;
make a highway for him who rides on the clouds.
Rejoice in the Lord, exult at his presence.

Father of the orphan, defender of the widow,
such is God in his holy place.
God gives the lonely a home to live in;
he leads the prisoners forth into freedom:
but rebels must dwell in a parched land.

When you went forth, O God, at the head of
    your people,
when you marched across the desert, the earth trembled:
the heavens melted at the presence of God,
at the presence of God, Israel's God.

You poured down, O God, a generous rain:
when your people were starved you gave them new life.
It was there that your people found a home,
prepared in your goodness, O God, for the poor.

Glory to the Father....

Word of God   Matthew 6:26

L OOK AT THE BIRDS in the
    sky; they do not sow or reap,
they gather nothing into barns, yet your heavenly

Father feeds them. Are not you more important than they?

> *Father of the orphan, defender of the widow,/*
> *such is God in his holy place.*
> *(Ps 68:6)*

CANTICLE OF MARY   (Text, back cover A)

Just as the living Father sent me and I have life because of the Father, so also the one who feeds on me will have life because of me. (Jn 6:57)

INTERCESSIONS

With confidence in God our Father, let us pray:

℟   Father, hear us!

Protect the orphaned from abandonment and ill-treatment, we pray: ℟

Defend the widowed from isolation, we pray: ℟

Give the homeless a home to live in, we pray: ℟

Feed the hungry, we pray: ℟

Personal intentions

Our Father....

Grace to us and peace from God our Father and the Lord Jesus Christ. Amen. (cf. 2 Cor 1:2)

MARIAN ANTIPHON   (page 12 or 13)

❧ ❧ ❧

SAINT WHO?

Saints Who Were Visionaries

Saint Ercongota
Virgin († c. 660)   Feast: February 23

Ercongota's father, King Erconbert, ruled in what today is southeast England. Her mother, Sexburgh, eventually became abbess at Ely, succeeding her sister, Saint Etheldreda. According to Saint Bede, who tells the story in his *Ecclesiastical History*, Ercongota desired to enter religious life as well. She went to the monastery of Faremoutiers-en-Brie in France, where her aunts, Sethrida and Ethelburga, were already nuns.

Bede tells us that "many wonderful works and miracles" were reported of the virgin Ercongota, and he shares with us the unusual circumstances of her death. One night Ercongota unexpectedly paid visits to the cells of the older nuns in the monastery, asking them for their prayers. She told them of a vision she had received of a host of white clad men arriving at the monastery from Kent, her homeland. When she asked them why they had come to the monastery, the men said that they were there to reclaim "the golden coin that was brought here from Kent." Ercongota took this to mean that her death was imminent.

Indeed, Ercongota died that very night. At the exact moment of her passing, a chorus of angelic voices was suddenly heard in the monastery. The nuns then beheld a bright light in the sky escorting Ercongota's soul heavenward.

Father in heaven, through the intercession
of Saint Ercongota, prepare me
for the moment of death.

WEDNESDAY, MAY 8

Prayer for the Morning

Let us praise the God of mystery and love, alleluia!

Glory to the Father.... Alleluia!

HYMN
Meter: 10 10 10 10
This hymn can be sung to the tune used for
Abide with Me

Christ was of old, yet Christ is of today;
Timeless he lives in everlasting day.
He is the Lord on whom all things depend,
Their one Beginning and their only End.

Christ is the Alpha, Fount of all that is,
The End, the Omega, for all is his.
He rules all time, each age and every hour;
To him belong eternal praise and power.

Christ by his glorious wounds in safety keep
His little flock, true Shepherd of his sheep.
May he who rose to glory from death's night
Shine on our hearts and minds with Easter light.

CANTICLE OF ISAIAH
40:10-14

The light shines in the darkness,/ and the darkness has not overcome it. (Jn 1:5)

God is mystery. The maker of the universe dwells in light inaccessible, so bright that it blinds the probing eye, the questioning mind.
Yet this awesome God has taken on a human face and a human
name in Jesus. He is the Son of the Father and the Word made flesh,
the mystery hidden in God for all ages.

Here comes with power
the Lord God,

who rules by his strong arm;
here is his reward with him,
his recompense before him.

Like a shepherd he feeds his flock;
in his arms he gathers the lambs,
carrying them in his bosom,
and leading the ewes with care.

Who has cupped in his hand the waters of the sea,
and marked off the heavens with a span?
Who has held in a measure the dust of the earth,
weighed the mountains in scales
and the hills in a balance?

Who has directed the spirit of the Lord,
or has instructed him as his counselor?
Whom did he consult to gain knowledge?
Who taught him the path of judgment,
or showed him the way of understanding?

Glory to the Father....

Word of God   Isaiah 55:8-9

M Y THOUGHTS are not your thoughts,/ nor are your ways my ways, says the LORD./ As high as the heavens are above the earth,/ so high are my ways above your ways/ and my thoughts above your thoughts.

Look up to the skies and behold;/
regard the heavens high above you.
(Jb 35:5)

CANTICLE OF ZECHARIAH   (Text, back cover B)

The LORD, your God, who is in your midst, is a great and awesome God. (Dt 7:21)

INTERCESSIONS

With reverence and love, let us lay before our God the needs of the world.

℟   Hear us, O God our Savior!

For those who are powerless,
– that they may experience your power employed on their behalf. ℟

For those who have abandoned hope,
– that they may know your mercy. ℟

For those who fail to see you in mystery,
– that they may come to feel your gentle love. ℟

Personal intentions

Our Father....

O God, hidden in light inaccessible, you have revealed the face of your love in Jesus Christ, our Lord. Grant us the grace to worship you with reverence and to entrust ourselves to you in love, through the same Christ our Lord. Amen.

MASS

Wednesday of the Third Week of Easter

"A severe persecution" broke out and "all were scattered throughout the countryside." But that crisis—that cross—was a blessing in disguise, for "those who had been scattered went about preaching the word." Thanks to that scattering, the Bread of Life is also brought to "many possessed people, and many paralyzed and crippled people." Those rejected by the world find in Jesus the one who loves with divine plenitude: "I will not reject anyone who comes to me," and "Whoever comes to me will never hunger."

ENTRANCE ANTIPHON   Cf. Ps 71 (70):8, 23

Let my mouth be filled with your praise, that I may sing aloud;/ my lips shall shout for joy, when I sing to you, alleluia.

COLLECT

Be present to your family, O Lord, we pray,
and graciously ensure
those you have endowed with the grace of faith
an eternal share in the Resurrection of your
　　Only Begotten Son.
Who lives and reigns with you in the unity
　　of the Holy Spirit,
one God, for ever and ever.

● *They went about preaching the word.* ●

A reading from
the Acts of the Apostles   8:1b-8

T HERE BROKE OUT a severe persecution of the Church in Jerusalem, and all were scattered throughout the countryside of Judea and Samaria, except the Apostles. Devout men buried Stephen and made a loud lament over him. Saul, meanwhile, was trying to destroy the Church; entering house after house and dragging out men and women, he handed them over for imprisonment.

Now those who had been scattered went about preaching the word. Thus Philip went down to the city of Samaria and proclaimed the Christ to them. With one accord, the crowds paid attention to what was said by Philip when they heard it and saw the signs he was doing. For unclean spirits, crying out in a loud voice, came out of many possessed people, and many paralyzed and crippled people were cured. There was great joy in that city.

The word of the Lord.

———• PSALM 66 •———

℟ (1) **Let all the earth cry out to God with joy.**

Or: Alleluia.

Shout joyfully to God, all the earth,
  sing praise to the glory of his name;
  proclaim his glorious praise.
Say to God, "How tremendous are your deeds!" ℟

"Let all on earth worship and sing praise to you,
  sing praise to your name!"
Come and see the works of God,
  his tremendous deeds among the children of
    Adam. ℟

He has changed the sea into dry land;
  through the river they passed on foot;
  therefore let us rejoice in him.
He rules by his might forever. ℟

Alleluia, alleluia. Everyone who believes in the Son has
eternal life,/ and I shall raise him on the last day, says
the Lord. Alleluia, alleluia.

> • *This is the will of my Father, that all who see the
> Son may have eternal life.* •

A reading from
the holy Gospel according to John   6:35-40
_____

JESUS SAID to the crowds,
  "I am the bread of life; who-
ever comes to me will never hunger, and whoever believes in me will never thirst. But I told you
that although you have seen me, you do not believe.
Everything that the Father gives me will come to me,
and I will not reject anyone who comes to me, because

I came down from heaven not to do my own will but the will of the one who sent me. And this is the will of the one who sent me, that I should not lose anything of what he gave me, but that I should raise it on the last day. For this is the will of my Father, that everyone who sees the Son and believes in him may have eternal life, and I shall raise him on the last day."
The Gospel of the Lord.

Prayer over the Offerings
Grant, we pray, O Lord,
that we may always find delight in these paschal mysteries,
so that the renewal constantly at work within us
may be the cause of our unending joy.
Through Christ our Lord.

Preface I-V of Easter ———————— pages 218 to 219

Communion Antiphon
The Lord has risen and shone his light upon us,/ whom he has redeemed by his Blood, alleluia.

Prayer after Communion
Hear, O Lord, our prayers,
that this most holy exchange,
by which you have redeemed us,
may bring your help in this present life
and ensure for us eternal gladness.
Through Christ our Lord.

MEDITATION OF THE DAY

The Life-Giving Will of the Father

In this loving and faithful obedience to the Father, our Lord and Master teaches us the most fundamental lesson we have to learn as children of God. He has demonstrated for us what the filial turning toward the

Father means in terms of human life…. There is no reluctance to do the Father's will: instead his child lives on it, and desires that others should know, love, and obey the Father too. He gives each of his adopted children a task to do and complete in the circumstances of his own life; there is a particular one for each, just as our Master had his. We must have therefore something of his desire to glorify the Father, to spend our lives in doing this, in union with his Son.

It does not matter what kind of task we have, or whether it seems important or not. Our Lord could have brought more tangible results out of his work at once, and made a stir in the world as a whole, but this was not his task. He did only what the Father wanted. Some people have more spectacular tasks than others, but we must not assess the value of our lives in the sight of God by the world's values. We may not even be meant to use all our talents in this life, for some may be meant to lie fallow, so let us not fret if our lives do not seem to provide us with much opportunity to display them. We only have to do what we are asked, just as our Lord did: He lived in a corner of Palestine, putting up with the scribes and Pharisees. He saw infinite possibilities in his work, but some were left undone during his lifetime because he concentrated everything on doing precisely what the Father wanted.

The only way to glorify God is our Lord's way. That is, we the adopted children have to become as much like the Only Begotten Son as possible, and so in our own little way reflect the loving relationship of the Son and his Father. We can only do this if we grow in sensitivity to our Father's will. His will must become our food, as it was for our Lord: it must sustain and nourish us, give us life, knowledge, and love. But it cannot become our real nourishment until and unless we make frequent acts of union with our Father's will. Thus our wills, through these acts, will become more and more united to his will and endowed with all the perfections of his. Our will too will become wise, faithful, strong, beautiful, just, and, above all, loving, a flame of love.

FATHER BONAVENTURE PERQUIN, O.P.

Father Perquin († 1970) was a Dominican priest, theologian, and spiritual writer.

Prayer for the Evening

In peace and in patience,
let us pray to the Lord, alleluia!

Glory to the Father, and to the Son,
and to the Holy Spirit, as it was in the beginning,
is now, and will be for ever. Amen. Alleluia!

HYMN

Meter: SM
This hymn can be sung to the tune used for
Rise Up, O Men of God

When on the cruèl cross
The Lord was lifted high,
Affrighted earth in terror quailed
To see its Maker die.

Then had the yawning caves
Devoured the murderous band,
Had not the Crucified in love
Stretched forth his saving hand.

Thou gave thyself to die,
Dark Hades to explore,
To bring to souls in prison bound
New life for evermore.

O Lover of mankind,
To thee all glory be,
For thou did give not death, but life,
When hanging on the tree.

PSALM 37   5-11

Peace I leave with you; my peace I give to you. Not as the world gives do I give it to you. Do not let your hearts be troubled or afraid. (Jn 14:27)

Jesus Christ gives peace not through the conquest of armies but through his surrender to death. Through his Death and Resurrection, he established the definitive reign of peace into which all are invited to enter, by joyful self-surrender to God in every part of our lives. Through this self-surrender, we become like Christ, who is our peace.

Commit your life to the Lord,
trust in him and he will act,
so that your justice breaks forth like the light,
your cause like the noon-day sun.

Be still before the Lord and wait in patience;
do not fret at the man who prospers;
a man who makes evil plots
to bring down the needy and the poor.

Calm your anger and forget your rage;
do not fret, it only leads to evil.
For those who do evil shall perish;
the patient shall inherit the land.

A little longer—and the wicked shall have gone.
Look at his place, he is not there.
But the humble shall own the land
and enjoy the fullness of peace.

Glory to the Father....

Word of God   Ephesians 4:31-32

ALL BITTERNESS, fury, anger, shouting, and reviling must be removed from you, along with all malice.

[And] be kind to one another, compassionate, forgiving one another as God has forgiven you in Christ.

> *The Lord will give strength to his people,/*
> *the Lord will bless his people with peace.*
> *(Ps 29:11)*

Canticle of Mary   (Text, back cover A)

Put on then, as God's chosen ones, holy and beloved, heartfelt compassion, kindness, humility, gentleness, and patience. (Col 3:12)

Intercessions

Let us pray to the Lord Jesus Christ, who is our peace:

℟   Hear us, we pray.

In lands torn by war,
– bring new life through peace. ℟

To families and communities wounded by division,
– bring new life through peace. ℟

To the dying and the bereaved suffering under the threat of death,
– bring new life through peace. ℟

Personal intentions

Our Father….

May the Lord deliver us from all evil and bring us to life everlasting! Amen.

Marian Antiphon   (page 12 or 13)

SAINT WHO?

Saints Who Were Visionaries

Saint John of Sahagún
Priest († 1479)   Feast: June 12

John was the eldest of seven children born to pious parents in Sahagún, in the kingdom of León, Spain. He was educated among the Benedictines and sought ordination. Although it was normal at this time for priests from fine families to be assigned several benefices, thus ensuring a comfortable lifestyle, John resigned the additional benefices he was presented with and insisted on living on one benefice alone, at Saint Agnes in Burgos. After a time, he received permission to further his education at Salamanca.

While serving at a church near the city, John began to suffer from gallstones. Facing a surgery that was very risky at the time, he promised God that, were he to survive, he would enter religious life. He made it through the surgery, and shortly thereafter entered the Order of Saint Augustine.

Among the Augustinians, John preached with fervor. For a time he was forbidden by his superior from saying Mass because he was taking so long. After John admitted to the superior that he was receiving visions of the crucified Christ at the moment of the consecration, he was permitted to resume.

When John died in 1479, some suspected that he had been poisoned by a woman who was once the mistress of a prominent man in Salamanca: John persuaded the man to end the scandalous affair and the woman may have sought revenge on the preacher. In the Church's art, John usually holds a luminescent chalice.

Father of mercies, through the intercession of Saint John of Sahagún, grant that I might enter more deeply into the prayer of the Mass.

THURSDAY, MAY 9

Prayer for the Morning

Let us cry out to the Lord our God:
in mercy, he will hear us, alleluia!

Glory to the Father, and to the Son,
and to the Holy Spirit, as it was in the beginning,
is now, and will be for ever. Amen. Alleluia!

HYMN   Meter: 87 87 87
This hymn can be sung to the tune used for
Praise, My Soul, the King of Heaven

Let us rise in early morning,
And, instead of ointments, bring
Hymns of praises to our Master,
And his Resurrection sing:
We shall see the Sun of Justice
Ris'n with healing on his wing.

Go ye forth, his saints, to meet him!
Go with lamps in every hand!
From the sepulcher he riseth:
Ready for the Bridegroom stand:
And the Pascha of salvation
Hail, with his triumphant band.

PSALM 33   1-9

Be attentive to the Word, as to a lamp shining in a dark place, until
day dawns and the morning star rises in your hearts. (cf. 2 Pt 1:19)

Obedient to God's word, we offer our praise and prayer, that we
may share in the joy of the risen Christ, the Light of God's justice
that has dawned in our darkness.

Ring out your joy to the Lord, O you just;
for praise is fitting for loyal hearts.

Give thanks to the Lord upon the lyre,
with a ten-stringed harp sing him songs.
O sing him a song that is new,
play loudly, with all your skill.

For the word of the Lord is faithful
and all his works to be trusted.
The Lord loves justice and right
and fills the earth with his love.

By his word the heavens were made,
by the breath of his mouth all the stars.
He collects the waves of the ocean;
he stores up the depths of the sea.

Let all the earth fear the Lord,
all who live in the world revere him.
He spoke; and it came to be.
He commanded; it sprang into being.

Glory to the Father....

Word of God   Isaiah 26:8-9, 12

For your way and your judgments, O LORD,/ we look to you;/ Your name and your title/ are the desire of our souls./ My soul yearns for you in the night,/ yes, my spirit within me keeps vigil for you;/ When your judgment dawns upon the earth,/ the world's inhabitants learn justice./ O LORD, you mete out peace to us,/ for it is you who have accomplished all we have done.

*The LORD is waiting to show you favor,/
and he rises to pity you;/ For the LORD is a God
of justice:/ blessed are all who wait for him! (Is 30:18)*

CANTICLE OF ZECHARIAH (Text, back cover B)

What came to be through him was life,/ and this life was the light of the human race. (Jn 1:3-4)

INTERCESSIONS

To God whose word is life and light, we pray:

℟   Your word is faithful, O Lord!

In place of our empty silences,
– fill us with songs of praise: ℟

In place of our deserts of lovelessness,
– fill the earth with your love: ℟

In place of our self-seeking,
– fill us with praise of your glory: ℟

Personal intentions

Our Father....

God our Father, you have spoken into the chaos of sin the one all-powerful Word of salvation, your Son, our Lord Jesus Christ. His Death and Resurrection have brought light out of darkness. Grant us the grace to live by his light, through the same Christ our Lord. Amen.

MASS
Thursday of the Third Week of Easter

"Everyone who listens to my Father comes to me." The Father guarantees our ability to listen to him through Church's preaching and teaching, and by giving us every day "the bread of life." The Ethiopian asks, "How can I understand unless someone instructs me?" The God-sent Philip gives life to the man's soul by "proclaiming Jesus to him."

ENTRANCE ANTIPHON   Cf. Ex 15:1-2
Let us sing to the Lord, for he has gloriously triumphed./
The Lord is my strength and my might;/ he has become my
salvation, alleluia.

COLLECT
　　Almighty ever-living God,
　　let us feel your compassion more readily
　　during these days when, by your gift,
　　we have known it more fully,
　　so that those you have freed from the darkness of error
　　may cling more firmly to the teachings of your truth.
　　Through our Lord Jesus Christ, your Son,
　　who lives and reigns with you in the unity
　　　　of the Holy Spirit,
　　one God, for ever and ever.

　　● *Look, there is water. What is to prevent my being
　　baptized?* ●

A reading from
the Acts of the Apostles   8:26-40

T HE ANGEL of the Lord spoke
to Philip, "Get up and head
south on the road that goes down from Jerusalem to
Gaza, the desert route." So he got up and set out. Now
there was an Ethiopian eunuch, a court official of the
Candace, that is, the queen of the Ethiopians, in charge
of her entire treasury, who had come to Jerusalem to
worship, and was returning home. Seated in his chariot, he was reading the prophet Isaiah. The Spirit said
to Philip, "Go and join up with that chariot." Philip
ran up and heard him reading Isaiah the prophet and
said, "Do you understand what you are reading?" He
replied, "How can I, unless someone instructs me?" So
he invited Philip to get in and sit with him. This was the
Scripture passage he was reading:

Like a sheep he was led to the slaughter,/ and as a lamb before its shearer is silent,/ so he opened not his mouth./ In his humiliation justice was denied him./ Who will tell of his posterity?/ For his life is taken from the earth.

Then the eunuch said to Philip in reply, "I beg you, about whom is the prophet saying this? About himself, or about someone else?" Then Philip opened his mouth and, beginning with this Scripture passage, he proclaimed Jesus to him. As they traveled along the road they came to some water, and the eunuch said, "Look, there is water. What is to prevent my being baptized?" Then he ordered the chariot to stop, and Philip and the eunuch both went down into the water, and he baptized him. When they came out of the water, the Spirit of the Lord snatched Philip away, and the eunuch saw him no more, but continued on his way rejoicing. Philip came to Azotus, and went about proclaiming the good news to all the towns until he reached Caesarea.

The word of the Lord.

—— • PSALM 66 • ——

℟ (1) Let all the earth cry out to God with joy.

Or: Alleluia.

Bless our God, you peoples,
  loudly sound his praise;
He has given life to our souls,
  and has not let our feet slip. ℟

Hear now, all you who fear God, while I declare
  what he has done for me.
When I appealed to him in words,
  praise was on the tip of my tongue. ℟

Blessed be God who refused me not
  my prayer or his kindness! ℟

Alleluia, alleluia. I am the living bread that came down from heaven, says the Lord;/ whoever eats this bread will live forever. Alleluia, alleluia.

● *I am the living bread that came down from heaven.* ●

A reading from
the holy Gospel according to John
6:44-51

JESUS SAID TO the crowds: "No one can come to me unless the Father who sent me draw him, and I will raise him on the last day. It is written in the prophets:

They shall all be taught by God.

Everyone who listens to my Father and learns from him comes to me. Not that anyone has seen the Father except the one who is from God; he has seen the Father. Amen, amen, I say to you, whoever believes has eternal life. I am the bread of life. Your ancestors ate the manna in the desert, but they died; this is the bread that comes down from heaven so that one may eat it and not die. I am the living bread that came down from heaven; whoever eats this bread will live forever; and the bread that I will give is my Flesh for the life of the world."

The Gospel of the Lord.

PRAYER OVER THE OFFERINGS

O God, who by the wonderful exchange effected in
    this sacrifice
have made us partakers of the one supreme Godhead,
grant, we pray,
that, as we have come to know your truth,
we may make it ours by a worthy way of life.
Through Christ our Lord.

PREFACE I-V OF EASTER ———————— pages 218 to 219

COMMUNION ANTIPHON   2 Cor 5:15
Christ died for all, that those who live/ may live no longer
for themselves,/ but for him, who died for them and is risen,
alleluia.

PRAYER AFTER COMMUNION
>Graciously be present to your people, we pray,
>O Lord,
>and lead those you have imbued with heavenly
>mysteries
>to pass from former ways to newness of life.
>Through Christ our Lord.

MEDITATION OF THE DAY

"The bread that I will give"

Once again, he makes the shadow of the cross appear. Bread must be broken; and he who had come from God must be a sacrificial Victim that men might truly feed on him. Hence, it would be a Bread that would result from the voluntary offering of his own flesh to rescue the world from the slavery of sin unto the newness of life....

He not only pictured himself as one who had come down from heaven but as one who had come down to *give* himself, or to die. It would only be in the slain Christ that they would come to understand the glory of a Bread that nourishes unto eternity. He was here referring to his death; for the word "giving" expressed the sacrificial act. The flesh and blood of the Incarnate Son of God, which would be severed in death, would become the source of everlasting life. When he said, "my flesh," he meant his human nature, as "the Word became Flesh" meant that God the Word or the Son assumed to himself a human nature. But it was only because that human nature would be linked to a divine Person for all eternity that he could give eternal life to those who received it. And when he said that he would give that for the life of the world, the Greek word used meant "all mankind"....

As they had communion with the flesh and blood of the Paschal Lamb, so they would now have communion with the flesh and blood of the true Lamb of God. He, who was born in Bethlehem, the "House of Bread," and was laid in a manger, a place of food for lower animals, would now be to men, so inferior to him, their Bread of Life.

VENERABLE FULTON J. SHEEN

Archbishop Sheen († 1979) was a great American preacher and author of numerous books.

Prayer for the Evening

*Strong is God's love for us;/ he is faithful for ever:
come, let us give thanks and praise, alleluia!*
(cf. Ps 117:2)

*Glory to the Father, and to the Son,
and to the Holy Spirit, as it was in the beginning,
is now, and will be for ever. Amen. Alleluia!*

HYMN
                                    Meter: SM
              This hymn can be sung to the tune used for
                          'Tis Good, Lord, to Be Here

Rejoice, you pure in heart,
Rejoice, give thanks and sing;
Your festal banner wave on high,
The cross of Christ your King.

Bright youth and snow-crowned age,
All those for truth do seek;
Raise high your free, exulting song,
God's wondrous praises speak.

Yes, on through life's long path,
Still chanting as you go;
From youth to age, by night and day,
In gladness and in woe.

Then on, you pure in heart,
Rejoice, give thanks and sing;
Your glorious banner wave on high,
The cross of Christ your King.

PSALM 71   5-6, 16-22a, 23

You have kept the promise you made to your servant. With your
own mouth you spoke it, and by your own hand you have brought
it to fulfillment this day. (cf. 2 Chr 6:15)

If you are young, look forward to God's fidelity to you throughout
your life; if you are older, look back on God's fidelity to you through
all that is past. Whatever your age, know that God's love is the
foundation upon which all our hope stands firm. His guarantee is
the Death and Resurrection of Jesus Christ, a deed deep, high, and
unsearchable that exceeds all our praise.

It is you, O Lord, who are my hope,
my trust, O Lord, since my youth.
On you I have leaned from my birth,
from my mother's womb you have been my help.
My hope has always been in you.

I will declare the Lord's mighty deeds
proclaiming your justice, yours alone.
O God, you have taught me from my youth
and I proclaim your wonders still.

Now that I am old and grey-headed,
do not forsake me, God.
Let me tell of your power to all ages,
praise your strength and justice to the skies,
tell of you who have worked such wonders.
O God, who is like you?

You have burdened me with bitter troubles
but you will give me back my life.
You will raise me from the depths of the earth;
you will exalt me and console me again.

So I will give you thanks on the lyre
for your faithful love, my God.
When I sing to you my lips shall rejoice
and my soul, which you have redeemed.

Glory to the Father....

Word of God   Deuteronomy 26:18-19

TODAY THE LORD is making this agreement with you: you are to be a people peculiarly his own, as he promised you; and provided you keep all his commandments, he will then raise you high in praise and renown and glory above all other nations he has made, and you will be a people sacred to the LORD, your God, as he promised.

Faithful is God, faithful and true!
(cf. Is 25:1)

CANTICLE OF MARY   (Text, back cover A)

Look down, then, from heaven, your holy abode, and bless your people Israel and the soil you have given us in the land flowing with milk and honey which you promised on oath to our fathers. (Dt 26:15)

INTERCESSIONS

Lord Jesus, you died and rose in fulfillment of God's promise of life to all people. Bring us into the everlasting land of your glory as we pray:

℟   Come to us, O risen Savior!

You are the faithful physician of our bodies and our souls:
– grant relief to the sick and aging who suffer. ℟

You are the faithful sustainer of all who are burdened with bitter troubles:
– grant hope and help to those who suffer. ℟

You are the faithful consolation of all who are grieved:
– abide with those who suffer trial and bereavement. ℟

Personal intentions

Our Father....

May the LORD, the God of our fathers, increase us a thousand times over, and bless us as he promised! Amen.
(cf. Dt 1:11)

MARIAN ANTIPHON

(page 12 or 13)

SAINT WHO?

Saints Who Were Visionaries

Saint Marie Alphonsine Danil Ghattas

Foundress († 1927)   Feast: March 25

Marie Alphonsine was born in Jerusalem in 1843. Her parents named her Soultaneh Maria, "Mary the Queen," after the Mother of God. Daily recitation of the rosary with her family prepared her at fourteen to freely choose to enter the Sisters of Saint Joseph of the Apparition.

The Blessed Mother first appeared to Marie Alphonsine while she was in Bethlehem serving as a teacher and catechist. A year later, Mary appeared again, this time asking her to found the Congregation of the Most Holy Rosary and instructing her to take Father Youssef Tannous as her spiritual director. With Father Tannous' help, Marie Alphonsine began the process of separating from her congregation. In 1885, she and eight other women professed vows in the new order. Her deep trust in Mary carried her forward in the foundation of schools and orphanages. While in Galilee, a girl under her care fell into a deep cistern. Without any other way of helping the girl, Marie Alphonsine tossed in her large fifteen-decade rosary. The girl emerged from the well soon afterward, guided, she said, by a ladder shaped like a rosary.

Marie Alphonsine was praying the rosary with her sister when she died in 1927. Her order, the only Catholic community of indigenous religious women in Palestine, has spread to Lebanon, Egypt, Syria, Kuwait, and the United Arab Emirates.

Eternal Father, through the intercession of Saint Marie Alphonsine Danil Ghattas, let me face every situation with deeper trust and unswerving courage.

FRIDAY, MAY 10
Saint Damien de Veuster

Prayer for the Morning

God is our guardian and our guide!
Let us give thanks and praise, alleluia!

Glory to the Father, and to the Son,
and to the Holy Spirit, as it was in the beginning,
is now, and will be for ever. Amen. Alleluia!

HYMN
Meter: 10 10 10 10
This hymn can be sung to the tune used for
Be Thou My Vision

O Bread of life, Food of our pilgrim way,
We hail you, Strength of this our earthly day,
Sign of God's love, our Bond of unity,
Our Hope and Pledge of immortality!

O Source of Love and Truth, eternal Quest,
In you alone our hearts can find their rest,
Our doubts be stilled, our restless yearnings cease,
Our souls' deep hunger find its truest peace.

O Bread of life, earth's Light and Jubilee,
Your form conceals your Godhead's majesty.
O be our justice, peace and joy most blest,
Our surest Guide to heaven's eternal rest!

PSALM 78
13-19, 23-25

He filled them with bread from heaven. (Ps 105:40)

Lest we grow faint on the daily road from death to life, Jesus promises us food for the journey: the bread of life and the cup of salvation, his own flesh and blood.

God divided the sea and led them through
and made the waters stand up like a wall.
By day he led them with a cloud:
by night, with a light of fire.

He split the rocks in the desert.
He gave them plentiful drink as from the deep.
He made streams flow out from the rock
and made waters run down like rivers.

Yet still they sinned against him;
they defied the Most High in the desert.
In their heart they put God to the test
by demanding the food they craved.

They even spoke against God.
They said: "Is it possible for God
to prepare a table in the desert?"

Yet he commanded the clouds above
and opened the gates of heaven.
He rained down manna for their food,
and gave them bread from heaven.

Mere men ate the bread of angels.
He sent them abundance of food.

Glory to the Father….

Word of God   Isaiah 48:20b-21

WITH SHOUTS of joy proclaim
this, make it known;/ Publish
it to the ends of the earth, and say,/ "The LORD has redeemed his servant Jacob./ They did not thirst/ when
he led them through dry lands;/ Water from the rock

he set flowing for them;/ he cleft the rock, and waters welled forth."

Strong is God's love for us! (cf. Ps 117:2)

CANTICLE OF ZECHARIAH
(Text, back cover B)

This is the bread that came down from heaven. Unlike your ancestors who ate and still died, whoever eats this bread will live forever. (Jn 6:58)

INTERCESSIONS

What father would give his children stones when they asked for bread? How much more, then, will our heavenly Father give good things to those who ask him? Let us pray:

℟   We put our trust in you!

You led your people through the sea dry-shod:
– let us put our trust in you as you lead us through this day's challenges. ℟

You fed them in the desert:
– let us hear your word of life amid the noise of our busy lives today. ℟

You gave them water from the rock:
– let us drink from the fountain of life, and not from bitter and polluted waters. ℟

Personal intentions

Our Father....

O Lord our God, you sent into the midst of faithless humanity the living Bread, your risen Son, our Lord Jesus Christ, to nourish and strengthen us on the road. Through the mystery of the cross, you poured forth upon us the Spirit, the water of life. Have mercy on our lack of trust, and lead us in your ways today, through the same Christ our Lord. Amen.

MASS

Friday of the Third Week of Easter

ENTRANCE ANTIPHON   Rv 5:12
Worthy is the Lamb who was slain,/ to receive power and divinity,/ and wisdom and strength and honor, alleluia.

COLLECT
> Grant, we pray, almighty God,
> that we, who have come to know
> the grace of the Lord's Resurrection,
> may, through the love of the Spirit,
> ourselves rise to newness of life.
> Through our Lord Jesus Christ, your Son,
> who lives and reigns with you in the unity
>   of the Holy Spirit,
> one God, for ever and ever.

● *This man is a chosen instrument of mine to carry my name before the Gentiles.* ●

A reading from
the Acts of the Apostles   9:1-20

SAUL, STILL breathing murderous threats against the disciples of the Lord, went to the high priest and asked him for letters to the synagogues in Damascus, that, if he should find any men or women who belonged to the Way, he might bring them back to Jerusalem in chains. On his journey, as he was nearing Damascus, a light from the sky suddenly flashed around him. He fell to the ground and heard a voice saying to him, "Saul, Saul, why are you persecuting me?" He said, "Who are you, sir?" The reply came, "I am Jesus, whom you are persecuting. Now get up and go into the city and you will be told what you must do." The men who were traveling with him stood speechless, for they heard the voice but could see no one. Saul got up from the ground, but when he opened his eyes he could see nothing; so they led him by the hand and brought him to Damascus. For three days he was unable to see, and he neither ate nor drank.

There was a disciple in Damascus named Ananias, and the Lord said to him in a vision, "Ananias." He answered, "Here I am, Lord." The Lord said to him, "Get up and go to the street called Straight and ask at the house of Judas for a man from Tarsus named Saul. He is there praying, and in a vision he has seen a man named Ananias come in and lay his hands on him, that he may regain his sight." But Ananias replied, "Lord, I have heard from many sources about this man, what evil things he has done to your holy ones in Jerusalem. And here he has authority from the chief priests to imprison all who call upon your name." But the Lord said to him, "Go, for this man is a chosen instrument of mine to carry my name before Gentiles, kings, and children of Israel, and I will show him what he will have to suffer for my name." So Ananias went and entered the house; laying his hands on him, he said, "Saul, my brother, the Lord has sent me, Jesus who appeared to you on the way by which you came, that you may regain your sight and be filled with the Holy Spirit." Immediately things like scales fell from his eyes and he regained his sight. He got up and was baptized, and when he had eaten, he recovered his strength.

He stayed some days with the disciples in Damascus, and he began at once to proclaim Jesus in the synagogues, that he is the Son of God.

The word of the Lord.

━━•PSALM 117•━━

℟ (Mk 16:15) **Go out to all the world and tell the Good News.**

Or: **Alleluia.**

Praise the LORD, all you nations;
  glorify him, all you peoples! ℟

For steadfast is his kindness toward us,
  and the fidelity of the LORD endures forever. ℟

Alleluia, alleluia. Whoever eats my Flesh and drinks my Blood,/ remains in me and I in him, says the Lord. Alleluia, alleluia.

● *My Flesh is true food, and my Blood is true drink.* ●

A reading from
the holy Gospel according to John   6:52-59

THE JEWS QUARRELED among themselves, saying, "How can this man give us his Flesh to eat?" Jesus said to them, "Amen, amen, I say to you, unless you eat the Flesh of the Son of Man and drink his Blood, you do not have life within you. Whoever eats my Flesh and drinks my Blood has eternal life, and I will raise him on the last day. For my Flesh is true food, and my Blood is true drink. Whoever eats my Flesh and drinks my Blood remains in me and I in him. Just as the living Father sent me and I have life because of the Father, so also the one who feeds on me will have life because of me. This is the bread that came down from heaven. Unlike your ancestors who ate and still died, whoever eats this bread will live forever." These things he said while teaching in the synagogue in Capernaum.
The Gospel of the Lord.

PRAYER OVER THE OFFERINGS
    Graciously sanctify these gifts, O Lord, we pray,
    and, accepting the oblation of this spiritual sacrifice,
    make of us an eternal offering to you.
    Through Christ our Lord.

PREFACE I-V OF EASTER ———————— pages 218 to 219

COMMUNION ANTIPHON
The Crucified is risen from the dead/ and has redeemed us,
alleluia.

PRAYER AFTER COMMUNION
    We have partaken of the gifts of this sacred mystery,
    humbly imploring, O Lord,
    that what your Son commanded us to do
    in memory of him
    may bring us growth in charity.
    Through Christ our Lord.

SAINT DAMIEN DE VEUSTER   *Optional memorial*

    ● *Belgian-born Father Damien de Veuster, of the*
Fathers of the Sacred Hearts of Jesus and Mary, came
to minister to the victims of leprosy (Hansen's disease)
on the Hawaiian island of Molokai in 1873. For fifteen
years, Damien worked continually to improve the lot
of the lepers. After Damien died of leprosy himself in
1889, a Congregationist cleric's private criticisms of
his character were circulated in public, prompting
man of letters Robert Louis Stevenson to come to his
rescue. In a famous essay, Stevenson memorialized
the "intrusive and decisive heroism of Damien," the
priest's utter willingness to live and die among the
disfigured and forgotten. Damien was canonized in
2009. ●

ENTRANCE ANTIPHON
O chosen people, proclaim the mighty works of him/ who
called you out of darkness into his wonderful light, alleluia.

COLLECT
>Father of mercy,
>who gave us in Saint Damien
>a shining witness of love for the poorest and most
>   abandoned,
>grant that, by his intercession,
>as faithful witnesses of the heart of your Son Jesus,
>we too may be servants of the most needy and rejected.
>Through our Lord Jesus Christ, your Son,
>who lives and reigns with you in the unity
>   of the Holy Spirit,
>one God, for ever and ever.

PRAYER OVER THE OFFERINGS
>Look upon the sacrificial gifts we offer, almighty God,
>on the feast day of blessed Damien,
>and grant that we, who celebrate the mysteries of the
>   Lord's Passion,
>may imitate what we now do.
>Through Christ our Lord.

COMMUNION ANTIPHON   Ez 34:15
I will pasture my sheep;/ I myself will give them rest, says the
Lord, alleluia.

PRAYER AFTER COMMUNION
>By the power of this mystery, O Lord,
>confirm your servants in the true faith,
>that they may everywhere profess in word and deed
>the faith for which blessed Damien never ceased to labor
>and for which he spent his whole life.
>Through Christ our Lord.

• ───────────────────────────────── •

M E D I T A T I O N   O F   T H E   D A Y

• ───────────────────────────────── •

Living on True Food and True Drink

In the beginning people stayed away from him and
were afraid of him because they thought he was severe,
but later they lost any fear and loved him…. People
spoke well of Father Damien before and after his death
due to his benevolence to all….

I never heard him talking about his suffering or complaining about the disease. He was a man of will and of strong character. In spite of the pain in his fingers, he worked with the boys and others tilling the land....

He never wasted food nor would see others waste it. I and others of my family helped Father Damien as he was poor. We gave him food as we knew he was in need. He didn't eat too much, but cooked taro, the principal food of the Hawaiians. Sometimes I asked Father Damien, "Is the food enough?" He answered, "Even too much! Look, I have some taro and some fish." I sometimes said to the Father to throw something away as it was old. He answered, "No, it is still good for me." Father Damien warmed up his food a few times to make another meal rather than throw anything away.

Father Damien prayed very often. Often I saw him pray.... He called the boys to pray, showing them how to pray. Before entering in my boat he used to recite a prayer and when we were near landing to another bank, the first thing he did was kneel and pray. When he arrived at my house where he used to stay when in Pelekunu, he prayed again. He used to celebrate Mass in my house until he built a small chapel. In the beginning there were only eight Catholics coming to Mass, but very early he converted half of the population and built a chapel. I was his altar boy and I noticed he said Mass slowly and with devotion....

He had a lot of trust in God and in spite of his difficulties he did not lose courage or trust. He tried to encourage the patients to have hope in God....

I have a great affection and love for him as he was my spiritual father and my friend. Every night I pray to Father Damien for his help and his assistance.

JOSEPH MANU

Joseph Manu met Father Damien in 1873 when he was about sixteen years old. Many years later, Joseph described his friend's simple lifestyle and great devotion to God and the people of Kalawao.

Prayer for the Evening

Blessed in the name of the Lord is he who comes.
Let us greet him with praise and thanksgiving, alleluia!

Glory to the Father, and to the Son,
and to the Holy Spirit, as it was in the beginning,
is now, and will be for ever. Amen. Alleluia!

HYMN

Meter: LM
This hymn can be sung to the tune used for
On Jordan's Bank

O God, our light in work or rest,
We bear your image, bright, restored!
In raising Christ from death and grave
You raise us, too, in him, our Lord.

O God, our milk and honey now,
Yours is the feast for all to share:
Christ trod the winepress all alone;
The wedding feast is now prepared.

O God, our rainbow, ark, dry land,
Whose rage, repented, now is stilled:
Christ, raised, the firstfruits of the dead,
Has blessed all earth as you had willed.

PSALM 118

13-18, 25-27

The victor will inherit these gifts, and I shall be his God, and he will
be my son. (Rv 21:7)

The poetic images of Easter are themselves a feast for the imagination. Central is the image of light risen from the darkness of death.
In the light of the triumphant Christ, we, like Saul, see the world
anew and grasp new possibilities for our own lives, transformed by
the victory of the cross and fed at the table of life.

I was hard pressed and was falling
but the Lord came to help me.

The Lord is my strength and my song;
he is my savior.
There are shouts of joy and victory
in the tents of the just.

The Lord's right hand has triumphed;
his right hand raised me.
The Lord's right hand has triumphed;
I shall not die, I shall live
and recount his deeds.
I was punished, I was punished by the Lord,
but not doomed to die.

O Lord, grant us salvation;
O Lord, grant success.
Blessed in the name of the Lord
is he who comes.
We bless you from the house of the Lord;
the Lord God is our light.

Glory to the Father....

Word of God   Tobit 13:11

A BRIGHT LIGHT will shine to all parts of the earth;/ many nations shall come to you from afar,/ And the inhabitants of all the limits of the earth,/ drawn to you by the name of the Lord God,/ Bearing in their hands their gifts for the King of heaven./ Every generation shall give joyful praise in you,/ and shall call you the chosen one,/ through all ages forever.

On his journey, as Saul was nearing Damascus,
a light from the sky suddenly flashed around him.
                                      (cf. Acts 9:3)

CANTICLE OF MARY   (Text, back cover A)

The people who sit in darkness/ have seen a great light,/ on those dwelling in a land overshadowed by death/ light has arisen. (Mt 4:16)

INTERCESSIONS

With joy we pray to the risen Lord who shines in our midst:

℟   Light our way!

You arose out of the darkness of the tomb:
– grant the light of hope to those who live under threat of death. ℟

You appeared to Saul in a blaze of light:
– grant the light of faith to those who walk in the darkness of disbelief. ℟

You sent Paul, blinded and then made to see, to bring the light of the Gospel to the Gentiles:
– grant the light of love to those who labor in your name. ℟

Personal intentions

Our Father....

The LORD bless us and keep us!/ The LORD let his face shine upon us, and be gracious to us!/ The LORD look upon us kindly and give us peace! Amen. (cf. Nm 6:24-26)

MARIAN ANTIPHON   (page 12 or 13)

❧ ❧ ❧

SAINT WHO?

Saints Who Were Visionaries

Saint Aleydis of Schaerbeek
Virgin († 1250)   Feast: June 15

When she was seven, Aleydis (or Alice) was sent by her parents to be raised among the Cistercian nuns at Camera Sanctae Mariae Convent near Brussels, Belgium. She freely embraced the austerities of convent life. At a young age before she had even made vows, Aleydis was struck with leprosy. Fearing contagion, the other nuns required Aleydis to live segregated from them.

Alone and in pain, Aleydis gave herself over to prayer. Gradually, she began to embrace the value of her suffering. She offered her pains for the souls in purgatory. Still, the impossibility of receiving the Blood of Christ from the chalice—forbidden to a leper for hygiene reasons—was almost unbearable. Aleydis was certain she was not receiving the whole Christ. But our Lord relieved her suffering, one day in prayer: "Where there is part, there is also the whole."

In 1249, Aleydis' suffering intensified. The disease ravaged first one eye and then the other. Aleydis made bold to offer her blindness for the success of the Crusade being waged by Louis IX. Having lost earthly sight, she was consoled by visions. Christ appeared to her and revealed his five wounds. She died on the feast of Saint Barnabas in the year 1250. In 1907, veneration of her was approved by Pope Pius X.

Loving Father, through the intercession of Saint Aleydis of Schaerbeek, have mercy on me in my affliction. Speak softly to my soul.

SHE PONDERED THESE THINGS IN HER HEART (SEE LK 2:51)

There's No Place Like Home

Sonja Corbitt

Since I have a demanding speaking schedule that sends me traveling every week during peak seasons, my Southern home is a place of deep comfort. I need the land's silence and greenness, perhaps because I am introvert and extrovert in almost equal measure.

My husband and I spend mornings together with our coffee, on the porch or by the fire, in quiet meditation, savoring home and children, and bathing them in prayer. "There's no place like home."

Although the classic movie line expresses my heart exactly, I never thought the sentiment could also be a matter of faith until a recent pilgrimage to the Holy Land.

Back home I had just done a radio show on the "place" of the Bible—the climate, agriculture, geography, and topography of the Holy Land. I knew the land, but by faith, not sight.

Now, walking his paths and seeing his sites, I realized Jesus loves his "place" too. With profound appreciation I received his words from a fishing boat on the Sea of Galilee.

On the bow of a "Jesus boat" (as these replicas of ancient vessels are called), my arms thrown wide in thanksgiving and praise pounding through my heart at the beauty of the landscape, I felt Jesus speak into my heart a gift and sentiment I deeply appreciate: "See? I wanted to share *my* home with you, Sonja."

Immediately I remembered his words, *I go and prepare a place for you* (Jn 14:3). If earthly homes are so satisfying to us, I can only anticipate what heaven will be like.

(*Sonja Corbitt* is the Bible Study Evangelista and a best-selling author. Find her and her Bible study resources at biblestudyevangelista.com.

SATURDAY, MAY 11

Prayer for the Morning

In God is our joy:
let us give thanks and praise, alleluia!

Glory to the Father.... Alleluia!

Hymn   Meter: 77 77 with alleluias
This hymn can be sung to the tune used for
Jesus Christ Is Risen Today

Hail, O Queen of heav'n enthroned, alleluia!
Hail by angels mistress owned, alleluia!
Root of Jesse, Gate of Morn, alleluia!
When the world's true Light was born, alleluia!

Glorious Virgin, joy to thee, alleluia!
Loveliest whom in heaven they see, alleluia!
Fairest thou, where all are fair, alleluia!
Plead with Christ our sins to spare, alleluia!

Canticle of Isaiah   61:10; 62:2-3

I wore my honesty like a garment;/ justice was my robe and my
turban. (Jb 29:14)

Mary has been made a full sharer in the Resurrection of her Son.
She is clothed with the beauty of his risen glory. Through her intercession as mediatrix of all graces, the Church is robed in Christ
through baptism.

I rejoice heartily in the Lord,
in my God is the joy of my soul;
for he has clothed me with a robe of salvation,
and wrapped me in a mantle of justice,
like a bridegroom adorned with a diadem,
like a bride bedecked with her jewels.

Nations shall behold your vindication,
and all kings your glory;
you shall be called by a new name
pronounced by the mouth of the LORD.
You shall be a glorious crown in the hand of the LORD,
a royal diadem held by your God.

Glory to the Father....

Word of God   Revelation 21:2; 19:8

I ALSO SAW the holy city, a new Jerusalem, coming down out of heaven from God, prepared as a bride adorned for her husband. [...]

She was allowed to wear/ a bright, clean linen garment./ (The linen represents the righteous deeds of the holy ones.)

And over all these put on love, that is,
the bond of perfection. (Col 3:14)

CANTICLE OF ZECHARIAH   (Text, back cover B)

All of you who were baptized into Christ have clothed yourselves with Christ. (Gal 3:27)

INTERCESSIONS

The Lord has robed us in the light of salvation. Through the intercession of the Blessed Virgin Mary, let us pray:

℞   Clothe your people in love.

Inspire in all hearts the desire to do good in simple, everyday ways,
– that your Church may always be robed in the righteous deeds of the holy. ℞

Move those who are well-clothed and fed to provide clothing, food, and shelter to refugees, the homeless, and the poor,
– that those deprived of life's necessities may rejoice in you. ℟

Convert the hearts of those who are clad in deeds of darkness,
– that they may divest themselves of their evil and be robed in your light. ℟

Personal intentions

Our Father....

O God, through the faithful obedience of the Blessed Virgin Mary, you have clothed your people in the glory of salvation. Through her constant prayer, let us live according to your love in Jesus Christ, your risen Son, our Lord. Amen.

Mass

Saturday of the Third Week of Easter

"To whom shall we go?" This question remains the deepest expression of our life for us who are God's servants, who have faith that Jesus is the Holy One of God. Peter's attachment to Christ in turn becomes a powerful grace for others in trouble who beg him, "Please come to us without delay." May the grace of faith overcome all murmuring within us.

Entrance Antiphon
Col 2:12
You have been buried with Christ in Baptism,/ through which you also rose again/ by faith in the working of God,/ who raised him from the dead, alleluia.

Collect
O God, who in the font of Baptism
have made new those who believe in you,
keep safe those reborn in Christ,

that, defeating every onslaught of error,
they may faithfully preserve the grace of your blessing.
Through our Lord Jesus Christ, your Son,
who lives and reigns with you in the unity
    of the Holy Spirit,
one God, for ever and ever.

● *The Church was being built up, and with the
consolation of the Holy Spirit she grew in numbers.* ●

A reading from
the Acts of the Apostles   9:31-42

THE CHURCH throughout all
Judea, Galilee, and Samaria
was at peace. She was being built up and walked in the
fear of the Lord, and with the consolation of the Holy
Spirit she grew in numbers.

As Peter was passing through every region, he went
down to the holy ones living in Lydda. There he found
a man named Aeneas, who had been confined to bed
for eight years, for he was paralyzed. Peter said to
him, "Aeneas, Jesus Christ heals you. Get up and make
your bed." He got up at once. And all the inhabitants
of Lydda and Sharon saw him, and they turned to the
Lord.

Now in Joppa there was a disciple named Tabitha
(which translated is Dorcas). She was completely oc-
cupied with good deeds and almsgiving. Now during
those days she fell sick and died, so after washing her,
they laid her out in a room upstairs. Since Lydda was
near Joppa, the disciples, hearing that Peter was there,
sent two men to him with the request, "Please come to
us without delay." So Peter got up and went with them.
When he arrived, they took him to the room upstairs
where all the widows came to him weeping and showing him the tunics and cloaks that Dorcas had made

while she was with them. Peter sent them all out and knelt down and prayed. Then he turned to her body and said, "Tabitha, rise up." She opened her eyes, saw Peter, and sat up. He gave her his hand and raised her up, and when he had called the holy ones and the widows, he presented her alive. This became known all over Joppa, and many came to believe in the Lord.
The word of the Lord.

—— • Psalm 116 • ——

℟ (12) **How shall I make a return to the Lord for all the good he has done for me?**

Or: **Alleluia.**

How shall I make a return to the Lord
   for all the good he has done for me?
The cup of salvation I will take up,
   and I will call upon the name of the Lord. ℟

My vows to the Lord I will pay
   in the presence of all his people.
Precious in the eyes of the Lord
   is the death of his faithful ones. ℟

O Lord, I am your servant;
   I am your servant, the son of your handmaid;
   you have loosed my bonds.
To you will I offer sacrifice of thanksgiving,
   and I will call upon the name of the Lord. ℟

Alleluia, alleluia. Your words, Lord, are Spirit and life;/ you have the words of everlasting life. Alleluia, alleluia.

> • *To whom shall we go? You have the words of eternal life.* •

A reading from
the holy Gospel according to John   6:60-69

MANY OF THE disciples of Jesus who were listening said, "This saying is hard; who can accept it?" Since Jesus knew that his disciples were murmuring about this, he said to them, "Does this shock you? What if you were to see the Son of Man ascending to where he was before? It is the Spirit that gives life, while the flesh is of no avail. The words I have spoken to you are Spirit and life. But there are some of you who do not believe." Jesus knew from the beginning the ones who would not believe and the one who would betray him. And he said, "For this reason I have told you that no one can come to me unless it is granted him by my Father."

As a result of this, many of his disciples returned to their former way of life and no longer walked with him. Jesus then said to the Twelve, "Do you also want to leave?" Simon Peter answered him, "Master, to whom shall we go? You have the words of eternal life. We have come to believe and are convinced that you are the Holy One of God."

The Gospel of the Lord.

PRAYER OVER THE OFFERINGS
Accept in compassion, Lord, we pray,
the offerings of your family,
that under your protective care
they may never lose what they have received,
but attain the gifts that are eternal.
Through Christ our Lord.

PREFACE I-V OF EASTER ——————— pages 218 to 219

COMMUNION ANTIPHON   Jn 17:20-21
Father, I pray for them, that they may be one in us,/ so that the world may believe it was you who sent me,/ says the Lord, alleluia.

PRAYER AFTER COMMUNION

Keep safe, O Lord, we pray,
those whom you have saved by your kindness,
that, redeemed by the Passion of your Son,
they may rejoice in his Resurrection.
Who lives and reigns for ever and ever.

MEDITATION OF THE DAY

"To whom shall we go?"

When Jesus one day showed his Apostles how to bring in an overwhelming catch of fish, Peter's reaction was to fall down at Jesus' knees and exclaim: *Depart from me, for I am a sinful man, O Lord*. But Peter's reaction was very different on the occasion when Jesus presented himself to the world as the Bread of Life and many found the teaching difficult and began to turn their backs on him. As the Lord pointedly asked the Twelve, *Will you also go away?* Simon Peter answered him, *Lord, to whom shall we go? You have the words of eternal life*. These are indeed the two apparently opposite impulses that define the essence of discipleship: on the one hand, the consciousness of one's utter unworthiness to abide in the presence of the holy God and, simultaneously, one's desperate need precisely to abide in that presence, only source of lasting life and joy....

The passion for simply abiding in the company of Jesus, the need continually *to be with him* in every sense of that verb, is the very heart of discipleship.

ERASMO LEIVA-MERIKAKIS

Erasmo Leiva-Merikakis, now known as Father Simeon, is a Cistercian monk serving in Rome. He is the author of Fire of Mercy, Heart of the Word, *a three-volume commentary on Matthew's Gospel.*

Prayer for the Evening

Vigil of the Fourth Sunday of Easter

Christ is our shepherd:
come, let us adore, alleluia!

Glory to the Father, and to the Son,
and to the Holy Spirit, as it was in the beginning,
is now, and will be for ever. Amen. Alleluia!

HYMN Meter: 76 76 D
This hymn can be sung to the tune used for
I Sing the Mighty Power of God

Wherever Christ may guide me,
No want shall turn me back;
My Shepherd is beside me,
And nothing can I lack.
His wisdom ever waking,
His sight is never dim;
He knows the way he's taking
And I will walk with him.

Green pastures are before me,
Which yet I have not seen;
Bright skies will soon be o'er me,
Where the dark clouds have been.
My hope I cannot measure,
The path to life is free;
My Savior has my treasure,
And he will walk with me.

PSALM 67 4-8

If you hearken to my voice and keep my covenant, you shall be my
special possession, dearer to me than all other people, though all the
earth is mine. (Ex 19:5)

Our Good Shepherd holds us by the hand and leads us through the darkness by the sound of his voice. Let us follow with joy into the new day of eternal life.

Let the peoples praise you, O God;
let all the peoples praise you.

Let the nations be glad and exult
for you rule the world with justice.
With fairness you rule the peoples,
you guide the nations on earth.

Let the peoples praise you, O God;
let all the peoples praise you.

The earth has yielded its fruit
for God, our God, has blessed us.
May God still give us his blessing
till the ends of the earth revere him.

Let the peoples praise you, O God;
let all the peoples praise you.

Glory to the Father....

Word of God   Ezekiel 34:11-13

THUS SAYS the Lord GOD:
I myself will look after and
tend my sheep. As a shepherd tends his flock when he
finds himself among his scattered sheep, so will I tend
my sheep. I will rescue them from every place where
they were scattered when it was cloudy and dark. I will
lead them out from among the peoples and gather them
from the foreign lands; I will bring them back to their
own country and pasture them upon the mountains of
Israel [in the land's ravines and all its inhabited places].

I give them eternal life, and they shall never perish.
No one can take them out of my hand. (Jn 10:28)

Canticle of Mary   (Text, back cover A)

The Lamb who is in the center of the throne will shepherd them and lead them to springs of life-giving water, and God will wipe away every tear from their eyes. (Rv 7:17)

Intercessions

In this evening hour we pray:

℟   Loving shepherd, hear our prayer.

For all those who seek rest after turmoil,
– that they may find peace in you, we pray: ℟

For all those who walk in the valley of approaching death,
– that they may find freedom from fear in you, we pray: ℟

For all those who desire the life-giving waters of baptism,
– that they may find life in you, we pray: ℟

                                        Personal intentions

Our Father....

May the God of peace, who brought up from the dead the great shepherd of the sheep, Jesus our Lord, furnish us with all that is good, so that we may do his will. Amen. (cf. Hb 13:20-21)

Marian Antiphon   (page 12 or 13)

❧ ❧ ❧

SAINT WHO?

Saints Who Were Visionaries

Saint Basilides of Alexandria

Martyr († c. 205)   Feast: June 30

In Alexandria, Egypt, there lived a slave, Potamiana, who had been raised by a devout Christian mother, Marcella. When Potamiana's master conceived a desire for her, she refused his advances. Incensed, he turned the girl over to the Roman prefect.

The prefect threatened to have her boiled in oil if she did not obey her master. But Potamiana begged to be executed, asking only that she be lowered into the oil fully clothed. The prefect decided to grant her request, and he turned her over to the guard Basilides. He ushered the girl to the place of execution, taking care to shield her from the lewd insults of the crowds. In gratitude, Potamiana promised Basilides that she would obtain for him "the grace of salvation." The maiden was then executed in the boiling oil. Her mother Marcella was likewise killed.

A few days later, Basilides declared to his fellow guards that he had accepted Christ. He was immediately imprisoned and questioned. He then told of how Potamiana had come to him in a vision and placed a crown upon his head, the gift of God's grace. She told him that he too would soon enter into glory. Basilides was brought to the prison, where Christians baptized him. The next day he was brought out, repeated his profession of faith, and beheaded.

Eternal Father, through the intercession of Saint Basilides of Alexandria, protect me from everything that threatens my purity.

Good Shepherd

Jennifer Hubbard

The words are a living promise given to me the day we broke frozen earth to bury my little one: *The LORD is my shepherd; there is nothing I lack* (Ps 23:1). In those days the Good Shepherd carried me to still waters and gave me rest. In his peace I found refuge, in his goodness I found life.

It is the same Good Shepherd who knows my earthly journey must advance. For if it was confined to a lush meadow and still waters, the meadow would become overgrazed and its still waters would turn stagnant. Because of this forward momentum there will be steep cliffs, sharp crevasses, menacing crossings, and prowling predators that seek to rattle me and throw me off my balance. The Good Shepherd carried me to still waters and the Good Shepherd brings me to higher places through the darkest valleys. His eyes remain keen for that which lurks ahead and his rod is at the ready for that which comes to destroy. I am not shaken, for *the LORD is my shepherd; there is nothing I lack.*

It is this promise, six years later, that I continue to draw on, trust, and follow, even when paths are frightening and dark—even when I do not understand. It is in these moments I embrace his closeness and know it is in his protection that I am enabled to walk. In this promise I am shown again and again that when the storm has passed, when the danger is averted, I will emerge onto green pastures, still waters, and find rest in the loving tenderness of the Good Shepherd.

Jennifer Hubbard resides in Newtown, Conn. The younger of her two children, Catherine Violet, was a victim of the Sandy Hook Elementary School shooting in 2012.

Suggested Prayer of the Faithful

(Each local community should compose its own Universal Prayer, but may find inspiration in the texts proposed here.)

We entrust ourselves to God the Father who judges justly and holds us firmly in his hand. With hearts filled with confidence we now pray:

For the bishops, the shepherds of the Church: that they will be filled with the zeal and have the heart of Christ, the Good Shepherd.

That those who govern will favor truth, justice, and a commitment to peace.

For all mothers, that through the intercession of the Mother of God, the Lord will bless them and reward them for their sacrifices and love.

For those who have gone astray like sheep: that they will hear the voice of the Good Shepherd, the guardian of their souls.

For all of the faithful departed: that they may enjoy eternal life with Christ, risen from the dead.

For the grace this week to hear and follow the voice of Jesus in all we do.

Loving Father, you sent your Son and raised him from the dead so that we might have life and have it more abundantly. Keep us obedient to our new life in him. Through Christ our Lord. Amen. ∎

SUNDAY, MAY 12
Fourth Sunday of Easter

Prayer for the Morning

We, your people, the flock of your pasture,/
will give you thanks for ever and ever;/
we will tell your praise from age to age, alleluia!
(Ps 79:13)

Glory to the Father, and to the Son,
and to the Holy Spirit, as it was in the beginning,
is now, and will be for ever. Amen. Alleluia!

HYMN
Meter: 77 77 D
This hymn can be sung to the tune used for
At the Lamb's High Feast We Sing

Christ the Lord is risen today;
Christians, haste your vows to pay;
Offer ye your praises meet
At the Paschal Victim's feet.
For the sheep the Lamb has bled,
Sinless in the sinner's stead;
Christ the Lord is ris'n on high,
Now he lives no more to die.

Christ, who once for sinners bled,
Now the first-born from the dead,
Throned in endless might and power,
Lives and reigns forevermore.
Hail, eternal Hope on high!
Hail, thou King of victory!
Hail, thou Prince of life adored!
Help and save us, gracious Lord.

Pѕᴀʟᴍ 86   9-13

My sheep hear my voice; I know them, and they follow me. (Jn 10:27)

To follow in the footsteps of our Shepherd is to pass through the valley of death into the glory of life lived to the full in his presence. Let us pray always for the reassurance of his guiding hand and of his word, spoken through the word we will hear in today's Eucharistic liturgy and through those appointed to lead us in his name.

All the nations shall come to adore you
and glorify your name, O Lord:
for you are great and do marvelous deeds,
you who alone are God.

Show me, Lord, your way
so that I may walk in your truth.
Guide my heart to fear your name.

I will praise you, Lord my God, with all my heart
and glorify your name for ever;
for your love to me has been great:
you have saved me from the depths of the grave.

Glory to the Father....

Word of God   Numbers 27:15-17

Mᴏѕᴇѕ ѕᴀɪᴅ to the Lᴏʀᴅ, "May the Lᴏʀᴅ, the God of the spirits of all mankind, set over the community a man who shall act as their leader in all things, to guide them in all their actions; that the Lᴏʀᴅ's community may not be like sheep without a shepherd."

Be attentive to him and heed his voice.
(Ex 23:21)

Cᴀɴᴛɪᴄʟᴇ ᴏꜰ Zᴇᴄʜᴀʀɪᴀʜ   (Text, back cover B)

God brought forth his people like sheep;/ he guided his flock in the desert./ He led them safely with nothing to fear. (Ps 78:52-53)

INTERCESSIONS

Let us pray for all those who have been appointed to the task of shepherd in the Church:

℟ O Shepherd of Israel, hear us.

O Shepherd of all shepherds, guide and strengthen our Holy Father,
– that he may always shepherd your flock in the image of Christ: ℟

O Shepherd of all shepherds, inspire our local bishops,
– that they may lead your people safely with nothing to fear: ℟

O Shepherd of all shepherds, be with our local pastors,
– that they may care for the lost: ℟

Personal intentions

Our Father….

O God our Shepherd, you care for your flock across every desert and through every dark place. Through the intercession of the Blessed Virgin Mary, seek out and restore all those who have lost their way, that we may all come together into the glory of the Kingdom of your risen Son, our Lord Jesus Christ, who lives and reigns with you in the unity of the Holy Spirit, one God, for ever and ever. Amen.

MASS

Fourth Sunday of Easter

On this Good Shepherd Sunday the risen Christ consoles us: "My sheep hear my voice; they follow me." What fills Christ's disciples with joy and the Holy Spirit is this voice, which is identical with life. Like the converts whom Paul and Barnabas urged "to remain faithful to the grace of God," our happiness lies in our faithfulness to the the tender voice of the Shepherd. For this Shepherd is also the Lamb who lives to wipe every tear from our eyes. With Saint Gregory of Nyssa we say: "How could I not love you, who has loved me so much…so as to lay down your life for the sheep whose shepherd you are? There can be no greater love than this, to lay down your life for my salvation."

Eɴᴛʀᴀɴᴄᴇ Aɴᴛɪᴘʜᴏɴ   Cf. Ps 33 (32):5-6
The merciful love of the Lord fills the earth;/ by the word of
the Lord the heavens were made, alleluia.

Gʟᴏʀɪᴀ ————————————————————— page 212

Cᴏʟʟᴇᴄᴛ
        Almighty ever-living God,
        lead us to a share in the joys of heaven,
        so that the humble flock may reach
        where the brave Shepherd has gone before.
        Who lives and reigns with you in the unity
            of the Holy Spirit,
        one God, for ever and ever.

        ● *We now turn to the Gentiles.* ●

A reading from the Acts of the Apostles 13:14, 43-52

Pᴀᴜʟ ᴀɴᴅ Bᴀʀɴᴀʙᴀs con-
tinued on from Perga and
reached Antioch in Pisidia. On the sabbath they entered the synagogue and took their seats. Many Jews
and worshipers who were converts to Judaism followed
Paul and Barnabas, who spoke to them and urged them
to remain faithful to the grace of God.

    On the following sabbath almost the whole city gath-
ered to hear the word of the Lord. When the Jews saw
the crowds, they were filled with jealousy and with violent abuse contradicted what Paul said. Both Paul and
Barnabas spoke out boldly and said, "It was necessary

that the word of God be spoken to you first, but since you reject it and condemn yourselves as unworthy of eternal life, we now turn to the Gentiles. For so the Lord has commanded us, *I have made you a light to the Gentiles, that you may be an instrument of salvation to the ends of the earth.*"

The Gentiles were delighted when they heard this and glorified the word of the Lord. All who were destined for eternal life came to believe, and the word of the Lord continued to spread through the whole region. The Jews, however, incited the women of prominence who were worshipers and the leading men of the city, stirred up a persecution against Paul and Barnabas, and expelled them from their territory. So they shook the dust from their feet in protest against them, and went to Iconium. The disciples were filled with joy and the Holy Spirit.

The word of the Lord.

———• Psalm 100 •———

℟ (3c) **We are his people, the sheep of his flock.**

Or: **Alleluia.**

Sing joyfully to the Lord, all you lands;
    serve the Lord with gladness;
    come before him with joyful song. ℟

Know that the Lord is God;
    he made us, his we are;
    his people, the flock he tends. ℟

The Lord is good:
    his kindness endures forever,
    and his faithfulness, to all generations. ℟

● *The Lamb will shepherd them and lead them to springs of life-giving water.* ●

A reading from
the Book of Revelation   7:9, 14b-17

I, JOHN, HAD a vision of a great multitude, which no one could count, from every nation, race, people, and tongue. They stood before the throne and before the Lamb, wearing white robes and holding palm branches in their hands.

Then one of the elders said to me, "These are the ones who have survived the time of great distress; they have washed their robes and made them white in the blood of the Lamb.

"For this reason they stand before God's throne/ and worship him day and night in his temple./ The one who sits on the throne will shelter them./ They will not hunger or thirst anymore,/ nor will the sun or any heat strike them./ For the Lamb who is in the center of the throne will shepherd them/ and lead them to springs of life-giving water,/ and God will wipe away every tear from their eyes."
The word of the Lord.

Alleluia, alleluia. I am the good shepherd, says the Lord;/ I know my sheep, and mine know me. Alleluia, alleluia.

● *I give my sheep eternal life.* ●

A reading from
the holy Gospel according to John   10:27-30

JESUS SAID: "MY sheep hear my voice; I know them, and they follow me. I give them eternal life, and they shall

never perish. No one can take them out of my hand. My Father, who has given them to me, is greater than all, and no one can take them out of the Father's hand. The Father and I are one."
The Gospel of the Lord.

CREDO ———————————————————— page 214

PRAYER OVER THE OFFERINGS
Grant, we pray, O Lord,
that we may always find delight in these paschal mysteries,
so that the renewal constantly at work within us
may be the cause of our unending joy.
Through Christ our Lord.

PREFACE I-V OF EASTER ————————— pages 218 to 219

COMMUNION ANTIPHON
The Good Shepherd has risen,/ who laid down his life for his sheep/ and willingly died for his flock, alleluia.

PRAYER AFTER COMMUNION
Look upon your flock, kind Shepherd,
and be pleased to settle in eternal pastures
the sheep you have redeemed
by the Precious Blood of your Son.
Who lives and reigns for ever and ever.

A formula of Solemn Blessing, pages 78-79, may be used.

MEDITATION OF THE DAY

Hearing the Voice of the Good Shepherd

The shepherd is everything to his flock; their life, their sustenance, and their care is entirely in his hands, and if the shepherd is good, they will have nothing to fear under his protection, and they will want for nothing.

Jesus is preeminently the Good Shepherd: He not only loves, feeds, and guards his sheep, but he also gives them life at the cost of his own. In the mystery of the Incarnation, the Son of God comes to earth in search of men who, like stray sheep, have wandered away from the sheepfold and have become lost in the dark valley of sin. He comes as a most loving Shepherd who, in order to take better care of his flock, is not afraid to share their lot....

What could be a better synthesis of the whole work of the Redemption? It seems still more wonderful when we hear Jesus declare: *I am come that they may have life and may have it more abundantly* (Jn 10:10). In truth, he could well repeat to each one of us: *What more could I have done for you that I have not done?* (cf. Is 5:4). Oh, would that our generosity in giving ourselves to him had no limits, after the pattern of his own liberality in giving himself to us!

Again Jesus said: *I know mine, and mine know me, even as the Father knows me and I know the Father* (Jn 10:14-15). Although there is no question here of equality, but merely that of a simple comparison, it is nevertheless very consoling and glorious for us to see how Jesus likes to compare his relations with us to those he has with his Father. At the Last Supper also, he said: *As the Father hath loved me, I also have loved you,* and again: *as thou, Father, in me, and I in thee; that they also may be one in us* (Jn 15:9, 17:21). This shows that between us, the sheep, and Jesus, our Shepherd, there is not only a relation of acquaintance, but also one of love, and better, still, of a communion of life, similar to that which exists between the Son and the Father.

FATHER GABRIEL OF SAINT MARY MAGDALEN, O.C.D.

Father Gabriel of Saint Mary Magdalen († 1952) was a Belgian Carmelite priest, teacher, and spiritual director.

Prayer for the Evening

Come, let us worship the Lord our God, alleluia!

*Glory to the Father, and to the Son,
and to the Holy Spirit, as it was in the beginning,
is now, and will be for ever. Amen. Alleluia!*

HYMN   Meter: 77 77 D
This hymn can be sung to the tune used for
Come, Ye Thankful People, Come

Loving Shepherd of your sheep,
Keep us, Lord, in safety keep;
Nothing can your pow'r withstand,
None can pluck us from your hand.
Loving Shepherd, you did give
Your own life that we might live;
May we love you day by day,
Gladly all your will obey.

Loving Shepherd, ever near,
Teach us still your voice to hear;
Suffer not our step to stray
From the straight and narrow way.
Where you lead us we would go,
Walking in your steps below,
Till before your Father's throne
We shall know as we are known.

PSALM 80   2-4, 18-20

He is our God/ and we the people who belong to his pasture,/ the
flock that is led by his hand. (Ps 95:7)

Jesus Christ is the One whom God has chosen to shepherd his
people to salvation. All other shepherds serve in his name.

O shepherd of Israel, hear us,
you who lead Joseph's flock,

shine forth from your cherubim throne
upon Ephraim, Benjamin, Manasseh.
O Lord, rouse up your might,
O Lord, come to our help.

God of hosts, bring us back;
let your face shine on us and we shall be saved.

May your hand be on the man you have chosen,
the man you have given your strength.
And we shall never forsake you again:
give us life that we may call upon your name.

God of hosts, bring us back;
let your face shine on us and we shall be saved.

Glory to the Father....

Word of God
Jeremiah 31:10

HEAR THE WORD of the LORD, O nations,/ proclaim it on distant coasts, and say:/ He who scattered Israel, now gathers them together,/ he guards them as a shepherd his flock.

He is the Shepherd, the Rock of Israel!
(cf. Gn 49:24)

CANTICLE OF MARY
(Text, back cover A)

Tell me, you whom my heart loves,/ where you pasture your flock,/ where you give them rest,/ Lest I be found wandering/ after the flocks of your companions. (cf. Song 1:7)

INTERCESSIONS

Through the intercession of the Blessed Virgin Mary, Mother of the Church, let us pray:

℟   Shepherd your flock, O Lord.

For all who do not believe in God,
– that they may find their way into the Good
Shepherd's fold: ℟

For all who do not trust in Christ,
– that they may discover the Good Shepherd's love: ℟

For all who are mistrustful of sheepfolds,
– that they may find a welcome in the Good Shepherd's
flock: ℟

For all who have died,
– that they may be led into the presence of their
Shepherd in joy: ℟

Personal intentions

Our Father....

*May mercy, peace, and love be ours in abundance.
Amen. (cf. Jude 2)*

MARIAN ANTIPHON (page 12 or 13)

Is That in the Bible?

A Divine Menu

———————— Father Anthony Giambrone, o.p. ————————

Jewish dietary law is more curious than people imagine, and keeping kosher means more than avoiding honey baked ham. Rock badger bacon, camel jerky, pelican stew, shark steaks, blood pudding, chocolate-covered caterpillars, frog legs, lobsters, *lapin à la moutarde*, and cheeseburgers are just some of the gastronomic oddities and culinary delights denied to observant Jews. While a smorgasbord of specific foods to be thrown out of Israel's kitchen appears in several places in the Pentateuch, Christians have been freed from these biblical laws of non-consumption, as we read in Acts 11 (see also Mark 7:1-23 and Acts 10:12-15). The question thus arises: What is a chapter like Leviticus 11, and its tangled list of dietary taboos, doing in our Bibles?

We will look in vain for one, tidy historical or practical rationale, for neither an association with pagan cults, nor natural repugnance, nor specific hygienic risks, can explain all the various forbidden food groups. Limiting our main course to herbivores that stick within the proper domain— i.e., walking on land or swimming in water—helps predict that birds of prey, snakes, and shellfish are all unclean, for instance. But exceptions like ducks (an omnivorous, winged water creature deemed clean) always spoil the logic. Or perhaps canard is just God's concession to French cuisine. Whatever the case, the challenge faced when considering these dietary laws helps account for the ancient appeal of allegorical explanations—animals that chew the cud are clean, for instance, since they remind us of meditating (that is, chewing) on God's Law.

Yet, on a more general level, one easily sees that the regulation of eating habits has a didactic, moral purpose: it fosters self-control and creates public witness; it reinforces election, separating Jews from the surrounding pagan nations; above all, it displays God's dominion over living things and in every detail of daily life, something fallen man should be conscious of at every waking moment.

In fact, food laws mark every stage of salvation history. In the beginning, the Lord gave Adam and Eve a vegetarian diet, including a command of what not to eat. After the Flood, God granted permission to consume flesh, but not blood. The Mosaic Law slowly shepherds the chosen people back toward the original fare, working to tame and sanctify man's lust for flesh, the bloody effort to nourish life by causing death.

In the New Covenant, however, a new law is given—*slaughter and eat*, yes, but more importantly, *Take this, all of you, and eat of it. Take this, all of you, and drink from it.* Consumption of Christ's Body and Blood alone satisfies us, pacifies justice, calms the hunger for violence, and slakes humanity's thirst for unending life. It is a small but beautiful sign of the cosmic concord, the eschatological pact of peace that Jesus' death reestablishes, that on Fridays, in honor of his cross, Catholics have traditionally abstained from feeding on flesh. In truth, every time we follow Christ's command—*do this in memory of me*—we enter paradise and approach the Tree of Life.

Father Anthony Giambrone, O.P., is a Dominican priest of the Province of Saint Joseph and professor of the New Testament at the École biblique de Jérusalem.

MONDAY, MAY 13
Our Lady of Fatima

Prayer for the Morning

Let us sing to the Lord all our life, alleluia!

Glory to the Father, and to the Son,
and to the Holy Spirit, as it was in the beginning,
is now, and will be for ever. Amen. Alleluia!

HYMN   Meter: 76 76 D
This hymn can be sung to the tune used for
Good King Wenceslaus

Come, ye faithful, raise the strain
Of triumphant gladness!
God has brought his Israel
Into joy from sadness;
Loosed from Pharaoh's bitter yoke
Jacob's sons and daughters;
Led them with unmoistened foot
Through the Red Sea waters.

'Tis the spring of souls today;
Christ has burst his prison,
And from three days' sleep in death
As a sun has risen:
All the winter of our sins,
Long and dark, is flying
From his light, to whom we give
Laud and praise undying.

PSALM 77   14-21

Who shut within doors the sea,/ when it burst forth from the womb?
(Jb 38:8)

Life could not exist in the primal waters of chaos. By his passage through the tomb, Christ has tamed the waters of death and transformed them into the waters of life, from which a new world is reborn in baptism. Our Good Shepherd leads us to these waters to drink our fill of his peace.

Your ways, O God, are holy.
What god is great as our God?
You are the God who works wonders.
You showed your power among the peoples.
Your strong arm redeemed your people,
the sons of Jacob and Joseph.

The waters saw you, O God,
the waters saw you and trembled;
the depths were moved with terror.
The clouds poured down rain,
the skies sent forth their voice;
your arrows flashed to and fro.

Your thunder rolled round the sky,
your flashes lighted up the world.
The earth was moved and trembled
when your way led through the sea,
your path through the mighty waters
and no one saw your footprints.

You guided your people like a flock
by the hand of Moses and Aaron.

Glory to the Father....

Word of God Mark 4:35-41

On that day, as evening drew on, he said to them, "Let us cross to the other side." Leaving the crowd, they took him with them in the boat just as he was. And other boats were with him. A violent squall came up and waves were breaking over the boat, so that it was already filling up. Jesus was in the stern, asleep on a cushion. They woke him and said to him, "Teacher, do you not care that we are perishing?" He woke up, rebuked the wind, and said to the sea, "Quiet! Be still!" The wind ceased and there was great calm. Then he asked them, "Why are you terrified? Do you not yet have faith?" They were filled with great awe and said to one another, "Who then is this whom even wind and sea obey?"

The waters swirled about me, threatening my life;/
the abyss enveloped me. (Jon 2:6)

CANTICLE OF ZECHARIAH (Text, back cover B)

From on high he reached down and seized me;/ he drew me forth from the mighty waters. (Ps 18:17)

INTERCESSIONS

With faith in the God who gives life, we pray:

℟   Draw us to yourself!

You are Lord of wind and sea:
– stretch out your saving hand to those who are drowning in confusion and sin. ℟

You set limits that the waters might not pass:
– protect all those who are overwhelmed by the chaos of lives driven by need. ℟

You water the earth and bring forth food:
– teach us to use the tools devoted to works of death to give and protect life. ℟

Personal intentions

Our Father....

Lord God of earth and sea, yours is the dry land and yours the water. Protect us from the fear of death; draw us out of the ways of danger; and bring us to new life, through Jesus Christ our Lord. Amen.

MASS

Monday of the Fourth Week of Easter

ENTRANCE ANTIPHON Rom 6:9

Christ, having risen from the dead, dies now no more;/ death will no longer have dominion over him, alleluia.

COLLECT

    O God, perfect light of the blessed,

    by whose gift we celebrate the paschal mysteries on earth,

    bring us, we pray,

    to rejoice in the full measure of your grace

    for ages unending.

    Through our Lord Jesus Christ, your Son,

    who lives and reigns with you in the unity

       of the Holy Spirit,

    one God, for ever and ever.

   • *God has then granted life-giving repentance to the Gentiles too.* •

A reading from
the Acts of the Apostles

11:1-18

THE APOSTLES and the brothers who were in Judea heard that the Gentiles too had accepted the word of God. So when Peter went up to Jerusalem the circumcised believers confronted him, saying, "You entered the house of uncircumcised people and ate with them." Peter began and explained it to them step by step, saying, "I was at prayer in the city of Joppa when

in a trance I had a vision, something resembling a large sheet coming down, lowered from the sky by its four corners, and it came to me. Looking intently into it, I observed and saw the four-legged animals of the earth, the wild beasts, the reptiles, and the birds of the sky. I also heard a voice say to me, 'Get up, Peter. Slaughter and eat.' But I said, 'Certainly not, sir, because nothing profane or unclean has ever entered my mouth.' But a second time a voice from heaven answered, 'What God has made clean, you are not to call profane.' This happened three times, and then everything was drawn up again into the sky. Just then three men appeared at the house where we were, who had been sent to me from Caesarea. The Spirit told me to accompany them without discriminating. These six brothers also went with me, and we entered the man's house. He related to us how he had seen the angel standing in his house, saying, 'Send someone to Joppa and summon Simon, who is called Peter, who will speak words to you by which you and all your household will be saved.' As I began to speak, the Holy Spirit fell upon them as it had upon us at the beginning, and I remembered the word of the Lord, how he had said, 'John baptized with water but you will be baptized with the Holy Spirit.' If then God gave them the same gift he gave to us when we came to believe in the Lord Jesus Christ, who was I to be able to hinder God?" When they heard this, they stopped objecting and glorified God, saying, "God has then granted life-giving repentance to the Gentiles too."
The word of the Lord.

———• Psalms 42; 43 •———

℟ (see 3a) **Athirst is my soul for the living God.**

Or: **Alleluia.**

As the hind longs for the running waters,
  so my soul longs for you, O God.
Athirst is my soul for God, the living God.
  When shall I go and behold the face of God? ℟

Send forth your light and your fidelity;
  they shall lead me on
And bring me to your holy mountain,
  to your dwelling-place. ℟

Then will I go in to the altar of God,
  the God of my gladness and joy;
Then will I give you thanks upon the harp,
  O God, my God! ℟

Alleluia, alleluia. I am the good shepherd, says the Lord;/
I know my sheep, and mine know me. Alleluia, alleluia.

● *I am the gate for the sheep.* ●

A reading from
the holy Gospel according to John   10:1-10

JESUS SAID: "AMEN, amen, I say to you, whoever does not enter a sheepfold through the gate but climbs over elsewhere is a thief and a robber. But whoever enters through the gate is the shepherd of the sheep. The gatekeeper opens it for him, and the sheep hear his voice, as he calls his own sheep by name and leads them out. When he has driven out all his own, he walks ahead of them, and the sheep follow him, because they recognize his voice. But they will not follow a stranger; they will run away from him, because they do not realize the voice of strangers." Although Jesus used this figure of speech, they did not realize what he was trying to tell them.

So Jesus said again, "Amen, amen, I say to you, I am the gate for the sheep. All who came before me are

thieves and robbers, but the sheep did not listen to them. I am the gate. Whoever enters through me will be saved, and will come in and go out and find pasture. A thief comes only to steal and slaughter and destroy; I came so that they might have life and have it more abundantly."
The Gospel of the Lord.

PRAYER OVER THE OFFERINGS
Receive, O Lord, we pray,
these offerings of your exultant Church,
and, as you have given her cause for such great gladness,
grant also that the gifts we bring
may bear fruit in perpetual happiness.
Through Christ our Lord.

PREFACE I-V OF EASTER ———————— pages 218 to 219

COMMUNION ANTIPHON Jn 20:19
Jesus stood in the midst of his disciples/ and said to them: Peace be with you, alleluia.

PRAYER AFTER COMMUNION
Look with kindness upon your people, O Lord,
and grant, we pray,
that those you were pleased to renew by eternal
    mysteries
may attain in their flesh
the incorruptible glory of the resurrection.
Through Christ our Lord.

OUR LADY OF FATIMA *Optional memorial*

● *This feast commemorates the first of six appearances of the Blessed Virgin Mary to three Portuguese shepherd children in 1917. Mary exhorted them: "Pray, pray very much. Make sacrifices for sinners. Many souls go to hell, because no one is willing to help them with sacrifice." On her third appearance, she showed the children a vision of the state of eternal pain and despair, and she asked that Russia be consecrated to her Immaculate Heart. "In the end, my Immaculate Heart will triumph," she reassured the children. On October 31, 1942, Pope Pius XII consecrated "the whole world torn by bitter strife" to the Immaculate Heart.* ●

ENTRANCE ANTIPHON
Cf. Ps 30 (29):12

You have changed my mourning into dancing, O Lord,/ and have girded me with joy, alleluia.

COLLECT

O God, who chose the Mother of your Son to be
    our Mother also,
grant us that, persevering in penance and prayer
for the salvation of the world,
we may further more effectively each day
    the reign of Christ.
Who lives and reigns with you in the unity
    of the Holy Spirit,
one God, for ever and ever.

PRAYER OVER THE OFFERINGS

Receive, holy Father, this offering of our humility,
which we bring you with joy
as we commemorate the Blessed Virgin Mary,
and grant, we pray, that it may be for us,
who are joined to the sacrifice of Christ,
our consolation on earth and our eternal salvation.
Who lives and reigns for ever and ever.

COMMUNION ANTIPHON

Rejoice, O Virgin Mother,/ for Christ has risen from the tomb, alleluia.

PRAYER AFTER COMMUNION

Renewed by this paschal Sacrament,
we pray, O Lord,
that we, who honor the memory of the Mother
    of your Son,
may show forth in our mortal flesh the life of Jesus.
Who lives and reigns for ever and ever.

MEDITATION OF THE DAY

The More Abundant Life that Mary Leads Us To

We all have a desire to preserve our temporal life, which passes with the days, the years, work, joys, sorrows, and suffering. But how little we concern ourselves with eternal life! And yet, this is the only life that is truly decisive and that lasts forever.

When God created human beings, he destined them for eternal life by sharing in his divine life. Hence, *God created man in his own image, in the image of God he created him; male and female he created them* (Gn 1:27), and then went on to explain that *The Lord God formed man of dust from the ground, and breathed into his nostrils the breath of life; and man became a living being* (Gn 2:7). We see here that the human body was taken from the dust of the earth, but human beings received life itself from the very Being of God, from the creative breath of his lips. Hence, our soul is a spiritual being which participates in the life of God and is immortal. When the body becomes totally incapable of co-operating with the action of the soul, the soul leaves it and flies to its center of attraction, which is God.

But our participation in eternal life must be decided between two very different realities: heaven or hell.

In the call to devotion to the Immaculate Heart of Mary, we saw how there are two distinct progenies which are at loggerheads with each other: the progeny of Satan, which leads people into the way of sin, and the progeny of the Immaculate Heart of Mary who, as the Mother of the children of God, leads them in the way of truth, justice and love, since *God is Love*, and all his children are known by the way they love. And…the

children of God climb by the way of love to the possession of eternal happiness in the Kingdom of God.

Servant of God Sister Lucia of Fatima, o.c.d.

Sister Lucia († 2005) was a Carmelite nun and the oldest of the three children to whom Our Lady of Fatima appeared in 1917.

Prayer for the Evening

Give thanks to the Lord for he is good;
for his love endures for ever, alleluia!

Glory to the Father, and to the Son,
and to the Holy Spirit, as it was in the beginning,
is now, and will be for ever. Amen. Alleluia!

Hymn

Meter: 77 77 with alleluias
This hymn can be sung to the tune used for
Jesus Christ Is Risen Today

Vain the stone, the watch, the seal; alleluia!
Christ has burst the gates of hell; alleluia!
Death in vain forbids his rise; alleluia!
Christ has opened Paradise; alleluia!

Lives again our glorious King; alleluia!
Where, O death, is now thy sting? Alleluia!
Dying once, he all doth save; alleluia!
Where thy victory, O grave? Alleluia!

Soar we now where Christ has led; alleluia!
Following our exalted Head; alleluia!
Made like him, like him we rise; alleluia!
Ours the cross, the grave, the skies; alleluia!

Psalm 107

1-3, 10-16

He has sent me to proclaim liberty to captives,/ to let the oppressed
go free. (cf. Lk 4:18)

Christ, the Good Shepherd, leads us into the sheepfold, not to imprison us within walls of law but to set us free from captivity to the fear of all those predators, seen and unseen, who threaten us with the distress, darkness, and gloom of which the Psalmist speaks.

"O give thanks to the Lord for he is good;
for his love endures for ever."

Let them say this, the Lord's redeemed,
whom he redeemed from the hand of the foe
and gathered from far-off lands,
from east and west, north and south.

Some lay in darkness and in gloom,
prisoners in misery and chains,
having defied the words of God
and spurned the counsels of the Most High.
He crushed their spirit with toil;
they stumbled; there was no one to help.

Then they cried to the Lord in their need
and he rescued them from their distress.
He led them forth from darkness and gloom
and broke their chains to pieces.

Let them thank the Lord for his goodness,
for the wonders he does for men:
for he bursts the gates of bronze
and shatters the iron bars.

Glory to the Father....

Word of God   Romans 6:20-23

WHEN YOU WERE slaves of sin, you were free from righteousness. But what profit did you get then from the things of which you are now ashamed? For the end of those things is death. But now that you have been freed from sin and have become slaves of God, the benefit that you have leads to sanctification, and its end is eternal life. For the wages of sin is death, but the gift of God is eternal life in Christ Jesus our Lord.

Where the Spirit of the Lord is, there is freedom.
(2 Cor 3:17)

CANTICLE OF MARY   (Text, back cover A)

He has sent me to proclaim liberty to the captives/ and release to the prisoners. (cf. Is 61:1)

INTERCESSIONS

For freedom Christ set us free (Gal 5:1). In grateful trust, let us pray to him:

℟   We cry to you, O Lord, in our need.

For those who are in prison,
– that they may learn the way to true freedom. ℟

For those who are entrapped in addiction,
– that they may find the road to recovery. ℟

For those who live in defiance of your word,
– that they may discover the freedom of the Gospel. ℟

For those who have been sent to minister in your name to all who are captive in body or spirit,
– that they may be rewarded. ℟

Personal intentions

Our Father....

To the one who is able to keep us from stumbling and to present us unblemished and exultant, in the presence of his glory, to the only God, our savior, through Jesus Christ our Lord be glory, majesty, power, and authority from ages past, now, and for ages to come. Amen.
(cf. Jude 24-25)

MARIAN ANTIPHON   (page 12 or 13)

Saint Who?

Saints Who Were Visionaries

Saint Catherine de' Ricci
Virgin († 1590)   Feast: February 2

The daughter of a respected Florentine family, Catherine entered the Dominican convent at Prato at thirteen. For the first two years she had an illness that challenged the doctors. She learned to unite her sufferings to those of Christ.

When she was twenty, extraordinary graces were showered upon Catherine. For the next twelve years, she mystically participated in Christ's Passion every Friday. She received the stigmata, the wounds of Christ manifested in her own body. Christ united himself to her in a mystical marriage, complete with a wedding ring. Saint Philip Neri reported that she appeared to him while being at the same time in her convent, a phenomenon known as bilocation.

Catherine's mystical experiences in no way prevented her from leading the other nuns as prioress. She wrote at least a thousand letters of advice to persons of low estate as well as bishops and popes. She showered attention on the poor, and even brought daily snacks to the girls in the convent school.

Catherine died in 1590 at the age of sixty-eight. Her counsel: "Gather up all your worries and make a bundle of them and throw them all into those most holy wounds of Jesus Christ. You could not put them anywhere better than in Jesus and his most holy Mother. They are the ones who are perfectly capable of consoling and calming the human heart."

Compassionate Father, through the intercession of Saint Catherine de' Ricci, console my anxious heart.

TUESDAY, MAY 14
Saint Matthias
Prayer for the Morning

God's majesty is praised above the heavens:
in the faith of the Apostles, come, let us worship,
alleluia!

Glory to the Father, and to the Son,
and to the Holy Spirit, as it was in the beginning,
is now, and will be for ever. Amen. Alleluia!

Hymn   Meter: LM
This hymn can be sung to the tune used for
Creator of the Stars of Night

What wisdom and what wondrous love
Lay hidden in God's plan above,
That you, Matthias, should find place
Among the Twelve, and share their grace.

With dedicated strength and zeal
Christ's light to men you would reveal,
A martyr's glory, too, you claim
By dying for our Savior's Name.

Give us your energy and zest
To do for God our very best,
To follow where the Spirit leads,
Apostles by our words and deeds.

Psalm 19   2-7

With great power the apostles bore witness to the resurrection of
the Lord Jesus, and great favor was accorded them all. (Acts 4:33)

Matthias was chosen to join the apostolic band because he had been
a witness to the Resurrection of Jesus, and so could bear witness to
the utmost bounds of the world.

The heavens proclaim the glory of God
and the firmament shows forth the work of his hands.
Day unto day takes up the story
and night unto night makes known the message.

No speech, no word, no voice is heard
yet their span extends through all the earth,
their words to the utmost bounds of the world.

There he has placed a tent for the sun;
it comes forth like a bridegroom coming from his tent,
rejoices like a champion to run its course.

At the end of the sky is the rising of the sun;
to the furthest end of the sky is its course.
There is nothing concealed from its burning heat.

Glory to the Father....

Word of God   Acts 10:40-42

This man [Jesus] God raised [on] the third day and granted that he be visible, not to all the people, but to us, the witnesses chosen by God in advance, who ate and drank with him after he rose from the dead. He commissioned us to preach to the people and testify that he is the one appointed by God as judge of the living and the dead.

> *Many signs and wonders were done among*
> *the people at the hands of the apostles.*
> *(Acts 5:12)*

CANTICLE OF ZECHARIAH   (Text, back cover B)

I heard the voice of the Lord saying, "Whom shall I send? Who will go for us?" "Here I am," I said; "send me!" (Is 6:8)

INTERCESSIONS

Through the intercession of Saint Matthias, let us pray:

℟   Pour out your Spirit, O Lord, and make your
Church holy, as you are holy.

You chose Matthias, the faithful, to take the place of
Judas, the betrayer:
– make us faithful, O Lord. ℟

You sent your Apostles out to preach your word to the
ends of the earth:
– teach us to live the Gospel in our everyday world. ℟

You called your Apostles to follow you through death
to glory:
– inspire us to love the cross. ℟

Personal intentions

Our Father….

Pour forth upon your Church, O Lord, the gift of your
Holy Spirit, that our love for one another and for your
Word may set fire to our world as the Apostles set fire
to theirs, through Christ our Lord. Amen.

MASS

Feast of Saint Matthias

*Chosen by God to join the ranks of the Apostles after Judas'
betrayal and death, Matthias was present in the Upper Room
at Pentecost, when the Holy Spirit came down as tongues of fire.
He is said to have preached first in Judea. According to Greek
menologies, collections of the lives of the saints in the Eastern
Church, Matthias brought the Gospel to Cappadocia (present-
day Turkey) and the coasts of the Caspian Sea. Ethiopia also
claims his apostolic preaching. Matthias is often pictured with an
ax, which suggests that he was beheaded.*

ENTRANCE ANTIPHON   Jn 15:16
It was not you who chose me, says the Lord,/ but I who chose
you and appointed you to go and bear fruit,/ fruit that will
last, alleluia.

GLORIA ───────────────────────────── page 212

COLLECT
>   O God, who assigned Saint Matthias
>   a place in the college of Apostles,
>   grant us, through his intercession,
>   that, rejoicing at how your love has been allotted to us,
>   we may merit to be numbered among the elect.
>   Through our Lord Jesus Christ, your Son,
>   who lives and reigns with you in the unity
>   of the Holy Spirit,
>   one God, for ever and ever.

>   ● *The lot fell upon Matthias, and he was counted with*
>   *the Eleven Apostles.* ●

A reading from
the Acts of the Apostles   1:15-17, 20-26

PETER STOOD UP in the midst
of the brothers and sisters
(there was a group of about one hundred and twenty
persons in the one place). He said, "My brothers and
sisters, the Scripture had to be fulfilled which the Holy
Spirit spoke beforehand through the mouth of David,
concerning Judas, who was the guide for those who ar-
rested Jesus. Judas was numbered among us and was
allotted a share in this ministry. For it is written in the
Book of Psalms:
>   *Let his encampment become desolate,/ and may no*
>   *one dwell in it.*
and:
>   *May another take his office.*

Therefore, it is necessary that one of the men who accompanied us the whole time the Lord Jesus came and went among us, beginning from the baptism of John until the day on which he was taken up from us, become with us a witness to his resurrection." So they proposed two, Joseph called Barsabbas, who was also known as Justus, and Matthias. Then they prayed, "You, Lord, who know the hearts of all, show which one of these two you have chosen to take the place in this apostolic ministry from which Judas turned away to go to his own place." Then they gave lots to them, and the lot fell upon Matthias, and he was counted with the Eleven Apostles. The word of the Lord.

———• PSALM 113 •———

℟ (8) The Lord will give him a seat with the leaders of his people.

Or: Alleluia.

Praise, you servants of the LORD,
  praise the name of the LORD.
Blessed be the name of the LORD
  both now and forever. ℟

From the rising to the setting of the sun
  is the name of the LORD to be praised.
High above all nations is the LORD;
  above the heavens is his glory. ℟

Who is like the LORD, our God, who is enthroned
    on high
  and looks upon the heavens and the earth below? ℟

He raises up the lowly from the dust;
  from the dunghill he lifts up the poor

To seat them with princes,
    with the princes of his own people. ℟

Alleluia, alleluia. I chose you from the world,/ to go and
bear fruit that will last, says the Lord. Alleluia, alleluia.

• *It was not you who chose me, but I who chose you.* •

A reading from
the holy Gospel according to John   15:9-17

Jesus said to his disciples:
"As the Father loves me, so
I also love you. Remain in my love. If you keep my commandments, you will remain in my love, just as I have
kept my Father's commandments and remain in his
love.

"I have told you this so that my joy might be in you
and your joy might be complete. This is my commandment: love one another as I love you. No one has greater love than this, to lay down one's life for one's friends.
You are my friends if you do what I command you. I no
longer call you slaves, because a slave does not know
what his master is doing. I have called you friends, because I have told you everything I have heard from my
Father. It was not you who chose me, but I who chose
you and appointed you to go and bear fruit that will remain, so that whatever you ask the Father in my name he
may give you. This I command you: love one another."
The Gospel of the Lord.

Prayer over the Offerings
    Receive, O Lord, the offerings of your Church,
    reverently presented for the Feast of Saint Matthias,
    and through them strengthen us by the power
        of your grace.
    Through Christ our Lord.

Preface I or II of the Apostles————————— page 51

Communion Antiphon Jn 15:12
This is my commandment: Love one another/ as I love you,
says the Lord, alleluia.

Prayer after Communion
Never cease, O Lord, we pray,
to fill your family with divine gifts,
and, through blessed Matthias' intercession for us,
graciously admit us to a share in the lot of the Saints
in light.
Through Christ our Lord.

A formula of Solemn Blessing (p. 52) may be used.

MEDITATION OF THE DAY

Remaining in Christ's Love with Matthias

When we think of the negative role Judas played, we must consider it according to the lofty ways in which God leads events. His betrayal led to the death of Jesus, who transformed this tremendous torment into a space of salvific love by consigning himself to the Father.

The word "to betray" is the version of a Greek word that means "to consign." Sometimes the subject is even God in person: It was he who for love "consigned" Jesus for all of us. In his mysterious salvific plan, God assumes Judas' inexcusable gesture as the occasion for the total gift of the Son for the redemption of the world.

[And] we want to remember him who, after Easter, was elected in place of the betrayer. In the Church of Jerusalem two were proposed to the community, and then lots were cast for their names: *Joseph Barsabbas, who was surnamed Justus, and Matthias.*

Precisely the latter was chosen, hence, *he was enrolled with the eleven Apostles*. We know nothing else about him, if not that he had been a witness to all Jesus' earthly events, remaining faithful to him to the end. To the greatness of his fidelity was later added the divine call to take the place of Judas, almost compensating for his betrayal.

We draw from this a final lesson: While there is no lack of unworthy and traitorous Christians in the Church, it is up to each of us to counterbalance the evil done by them with our clear witness to Jesus Christ, our Lord and Savior.

POPE BENEDICT XVI

His Holiness Benedict XVI reigned as pope from 2005 to 2013.

Prayer for the Evening

The glorious Apostles sing God's praise:
come, let us worship, alleluia!

Glory to the Father, and to the Son,
and to the Holy Spirit, as it was in the beginning,
is now, and will be for ever. Amen. Alleluia!

HYMN   Meter: LM
This hymn can be sung to the tune used for
On Jordan's Bank

Let all on earth their voices raise,
Resounding heaven's joyful praise
To God who gave th'Apostles grace
To run on earth their glorious race.

Lord, in whose might they spoke the word
Which cured disease and health restored,

To us its healing power prolong,
Support the weak, confirm the strong.

And when the thrones are set on high,
And judgment's awesome hour draws nigh,
Then, Lord, with them pronounce us blest,
And take us to your endless rest.

CANTICLE   Ephesians 1:3-10

He gave some as apostles, others as prophets, others as evangelists, others as pastors and teachers. (Eph 4:11)

Through the faith and fidelity of the Apostles, even of those appointed "out of season," like Matthias, God has bestowed on all of us every spiritual blessing.

Praised be the God and Father
of our Lord Jesus Christ,
who has bestowed on us in Christ
every spiritual blessing in the heavens.

God chose us in him
before the world began
to be holy
and blameless in his sight.

He predestined us
to be his adopted sons through Jesus Christ,
such was his will and pleasure,
that all might praise the glorious favor
he has bestowed on us in his beloved.

In him and through his blood, we have been redeemed,
and our sins forgiven,
so immeasurably generous
is God's favor to us.

God has given us the wisdom
to understand fully the mystery,
the plan he was pleased
to decree in Christ.

A plan to be carried out
in Christ, in the fullness of time,
to bring all things into one in him,
in the heavens and on earth.

Word of God Ephesians 1:11-12

I N [CHRIST] WE WERE also chosen, destined in accord with the purpose of the One who accomplishes all things according to the intention of his will, so that we might exist for the praise of his glory, we who first hoped in Christ.

Since we have gifts that differ according to the grace given to us, let us exercise them.
(Rom 12:6)

CANTICLE OF MARY (Text, back cover A)

Beloved, remember the words spoken beforehand by the apostles of our Lord Jesus Christ. (Jude 17)

INTERCESSIONS

As we remember and give thanks for the gift of apostolic faith and preaching, let us pray:

℟ Give us wisdom, O God of light and truth.

You chose to keep us in the light of faith through the message of your Apostles:
– may the light of faith burn steadily in our minds and hearts. ℟

You chose to feed us with the Bread of life through the ministry of the Apostles:
– may your Word be food for our journey to you. ℟

You chose to entrust to us the promise of salvation through the work of your Apostles:
– may your promise be fulfilled in the resurrection of the dead. ℟

Personal intentions

Our Father....

May the LORD, our God, be with us as he was with our fathers and may he not forsake us nor cast us off. Amen.
(1 Kgs 8:57)

MARIAN ANTIPHON   (page 12 or 13)

WEDNESDAY, MAY 15
Saint Isidore

Prayer for the Morning

Glorious is God's name over all the earth:
come, let us sing praise, alleluia!

Glory to the Father, and to the Son,
and to the Holy Spirit, as it was in the beginning,
is now, and will be for ever. Amen. Alleluia!

HYMN
Meter: 87 87 D
This hymn can be sung to the tune used for
Joyful, Joyful, We Adore Thee

Word of God! your crucifixion
Has upraised me from the earth;
By your death and dereliction,
You have giv'n me nobler birth,
By your resurrection glorious,
Life immortal now I own:
Hence ascend my songs victorious
To your praise, O Christ the Son.

By your hand at the creation,
You did form me from the ground,
And, to mark my kingly station,
With your image I was crowned;
And that hand, when pierced and bleeding,
Raised me from corruption's mire;
And, though all this love unheeding,
Decked me with divine attire.

You who gave my soul its being,
Breathing in me life divine,
Did, by your all-wise decreeing,
Unto death your life resign;

And from death my soul defending,
You did sojourn with the dead,
That you might, my fetters rending,
Raise me up, O glorious Head!

PSALM 8

When God created man, he made him in the likeness of God. (Gn 5:1)

We have reason for praise: we are God's children, made in his image. When we were defaced by our sin, God renewed in us that image through the Incarnation, Death, and Resurrection of Jesus Christ, the light of the world. By his light, we see ourselves as we are and as we are intended to be. Our challenge is to grow toward the true humanity we see in him.

How great is your name, O Lord our God,
through all the earth!

Your majesty is praised above the heavens;
on the lips of children and of babes
you have found praise to foil your enemy,
to silence the foe and the rebel.

When I see the heavens, the work of your hands,
the moon and the stars which you arranged,
what is man that you should keep him in mind,
mortal man that you care for him?

Yet you have made him little less than a god;
with glory and honor you crowned him,
gave him power over the works of your hand,
put all things under his feet.

All of them, sheep and cattle,
yes, even the savage beasts,
birds of the air, and fish
that make their way through the waters.

How great is your name, O Lord our God,
through all the earth!

Glory to the Father....

Word of God

Genesis 1:27-28, 31a

G OD CREATED MAN in his image;/ in the divine image he created him;/ male and female he created them./ God blessed them, saying to them: "Be fertile and multiply; fill the earth and subdue it. Have dominion over the fish of the sea, the birds of the air, and all the living things that move on the earth." God looked at everything he had made, and he found it very good.

You have put on the new self, which is being renewed, for knowledge, in the image of its creator. (cf. Col 3:10)

CANTICLE OF ZECHARIAH (Text, back cover B)

All of us, gazing with unveiled face on the glory of the Lord, are being transformed into the same image from glory to glory, as from the Lord who is the Spirit. (2 Cor 3:18)

INTERCESSIONS

Let us praise the God whose mystery fills the universe with wonder:

℟ Hear your children's plea!

You made all human beings in your image:
– fill us with reverence for one another. ℟

You restored us in your image through the work of the cross:
– teach us to work to restore the dignity of all those degraded by works of evil. ℟

You raise us to newness of life in Jesus Christ:
– fill us always with Easter joy. ℟

Personal intentions

Our Father....

O God, you are over all, in all, beyond all. Open our
eyes to see the wonders that surround us; open our
hearts to know the wonders of our brothers and sisters;
open our lips to sing your praise. Restore all peoples in
your image, who is Jesus Christ, your Son and our Lord,
who lives and reigns with you in the unity of the Holy
Spirit, one God, for ever and ever. Amen.

MASS

Wednesday of the Fourth Week of Easter

ENTRANCE ANTIPHON   Cf. Ps 18 (17):50; 22 (21):23
I will praise you, Lord, among the nations;/ I will tell of your
name to my kin, alleluia.

COLLECT
O God, life of the faithful,
glory of the humble, blessedness of the just,
listen kindly to the prayers
of those who call on you,
that they who thirst for what you generously promise
may always have their fill of your plenty.
Through our Lord Jesus Christ, your Son,
who lives and reigns with you in the unity
of the Holy Spirit,
one God, for ever and ever.

● *Set apart for me Barnabas and Saul.* ●

A reading from
the Acts of the Apostles   12:24–13:5a

T HE WORD OF God contin-
ued to spread and grow.

After Barnabas and Saul completed their relief mission, they returned to Jerusalem, taking with them John, who is called Mark.

Now there were in the Church at Antioch prophets and teachers: Barnabas, Symeon who was called Niger, Lucius of Cyrene, Manaen who was a close friend of Herod the tetrarch, and Saul. While they were worshiping the Lord and fasting, the Holy Spirit said, "Set apart for me Barnabas and Saul for the work to which I have called them." Then, completing their fasting and prayer, they laid hands on them and sent them off.

So they, sent forth by the Holy Spirit, went down to Seleucia and from there sailed to Cyprus. When they arrived in Salamis, they proclaimed the word of God in the Jewish synagogues.

The word of the Lord.

——• Psalm 67 •——

℟ (4) O God, let all the nations praise you!

Or: Alleluia.

May God have pity on us and bless us;
    may he let his face shine upon us.
So may your way be known upon earth;
    among all nations, your salvation. ℟

May the nations be glad and exult
    because you rule the peoples in equity;
    the nations on the earth you guide. ℟

May the peoples praise you, O God;
    may all the peoples praise you!
May God bless us,
    and may all the ends of the earth fear him! ℟

Alleluia, alleluia. I am the light of the world, says the Lord;/ whoever follows me will have the light of life. Alleluia, alleluia.

● *I came into the world as light.* ●

A reading from
the holy Gospel according to John   12:44-50

JESUS CRIED OUT and said, "Whoever believes in me believes not only in me but also in the one who sent me, and whoever sees me sees the one who sent me. I came into the world as light, so that everyone who believes in me might not remain in darkness. And if anyone hears my words and does not observe them, I do not condemn him, for I did not come to condemn the world but to save the world. Whoever rejects me and does not accept my words has something to judge him: the word that I spoke, it will condemn him on the last day, because I did not speak on my own, but the Father who sent me commanded me what to say and speak. And I know that his commandment is eternal life. So what I say, I say as the Father told me."
The Gospel of the Lord.

PRAYER OVER THE OFFERINGS
    O God, who by the wonderful exchange effected in
        this sacrifice
    have made us partakers of the one supreme Godhead,
    grant, we pray,
    that, as we have come to know your truth,
    we may make it ours by a worthy way of life.
    Through Christ our Lord.

PREFACE I-V OF EASTER ———————— pages 218 to 219

Communion Antiphon Cf. Jn 15:16, 19

I have chosen you from the world, says the Lord,/ and have appointed you to go out and bear fruit,/ fruit that will last, alleluia.

Prayer after Communion

Graciously be present to your people, we pray,
O Lord,
and lead those you have imbued with heavenly mysteries
to pass from former ways to newness of life.
Through Christ our Lord.

Saint Isidore *Optional memorial*

● *Isidore, a peasant day laborer, tilled the soil on the estate of Juan de Vargas outside Madrid. He devoutly served at Mass every day before his daily labors. He and his wife served the poor. Angels were said to accompany him in his work. Shortly after his death in 1130, miracles were attributed to his intercession. In 1615, King Philip III of Spain, in danger of death, had Isidore's relics brought to his bedside. He was miraculously healed, and successfully petitioned for Isidore's formal canonization in 1622. Isidore is the patron saint of laborers, farmers, and several Spanish cities.* ●

Entrance Antiphon Cf. Ps 21 (20):2-3

In your strength, O Lord, the just one rejoices;/ how greatly your salvation makes him glad!/ You have granted him his soul's desire, alleluia.

Collect

Lord God, to whom belongs all creation,
and who call us to serve you
by caring for the gifts that surround us,
inspire us by the example of Saint Isidore
to share our food with the hungry
and to work for the salvation of all people.
Through our Lord Jesus Christ, your Son,

who lives and reigns with you in the unity
of the Holy Spirit,
one God, for ever and ever.

Prayer over the Offerings

Through the present oblation, O Lord,
which we offer in commemoration of blessed Isidore,
bestow on your faithful, we pray,
the gifts of unity and peace.
Through Christ our Lord.

Communion Antiphon   Cf. Mt 16:24

Whoever wishes to come after me,/ must deny himself, take
up his cross,/ and follow me, says the Lord, alleluia.

Prayer after Communion

May the Sacrament we have received, O Lord,
in commemoration of blessed Isidore,
sanctify our minds and hearts,
that we may merit to be made sharers in
the divine nature.
Through Christ our Lord.

MEDITATION OF THE DAY

Believing and Seeing Jesus

True faith is what may be called colorless, like air or
water, it is but the medium through which the soul
sees Christ; and the soul as little really rests upon it and
contemplates it as the eye can see the air…. As God's
grace elicits our faith, so his holiness stirs our fear, and
his glory kindles our love….

Divine worship is simply contemplating our Maker,
Redeemer, Sanctifier, and Judge…. The Ancients worshiped; they went out of their own selves into the Infinite
Temple which was around them. They saw Christ in the
Gospels, in the creed, in the sacraments and other rites;
in the visible structure and ornaments of his house, in
the altar, and in the cross; and, not content with giving

the service of their eyes, they gave him their voices, their bodies, and their time, gave up their rest by night and their leisure by day, all that could evidence the offering of their hearts to him....

Unwavering, unflagging, not urged by fits and starts, not heralding forth their feelings, but resolutely, simply, perseveringly, day after day, Sunday and weekday, fast day and festival, week by week, season by season, year by year, in youth and in age, through a life, thirty years, forty years, fifty years, in prelude of the everlasting chant before the Throne—so they went on *constant in prayer*, after the pattern of Psalmists and apostles, in the day with David, in the night with Paul and Silas, winter and summer, in heat and in cold, in peace and in danger, in a prison or in a cathedral, in the dark, in the daybreak, at sunrising, in the forenoon, at noon, in the afternoon, at eventide, and on going to rest, still they had Christ before them; his thought in their mind, his emblems in their eye, his name in their mouth, his service in their posture, magnifying him, and calling on all that lives to magnify him, joining with angels in heaven and saints in paradise to bless and praise him for ever and ever.

Blessed John Henry Newman

Blessed John Henry Newman († 1890), a cardinal, established the Oratory in Birmingham, England, and was a preacher of great eloquence.

Prayer for the Evening

The Lord will not abandon his people:
let us give thanks and praise, alleluia!

Glory to the Father, and to the Son,
and to the Holy Spirit, as it was in the beginning,
is now, and will be for ever. Amen. Alleluia!

HYMN   Meter: 67 67 66 66
                                This hymn can be sung to the tune used for
                                        Now Thank We All Our God

Graces in copious stream
From that pure fount are welling,
Where, in our heart of hearts,
Our God has set his dwelling.
His word our lantern is,
His peace our comfort still,
His sweetness all our rest,
Our law, our life, our will.

All praise and thanks to God
The Father now be given,
The Son, and Spirit blest
Who reigns in highest heaven;
Eternal Triune God,
Whom earth and heaven adore;
For thus it was, is now,
And shall be evermore.

PSALM 94   9-15, 22

If anyone hears my words and does not observe them, I do not condemn him, for I did not come to condemn the world but to save the
world. (Jn 12:47)

The God who made us and became one among us in Jesus Christ
hears and sees all the realities of the human heart. He has fashioned
a law for us that will train us for eternal happiness. It is the law of
love. Our life's work is to hear and choose this law of happiness over
the law of sin and death. Thus do we take part in the work of Easter.

Can he who made the ear, not hear?
Can he who formed the eye, not see?
Will he who corrects nations, not punish?
Will he who teaches men, not have knowledge?
The Lord knows the thoughts of men.
He knows they are no more than a breath.

Happy the man whom you teach, O Lord,
whom you train by means of your law:
to him you give peace in evil days
while the pit is being dug for the wicked.

The Lord will not abandon his people
nor forsake those who are his own:
for judgment shall again be just
and all true hearts shall uphold it.
As for me, the Lord will be a stronghold;
my God will be the rock where I take refuge.

Glory to the Father....

Word of God   Romans 7:22–8:2

I TAKE DELIGHT in the law of God, in my inner self, but I see in my members another principle at war with the law of my mind, taking me captive to the law of sin that dwells in my members. Miserable one that I am! Who will deliver me from this mortal body? Thanks be to God through Jesus Christ our Lord. Therefore, I myself, with my mind, serve the law of God but, with my flesh, the law of sin.

Hence, now there is no condemnation for those who are in Christ Jesus. For the law of the spirit of life in Christ Jesus has freed you from the law of sin and death.

God is faithful, and by him you were called to fellowship with his Son, Jesus Christ our Lord. (1 Cor 1:9)

CANTICLE OF MARY   (Text, back cover A)

I know that his commandment is eternal life. So what I say, I say as the Father told me. (Jn 12:50)

INTERCESSIONS

With faith in God, who keeps his promises, let us pray:

℟   Happy those whom you teach, O Lord!

For those who believe all law to be a burden:
– free them by your law of love. ℟

For those who seek salvation in laws other than your own:
– guide them into your way. ℟

For those who have abandoned themselves to the law of sin and death:
– raise them to new life in the Spirit. ℟

Personal intentions

Our Father....

*May the God in whose ways/ our fathers Abraham and Isaac walked,/ The God who has been our shepherd/ from our birth to this day,/ The Angel who has delivered us from all harm,/ bless us and keep us in peace. Amen.
(cf. Gn 48:15-16)*

MARIAN ANTIPHON   (page 12 or 13)

SAINT WHO?

Saints Who Were Visionaries

Saint Fursey
Abbot († c. 648)   Feast: January 16

Fursey was born at Lough Corrib in County Galway, Ireland. It is said that his great-uncle, Saint Brendan the Navigator, baptized him. He became a monk and was ordained a priest.

While still a young man, Fursey received a series of ecstatic visions that gave his preaching special urgency. In one, he beheld angels and demons locked in a struggle for his own soul. In another, he witnessed the blessedness of the just and the torments experienced by those in hell, with special punishments reserved for those who had committed specific sins.

With his brothers, Saints Foillan and Ultan, Fursey journeyed as a "pilgrim for Christ" to East Anglia in England. The king, Sigebert, gave him land for a monastery at Burgh Castle near Great Yarmouth in Suffolk. Eventually, war came to the land, and Fursey moved again, this time to Gaul (France), where he was well received by King Clovis II and his wife, Saint Bathild. He was granted land at Lagny-sur-Marne. Again, Fursey's zeal and devotion attracted a number of followers and he laid the foundations for a monastery.

Fursey died at Mezerolles around the year 648. His visions, communicated through Saint Bede's *Ecclesiastical History*, shaped medieval artistic depictions of heaven and hell. They may have influenced Dante's *Divine Comedy*.

All loving Father, through the intercession of Saint Fursey, free me from diversion and distraction. Help me to remain aware of my eternal destiny.

How the Church
Has Changed the World
Seeds of Life

———————— Anthony Esolen ————————

IN THE DAYS OF THE FATHER OF MICROBIOLOGY, Louis Pasteur (1822–1895), the atheistic view of the world and its organization and history was called "positivism." The positivists had a low ceiling over their heads. They believed in the finite, or rather they denied the Infinite. Such a belief or disbelief was not without some dire consequences, as we will see.

One of the great disputed questions of Pasteur's time was that of "spontaneous generation." If you leave raw meat in the open and wait a day or two, you will see worms crawling on it. Where did they come from? If you expose the juice of crushed grapes to the air, it will ferment. Why? Women in hospitals developed infections after childbirth. What could have infected them?

The positivists said that *inanimate material* in the objects themselves could produce, spontaneously, elementary forms of life. That is, life could come naturally out of non-life. The cause was, they thought, electricity or magnetism or some other generally active force.

Pasteur, wrote his son-in-law, "with his vision of the Infinite, showed himself as religious as [Isaac] Newton." Said the man himself, "Positivism does not take into account the most important of positive notions, the Infinite." We might say that the positivists viewed the world as less wondrous than it is by far, but for Pasteur it was more, always more.

■ Halls of death ■

In those days, the last place you wanted to be, if you were operated on, was a hospital. Since the scientific consensus was that disease was produced from within you, surgeons and nurses took no precautions to ensure that disease did not come from *outside of you*. But Pasteur, with his microscope and his dogged pursuit of truth, believed that the small organisms he saw in a droplet of blood or pus from a sick animal were themselves the cause, and that they came from without. At the most, surgeons thought that some "miasma" in the air was the culprit, so they used to throw open the windows of surgical wards to clear it out once a day.

What we might give to have been present on that summer day in 1881, when a Christian biochemist from Scotland got to meet Pasteur, whose work he had read about and learned from, and who was mocked and attacked in Britain, as Pasteur had often been mocked in France. The man's name was Joseph Lister, and he had come upon the idea that the *hands* of surgeons carried the germs—the word means "seeds"—of disease. At that time, surgeons took pride in how filthy their aprons were. But Lister treated wounds with carbolic acid, and found that infection did not develop. Yet it was a long time before Pasteur and Lister could persuade surgeons to do a couple of simple things: to *clean their hands*, for one. We have no idea how many women, especially, died in those halls of death called hospitals, just because of the stubbornness of people who put custom or ideology before truth.

This was nineteen years *after* Pasteur had proved by the simplest of experiments that "bad air" did not bring forth micro-organisms, presto, out of nothing. He took a beaker with a neck bent at more than 180 degrees, and filled its bowl with liquid. Then he heated the liquid to kill any germs in it, and let it sit. The liquid remained clean, because, even though it was exposed to air, any germs traveling in the air would get stuck along the bend in the glass. But bad ideas die harder than bad germs. There was Joseph Lister, still fighting, and Pasteur, suggesting an experiment on an animal limb that would demonstrate that nothing from *inside* the animal gave rise to infection.

The truth that Pasteur saw would win out, and Joseph Lister, to whom Pasteur himself paid a handsome tribute, would be called the father of modern surgery.

■ COMRADES IN SCIENCE ■

Louis Pasteur had a great capacity for friendship and love, and his friendships were bound up with his passionate pursuit of truth.

Many people know that Pasteur was the man who discovered the cause of rabies, that terrifying scourge of man's best friend, which claimed the lives of many a master or his children. If the disease developed, a horrible death would inevitably ensue. The only thing you could do if you were bitten by a mad dog was to amputate the limb within a few minutes and cauterize the wound. Of course that was impossible for most bites—to the trunk, the neck, the face, the upper leg or arm.

What they don't know is the danger to which Pasteur and his young friends exposed themselves to tear the veil off this disease. Imagine this scene. You have a mad dog, snapping and frothing. Two bold young men wearing leather gloves restrain the dog from behind and force its jaws open, while Louis Pasteur attempts to extract its saliva using a glass tube that he holds *between his teeth*. He was already an old man when he did that—an old man who had recovered from a stroke.

The first person Pasteur treated for bites from a rabid dog was a nine year old boy, Joseph Meister. The night before the final injection, which contained rabies germs that were powerful enough to kill rabbits in his laboratory, Pasteur could not sleep; he had embarked upon a voyage no one had taken before, and if the boy died—the boy whom he had come to love—he would be ruined. But Joseph Meister lived. The second person he treated was an older boy named Jean-Baptiste Jupille, who had heroically saved three small children from a mad dog and taken the mauling himself. You can see his bronze statue to this day in the gardens of the Pasteur Institute, in Paris, as you can find old photographs of Pasteur and Meister, one of them with the boy's arm resting upon the old man's shoulder. Meister became the doorkeeper to the Pasteur Institute.

Without a passionate love of mankind and of his native France, I don't believe that Pasteur would have done half of the things he did. Once there was a cholera outbreak in Egypt, claiming five hundred lives every day. Pasteur, who had gathered around him a group of young men of science, filled with high ideals and bound with the warmest friendship, agreed to send three of them to assist the physicians and to isolate and examine the infected water. He begged them to take every precaution, but soon received the devastating news that one of them had died. I cite this tribute from the *Cincinnati Lancet*: "Without having known Louis Thuillier, we love him; in this death, on the battle field of science, he appears to us, if not with the laurel of the victor, at least with the halo of the man, who passes through his life with a higher thought, to which he sacrifices all else." It is like a message from a different universe; from one wherein men have higher aims than those of lust, avarice, envy, and pride. Pasteur inspired such devotion.

▪ The faith of a peasant ▪

Pasteur kept his counsel in religious matters, but there is no question that he believed in God and walked in the ways of the faith he learned from his country parents. Here is what he had to say about Émile Littré, an elder scientist and, it is true, a positivist (though one who died in the Church after a later-in-life baptism): "Often have I fancied him seated by his wife, as in a picture of early Christian times; he, looking down upon earth, filled with compassion for human suffering; [...] she, by every divine grandeur, uniting in one impulse and in one heart the twofold holiness which forms the aureole of the Man-God, the one proceeding from devotion to humanity, the other emanating from ardent love for the divinity: she a saint in the canonic sense of the word; he a lay saint." The ideal that Pasteur drew of Littré's home was but a mirror of his own.

"Good, like evil," says his biographer, "is infectious." In his last days we find Pasteur reading the life of Saint Vincent de Paul. "He loved this son of poor peasants, proud to own his humble birth before a vainglorious society," who wanted no better than to become a chaplain to men in prison, who made a home for foundlings, and who worked all his life in the broad fields of charity. While Pasteur lay dying, he says, he seemed to see all those who went before him, who kept their firm faith in the life to come.

Louis Pasteur passed away, one hand in the hand of his dear wife, the other holding a crucifix.

Anthony Esolen is professor and writer-in-residence at *Thomas More College in N.H., translator and editor of Dante's* Divine Comedy *(Random House), and author of* The Beauty of the Word: A Running Commentary on the Roman Missal (Magnificat).

THE ORDER OF MASS

Greeting

- In the name of the Father, and of the Son,
  and of the Holy Spirit.
- Amen.
- The grace of our Lord Jesus Christ,
  and the love of God,
  and the communion of the Holy Spirit
  be with you all.

Or:

- Grace to you and peace from God our Father
  and the Lord Jesus Christ.

Or:

- The Lord be with you.
- And with your spirit.

Penitential Act

- Brethren (brothers and sisters), let us acknowledge our sins,
  and so prepare ourselves to celebrate the sacred mysteries.

A brief pause for silence follows.
Then all recite together the formula of general confession:

- I confess to almighty God
  and to you, my brothers and sisters,
  that I have greatly sinned,
  in my thoughts and in my words,
  in what I have done and in what I have failed to do,

And, striking their breast, they say:

through my fault, through my fault,
through my most grievous fault;

Then they continue:

therefore I ask blessed Mary ever-Virgin,
all the Angels and Saints,
and you, my brothers and sisters,
to pray for me to the Lord our God.

The absolution by the Priest follows:

■ May almighty God have mercy on us,
forgive us our sins,
and bring us to everlasting life.

■ Amen.

Or:

■ Brethren (brothers and sisters), let us acknowledge our sins,
and so prepare ourselves to celebrate the sacred mysteries.

A brief pause for silence follows.

■ Have mercy on us, O Lord.
■ For we have sinned against you.
■ Show us, O Lord, your mercy.
■ And grant us your salvation.

The absolution by the Priest follows:

■ May almighty God have mercy on us,
forgive us our sins,
and bring us to everlasting life.

■ Amen.

Or:

■ Brethren (brothers and sisters), let us acknowledge our sins,
and so prepare ourselves to celebrate the sacred mysteries.

A brief pause for silence follows.

*The Priest, or a Deacon or another minister,
then says the following or other invocations with
Kyrie, eleison (Lord, have mercy):*

■ You were sent to heal the contrite of heart:
Lord, have mercy. *Or:* Kyrie, eleison.
■ Lord, have mercy. *Or:* Kyrie, eleison.
■ You came to call sinners:
Christ, have mercy. *Or:* Christe, eleison.
■ Christ, have mercy. *Or:* Christe, eleison.
■ You are seated at the right hand of the Father
to intercede for us:
Lord, have mercy. *Or:* Kyrie, eleison.
■ Lord, have mercy. *Or:* Kyrie, eleison.

The absolution by the Priest follows:

- May almighty God have mercy on us,
  forgive us our sins,
  and bring us to everlasting life.
- Amen.

Kyrie

The Kyrie, eleison (Lord, have mercy) invocations follow, unless they have just occurred in a formula of the Penitential Act.

■ Lord, have mercy.	■ Kyrie, eleison.
■ Lord, have mercy.	■ Kyrie, eleison.
■ Christ, have mercy.	■ Christe, eleison.
■ Christ, have mercy.	■ Christe, eleison.
■ Lord, have mercy.	■ Kyrie, eleison.
■ Lord, have mercy.	■ Kyrie, eleison.

Then, when it is prescribed, this hymn is either sung or said:

Gloria

Glory to God in the highest,
and on earth peace to people of good will.

We praise you,
we bless you,
we adore you,
we glorify you,
we give you thanks for your great glory,
Lord God, heavenly King,
O God, almighty Father.

Lord Jesus Christ, Only Begotten Son,
Lord God, Lamb of God, Son of the Father,
you take away the sins of the world,
    have mercy on us;
you take away the sins of the world,
    receive our prayer;
you are seated at the right hand of the Father,
    have mercy on us.

For you alone are the Holy One,
you alone are the Lord,

you alone are the Most High,
Jesus Christ,
with the Holy Spirit,
in the glory of God the Father. Amen.

Gloria in excelsis Deo
et in terra pax hominibus bonae voluntatis.

Laudamus te,
benedicimus te,
adoramus te,
glorificamus te,
gratias agimus tibi propter magnam gloriam tuam,
Domine Deus, Rex caelestis,
Deus Pater omnipotens.

Domine Fili Unigenite, Iesu Christe,
Domine Deus, Agnus Dei, Filius Patris,
qui tollis peccata mundi, miserere nobis;
qui tollis peccata mundi, suscipe deprecationem nostram.
Qui sedes ad dexteram Patris, miserere nobis.

Quoniam tu solus Sanctus, tu solus Dominus,
     tu solus Altissimus,
Iesu Christe, cum Sancto Spiritu: in gloria Dei Patris. Amen.

Collect

LITURGY OF THE WORD

First Reading

Responsorial Psalm

Second Reading

Alleluia or Gospel Acclamation

Gospel

The Priest, bowing before the altar, says quietly:

Cleanse my heart and my lips, almighty God,
that I may worthily proclaim your holy Gospel.

- The Lord be with you.
- **And with your spirit.**
- A reading from the holy Gospel according to N.
- **Glory to you, O Lord.**

At the end of the Gospel:

- The Gospel of the Lord.
- **Praise to you, Lord Jesus Christ.**

Then the Priest [or the Deacon] kisses the book, saying quietly:

Through the words of the Gospel
may our sins be wiped away.

Homily

Profession of Faith

The Niceno-Constantinopolitan Creed

I believe in one God,
the Father almighty,
maker of heaven and earth,
of all things visible and invisible.

I believe in one Lord Jesus Christ,
the Only Begotten Son of God,
born of the Father before all ages.
God from God, Light from Light,
true God from true God,
begotten, not made, consubstantial with the Father;
through him all things were made.
For us men and for our salvation
he came down from heaven,

At the words that follow,
up to and including and became man, all bow.

and by the Holy Spirit was incarnate
   of the Virgin Mary,
and became man.

For our sake he was crucified under Pontius Pilate,
he suffered death and was buried,
and rose again on the third day

in accordance with the Scriptures.
He ascended into heaven
and is seated at the right hand of the Father.
He will come again in glory
to judge the living and the dead
and his kingdom will have no end.

I believe in the Holy Spirit, the Lord, the giver of life,
who proceeds from the Father and the Son,
who with the Father and the Son is adored and glorified,
who has spoken through the prophets.

I believe in one, holy, catholic and apostolic Church.
I confess one Baptism for the forgiveness of sins
and I look forward to the resurrection of the dead
and the life of the world to come. Amen.

Credo in unum Deum,
Patrem omnipotentem,
factorem caeli et terrae,
visibilium omnium et invisibilium.

Et in unum Dominum Iesum Christum,
Filium Dei Unigenitum,
et ex Patre natum ante omnia saecula.
Deum de Deo, lumen de lumine, Deum verum de Deo vero,
genitum, non factum, consubstantialem Patri:
per quem omnia facta sunt.
Qui propter nos homines et propter nostram salutem
descendit de caelis.

At the words that follow,
up to and including et homo factus est, all bow.

Et incarnatus est de Spiritu Sancto
ex Maria Virgine, et homo factus est.

Crucifixus etiam pro nobis sub Pontio Pilato;
passus et sepultus est,
et resurrexit tertia die, secundum Scripturas,
et ascendit in caelum, sedet ad dexteram Patris.
Et iterum venturus est cum gloria, iudicare vivos et mortuos,
cuius regni non erit finis.

Et in Spiritum Sanctum, Dominum et vivificantem:
qui ex Patre Filioque procedit.
Qui cum Patre et Filio simul adoratur et conglorificatur:
qui locutus est per prophetas.

Et unam, sanctam, catholicam et apostolicam Ecclesiam.
Confiteor unum baptisma in remissionem peccatorum.
Et exspecto resurrectionem mortuorum,
et vitam venturi saeculi. Amen.

The Apostles' Creed

I believe in God,
the Father almighty,
Creator of heaven and earth,
and in Jesus Christ, his only Son, our Lord,

At the words that follow,
up to and including the Virgin Mary, all bow.

who was conceived by the Holy Spirit,
born of the Virgin Mary,
suffered under Pontius Pilate,
was crucified, died and was buried;
he descended into hell;
on the third day he rose again from the dead;
he ascended into heaven,
and is seated at the right hand of God the Father almighty;
from there he will come to judge the living and the dead.

I believe in the Holy Spirit,
the holy catholic Church,
the communion of saints,
the forgiveness of sins,
the resurrection of the body,
and life everlasting. Amen.

Prayer of the Faithful
LITURGY OF THE EUCHARIST
Preparation of the altar and the offerings

■ Blessed are you, Lord God of all creation,
for through your goodness we have received

the bread we offer you:
fruit of the earth and work of human hands,
it will become for us the bread of life.

- **Blessed be God for ever.**

By the mystery of this water and wine
may we come to share in the divinity of Christ
who humbled himself to share in our humanity.

- **Blessed are you, Lord God of all creation,**
  for through your goodness we have received
  the wine we offer you:
  fruit of the vine and work of human hands,
  it will become our spiritual drink.
- **Blessed be God for ever.**

With humble spirit and contrite heart
may we be accepted by you, O Lord,
and may our sacrifice in your sight this day
be pleasing to you, Lord God.

Wash me, O Lord, from my iniquity
and cleanse me from my sin.

- **Pray, brethren (brothers and sisters),**
  that my sacrifice and yours
  may be acceptable to God,
  the almighty Father.
- **May the Lord accept the sacrifice at your hands**
  for the praise and glory of his name,
  for our good
  and the good of all his holy Church.

Prayer over the Offerings
Eucharistic Prayer

- **The Lord be with you.**
- **And with your spirit.**
- **Lift up your hearts.**
- **We lift them up to the Lord.**
- **Let us give thanks to the Lord our God.**
- **It is right and just.**

Preface I of Easter

The Paschal Mystery

It is truly right and just, our duty and our salvation,
at all times to acclaim you, O Lord,
but (on this night/ on this day/ in this time) above all
to laud you yet more gloriously,
when Christ our Passover has been sacrificed.

For he is the true Lamb
who has taken away the sins of the world;
by dying he has destroyed our death,
and by rising, restored our life.

Therefore, overcome with paschal joy,
every land, every people exults in your praise
and even the heavenly Powers, with the angelic hosts,
sing together the unending hymn of your glory,
as they acclaim: **Holy....**

Preface II of Easter

New life in Christ

It is truly right and just, our duty and our salvation,
at all times to acclaim you, O Lord,
but in this time above all to laud you yet more gloriously,
when Christ our Passover has been sacrificed.

Through him the children of light rise to eternal life
and the halls of the heavenly Kingdom
are thrown open to the faithful;
for his Death is our ransom from death,
and in his rising the life of all has risen.

Therefore, overcome with paschal joy,
every land, every people exults in your praise
and even the heavenly Powers, with the angelic hosts,
sing together the unending hymn of your glory,
as they acclaim: **Holy....**

Preface III of Easter

Christ living and always interceding for us

It is truly right and just, our duty and our salvation,
at all times to acclaim you, O Lord,

but in this time above all to laud you yet more gloriously,
when Christ our Passover has been sacrificed.

He never ceases to offer himself for us
but defends us and ever pleads our cause before you:
he is the sacrificial Victim who dies no more,
the Lamb, once slain, who lives for ever.

Therefore, overcome with paschal joy,
every land, every people exults in your praise
and even the heavenly Powers, with the angelic hosts,
sing together the unending hymn of your glory,
as they acclaim: Holy....

Preface IV of Easter

The restoration of the universe through the Paschal Mystery

It is truly right and just, our duty and our salvation,
at all times to acclaim you, O Lord,
but in this time above all to laud you yet more gloriously,
when Christ our Passover has been sacrificed.

For, with the old order destroyed,
a universe cast down is renewed,
and integrity of life is restored to us in Christ.

Therefore, overcome with paschal joy,
every land, every people exults in your praise
and even the heavenly Powers, with the angelic hosts,
sing together the unending hymn of your glory,
as they acclaim: Holy....

Preface V of Easter

Christ, Priest and Victim

It is truly right and just, our duty and our salvation,
at all times to acclaim you, O Lord,
but in this time above all to laud you yet more gloriously,
when Christ our Passover has been sacrificed.

By the oblation of his Body,
he brought the sacrifices of old to fulfillment
in the reality of the Cross

and, by commending himself to you for our salvation,
showed himself the Priest, the Altar, and the Lamb of sacrifice.

Therefore, overcome with paschal joy,
every land, every people exults in your praise
and even the heavenly Powers, with the angelic hosts,
sing together the unending hymn of your glory,
as they acclaim: Holy....

Preface I of the Ascension of the Lord
The mystery of the Ascension

It is truly right and just, our duty and our salvation,
always and everywhere to give you thanks,
Lord, holy Father, almighty and eternal God.

For the Lord Jesus, the King of glory,
conqueror of sin and death,
ascended (today) to the highest heavens,
as the Angels gazed in wonder.

Mediator between God and man,
judge of the world and Lord of hosts,
he ascended, not to distance himself from our lowly state
but that we, his members, might be confident of following
where he, our Head and Founder, has gone before.

Therefore, overcome with paschal joy,
every land, every people exults in your praise
and even the heavenly Powers, with the angelic hosts,
sing together the unending hymn of your glory,
as they acclaim: Holy....

Preface II of the Ascension of the Lord
The mystery of the Ascension

It is truly right and just, our duty and our salvation,
always and everywhere to give you thanks,
Lord, holy Father, almighty and eternal God,
through Christ our Lord.

For after his Resurrection
he plainly appeared to all his disciples

and was taken up to heaven in their sight,
that he might make us sharers in his divinity.

Therefore, overcome with paschal joy,
every land, every people exults in your praise
and even the heavenly Powers, with the angelic hosts,
sing together the unending hymn of your glory,
as they acclaim:

Holy, Holy, Holy Lord God of hosts.
Heaven and earth are full of your glory.
Hosanna in the highest.
Blessed is he who comes in the name of the Lord.
Hosanna in the highest.

Sanctus, Sanctus, Sanctus Dominus Deus Sabaoth.
Pleni sunt caeli et terra gloria tua.
Hosanna in excelsis.
Benedictus qui venit in nomine Domini.
Hosanna in excelsis.

Eucharistic Prayers

Eucharistic Prayer I (Roman Canon)

(In the first Eucharistic Prayer the words in brackets may be omitted.)

To you, therefore, most merciful Father,
we make humble prayer and petition
through Jesus Christ, your Son, our Lord:
that you accept
and bless ✠ these gifts, these offerings,
these holy and unblemished sacrifices,
which we offer you firstly
for your holy catholic Church.
Be pleased to grant her peace,
to guard, unite and govern her
throughout the whole world,

together with your servant N. our Pope
and N. our Bishop,
and all those who, holding to the truth,
hand on the catholic and apostolic faith.

Remember, Lord, your servants N. and N.
and all gathered here,
whose faith and devotion are known to you.
For them, we offer you this sacrifice of praise
or they offer it for themselves
and all who are dear to them:
for the redemption of their souls,
in hope of health and well-being,
and paying their homage to you,
the eternal God, living and true.

In communion with those whose memory we venerate,
especially the glorious ever-Virgin Mary,
Mother of our God and Lord, Jesus Christ,
† and blessed Joseph, her Spouse,
your blessed Apostles and Martyrs,
Peter and Paul, Andrew,
(James, John,
Thomas, James, Philip,
Bartholomew, Matthew,
Simon and Jude;
Linus, Cletus, Clement, Sixtus,
Cornelius, Cyprian,
Lawrence, Chrysogonus,
John and Paul,
Cosmas and Damian)
and all your Saints;
we ask that through their merits and prayers,
in all things we may be defended
by your protecting help.
(Through Christ our Lord. Amen.)

PROPER FORM OF "In communion with those…"
(Communicantes)

ON THE ASCENSION OF THE LORD

Celebrating the most sacred day
on which your Only Begotten Son, our Lord,
placed at the right hand of your glory
our weak human nature,
which he had united to himself,
and in communion with those whose memory we venerate,
especially the glorious ever-Virgin Mary,
Mother of our God and Lord, Jesus Christ, †

Therefore, Lord, we pray:
graciously accept this oblation of our service,
that of your whole family;
order our days in your peace,
and command that we be delivered from eternal damnation
and counted among the flock of those you have chosen.
(Through Christ our Lord. Amen.)

Be pleased, O God, we pray,
to bless, acknowledge,
and approve this offering in every respect;
make it spiritual and acceptable,
so that it may become for us
the Body and Blood of your most beloved Son,
our Lord Jesus Christ.

On the day before he was to suffer,
he took bread in his holy and venerable hands,
and with eyes raised to heaven
to you, O God, his almighty Father,
giving you thanks, he said the blessing,
broke the bread
and gave it to his disciples, saying:

TAKE THIS, ALL OF YOU, AND EAT OF IT,
FOR THIS IS MY BODY,
WHICH WILL BE GIVEN UP FOR YOU.

In a similar way, when supper was ended,
he took this precious chalice
in his holy and venerable hands,
and once more giving you thanks, he said the blessing
and gave the chalice to his disciples, saying:

TAKE THIS, ALL OF YOU, AND DRINK FROM IT,
FOR THIS IS THE CHALICE OF MY BLOOD,
THE BLOOD OF THE NEW AND ETERNAL COVENANT,
WHICH WILL BE POURED OUT FOR YOU AND FOR MANY
FOR THE FORGIVENESS OF SINS.
DO THIS IN MEMORY OF ME.

- The mystery of faith.
- We proclaim your Death, O Lord,
  and profess your Resurrection
  until you come again.

Or:

- When we eat this Bread and drink this Cup,
  we proclaim your Death, O Lord,
  until you come again.

Or:

- Save us, Savior of the world,
  for by your Cross and Resurrection
  you have set us free.

Therefore, O Lord,
as we celebrate the memorial of the blessed Passion,
the Resurrection from the dead,
and the glorious Ascension into heaven
of Christ, your Son, our Lord,
we, your servants and your holy people,
offer to your glorious majesty
from the gifts that you have given us,
this pure victim,
this holy victim,
this spotless victim,
the holy Bread of eternal life
and the Chalice of everlasting salvation.

Be pleased to look upon these offerings
with a serene and kindly countenance,
and to accept them,
as once you were pleased to accept
the gifts of your servant Abel the just,
the sacrifice of Abraham, our father in faith,
and the offering of your high priest Melchizedek,
a holy sacrifice, a spotless victim.

In humble prayer we ask you, almighty God:
command that these gifts be borne
by the hands of your holy Angel
to your altar on high
in the sight of your divine majesty,
so that all of us, who through this participation at the altar
receive the most holy Body and Blood of your Son,
may be filled with every grace and heavenly blessing.
(Through Christ our Lord. Amen.)

Remember also, Lord, your servants N. and N.,
who have gone before us with the sign of faith
and rest in the sleep of peace.

Grant them, O Lord, we pray,
and all who sleep in Christ,
a place of refreshment, light and peace.
(Through Christ our Lord. Amen.)

To us, also, your servants,
who, though sinners,
hope in your abundant mercies,
graciously grant some share
and fellowship with your holy Apostles and Martyrs:
with John the Baptist, Stephen,
Matthias, Barnabas,
(Ignatius, Alexander,
Marcellinus, Peter,
Felicity, Perpetua,
Agatha, Lucy,
Agnes, Cecilia, Anastasia)
and all your Saints;

admit us, we beseech you,
into their company,
not weighing our merits,
but granting us your pardon,
through Christ our Lord.

Through whom
you continue to make all these good things, O Lord;
you sanctify them, fill them with life,
bless them, and bestow them upon us.

Through him, and with him, and in him,
O God, almighty Father,
in the unity of the Holy Spirit,
all glory and honor is yours,
for ever and ever.

■ Amen.   *Communion Rite: page 234*

Eucharistic Prayer II

It is truly right and just, our duty and our salvation,
always and everywhere to give you thanks, Father most holy,
through your beloved Son, Jesus Christ,
your Word through whom you made all things,
whom you sent as our Savior and Redeemer,
incarnate by the Holy Spirit and born of the Virgin.

Fulfilling your will and gaining for you a holy people,
he stretched out his hands as he endured his Passion,
so as to break the bonds of death and manifest the resurrection.

And so, with the Angels and all the Saints
we declare your glory,
as with one voice we acclaim: **Holy….**

You are indeed Holy, O Lord,
the fount of all holiness.
Make holy, therefore, these gifts, we pray,
by sending down your Spirit upon them like the dewfall,
so that they may become for us
the Body and ✠ Blood of our Lord Jesus Christ.

At the time he was betrayed
and entered willingly into his Passion,

he took bread and, giving thanks, broke it,
and gave it to his disciples, saying:

TAKE THIS, ALL OF YOU, AND EAT OF IT,
FOR THIS IS MY BODY,
WHICH WILL BE GIVEN UP FOR YOU.

In a similar way, when supper was ended,
he took the chalice
and, once more giving thanks,
he gave it to his disciples, saying:

TAKE THIS, ALL OF YOU, AND DRINK FROM IT,
FOR THIS IS THE CHALICE OF MY BLOOD,
THE BLOOD OF THE NEW AND ETERNAL COVENANT,
WHICH WILL BE POURED OUT FOR YOU AND FOR MANY
FOR THE FORGIVENESS OF SINS.
DO THIS IN MEMORY OF ME.

- The mystery of faith.
- We proclaim your Death, O Lord,
  and profess your Resurrection
  until you come again.

Or:

- When we eat this Bread and drink this Cup,
  we proclaim your Death, O Lord,
  until you come again.

Or:

- Save us, Savior of the world,
  for by your Cross and Resurrection
  you have set us free.

Therefore, as we celebrate
the memorial of his Death and Resurrection,
we offer you, Lord,
the Bread of life and the Chalice of salvation,
giving thanks that you have held us worthy
to be in your presence and minister to you.

Humbly we pray
that, partaking of the Body and Blood of Christ,
we may be gathered into one by the Holy Spirit.

Remember, Lord, your Church,
spread throughout the world,
and bring her to the fullness of charity,
together with N. our Pope and N. our Bishop
and all the clergy.

Remember also our brothers and sisters
who have fallen asleep in the hope of the resurrection,
and all who have died in your mercy:
welcome them into the light of your face.
Have mercy on us all, we pray,
that with the Blessed Virgin Mary, Mother of God,
with blessed Joseph, her Spouse,
with the blessed Apostles,
and all the Saints who have pleased you throughout the ages,
we may merit to be coheirs to eternal life,
and may praise and glorify you
through your Son, Jesus Christ.

Through him, and with him, and in him,
O God, almighty Father,
in the unity of the Holy Spirit,
all glory and honor is yours,
for ever and ever.

■ Amen.

Communion Rite: page 234

Eucharistic Prayer III

You are indeed Holy, O Lord,
and all you have created
rightly gives you praise,
for through your Son our Lord Jesus Christ,
by the power and working of the Holy Spirit,
you give life to all things and make them holy,
and you never cease to gather a people to yourself,
so that from the rising of the sun to its setting
a pure sacrifice may be offered to your name.

Therefore, O Lord, we humbly implore you:
by the same Spirit graciously make holy
these gifts we have brought to you for consecration,
that they may become the Body and ✠ Blood

of your Son our Lord Jesus Christ,
at whose command we celebrate these mysteries.

For on the night he was betrayed
he himself took bread,
and, giving you thanks, he said the blessing,
broke the bread and gave it to his disciples, saying:

Take this, all of you, and eat of it,
for this is my Body,
which will be given up for you.

In a similar way, when supper was ended,
he took the chalice,
and, giving you thanks, he said the blessing,
and gave the chalice to his disciples, saying:

Take this, all of you, and drink from it,
for this is the chalice of my Blood,
the Blood of the new and eternal covenant,
which will be poured out for you and for many
for the forgiveness of sins.
Do this in memory of me.

■ The mystery of faith.
■ We proclaim your Death, O Lord,
and profess your Resurrection
until you come again.

Or:

■ When we eat this Bread and drink this Cup,
we proclaim your Death, O Lord,
until you come again.

Or:

■ Save us, Savior of the world,
for by your Cross and Resurrection
you have set us free.

Therefore, O Lord, as we celebrate the memorial
of the saving Passion of your Son,
his wondrous Resurrection
and Ascension into heaven,
and as we look forward to his second coming,

we offer you in thanksgiving
this holy and living sacrifice.

Look, we pray, upon the oblation of your Church
and, recognizing the sacrificial Victim by whose death
you willed to reconcile us to yourself,
grant that we, who are nourished
by the Body and Blood of your Son
and filled with his Holy Spirit,
may become one body, one spirit in Christ.

May he make of us
an eternal offering to you,
so that we may obtain an inheritance with your elect,
especially with the most Blessed Virgin Mary,
    Mother of God,
with blessed Joseph, her Spouse,
with your blessed Apostles and glorious Martyrs
(with Saint N.: the Saint of the day or Patron Saint)
and with all the Saints,
on whose constant intercession in your presence
we rely for unfailing help.

May this Sacrifice of our reconciliation,
we pray, O Lord,
advance the peace and salvation of all the world.
Be pleased to confirm in faith and charity
your pilgrim Church on earth,
with your servant N. our Pope and N. our Bishop,
the Order of Bishops, all the clergy,
and the entire people you have gained for your own.

Listen graciously to the prayers of this family,
whom you have summoned before you:
in your compassion, O merciful Father,
gather to yourself all your children
scattered throughout the world.

To our departed brothers and sisters
and to all who were pleasing to you
at their passing from this life,
give kind admittance to your kingdom.
There we hope to enjoy for ever the fullness of your glory

through Christ our Lord,
through whom you bestow on the world all that is good.

Through him, and with him, and in him,
O God, almighty Father,
in the unity of the Holy Spirit,
all glory and honor is yours,
for ever and ever.

■ **Amen.**

Communion Rite: page 234

Eucharistic Prayer IV

It is truly right to give you thanks,
truly just to give you glory, Father most holy,
for you are the one God living and true,
existing before all ages and abiding for all eternity,
dwelling in unapproachable light;
yet you, who alone are good, the source of life,
have made all that is,
so that you might fill your creatures with blessings
and bring joy to many of them by the glory of your light.

And so, in your presence are countless hosts of Angels,
who serve you day and night
and, gazing upon the glory of your face,
glorify you without ceasing.

With them we, too, confess your name in exultation,
giving voice to every creature under heaven,
as we acclaim: Holy....

We give you praise, Father most holy,
for you are great
and you have fashioned all your works
in wisdom and in love.
You formed man in your own image
and entrusted the whole world to his care,
so that in serving you alone, the Creator,
he might have dominion over all creatures.
And when through disobedience he had lost your friendship,
you did not abandon him to the domain of death.
For you came in mercy to the aid of all,
so that those who seek might find you.
Time and again you offered them covenants

and through the prophets
taught them to look forward to salvation.

And you so loved the world, Father most holy,
that in the fullness of time
you sent your Only Begotten Son to be our Savior.
Made incarnate by the Holy Spirit
and born of the Virgin Mary,
he shared our human nature
in all things but sin.
To the poor he proclaimed the good news of salvation,
to prisoners, freedom,
and to the sorrowful of heart, joy.
To accomplish your plan,
he gave himself up to death,
and, rising from the dead,
he destroyed death and restored life.

And that we might live no longer for ourselves
but for him who died and rose again for us,
he sent the Holy Spirit from you, Father,
as the first fruits for those who believe,
so that, bringing to perfection his work in the world,
he might sanctify creation to the full.

Therefore, O Lord, we pray:
may this same Holy Spirit
graciously sanctify these offerings,
that they may become
the Body and ✠ Blood of our Lord Jesus Christ
for the celebration of this great mystery,
which he himself left us
as an eternal covenant.

For when the hour had come
for him to be glorified by you, Father most holy,
having loved his own who were in the world,
he loved them to the end:
and while they were at supper,
he took bread, blessed and broke it,
and gave it to his disciples, saying:

TAKE THIS, ALL OF YOU, AND EAT OF IT,
FOR THIS IS MY BODY,
WHICH WILL BE GIVEN UP FOR YOU.

In a similar way,
taking the chalice filled with the fruit of the vine,
he gave thanks,
and gave the chalice to his disciples, saying:

TAKE THIS, ALL OF YOU, AND DRINK FROM IT,
FOR THIS IS THE CHALICE OF MY BLOOD,
THE BLOOD OF THE NEW AND ETERNAL COVENANT,
WHICH WILL BE POURED OUT FOR YOU AND FOR MANY
FOR THE FORGIVENESS OF SINS.
DO THIS IN MEMORY OF ME.

- The mystery of faith.
- We proclaim your Death, O Lord,
  and profess your Resurrection
  until you come again.

Or:

- When we eat this Bread and drink this Cup,
  we proclaim your Death, O Lord,
  until you come again.

Or:

- Save us, Savior of the world,
  for by your Cross and Resurrection
  you have set us free.

Therefore, O Lord,
as we now celebrate the memorial of our redemption,
we remember Christ's Death
and his descent to the realm of the dead,
we proclaim his Resurrection
and his Ascension to your right hand,
and, as we await his coming in glory,
we offer you his Body and Blood,
the sacrifice acceptable to you
which brings salvation to the whole world.

Look, O Lord, upon the Sacrifice
which you yourself have provided for your Church,
and grant in your loving kindness

to all who partake of this one Bread and one Chalice
that, gathered into one body by the Holy Spirit,
they may truly become a living sacrifice in Christ
to the praise of your glory.

Therefore, Lord, remember now
all for whom we offer this sacrifice:
especially your servant N. our Pope,
N. our Bishop, and the whole Order of Bishops,
all the clergy,
those who take part in this offering,
those gathered here before you,
your entire people,
and all who seek you with a sincere heart.

Remember also
those who have died in the peace of your Christ
and all the dead,
whose faith you alone have known.

To all of us, your children,
grant, O merciful Father,
that we may enter into a heavenly inheritance
with the Blessed Virgin Mary, Mother of God,
with blessed Joseph, her Spouse,
and with your Apostles and Saints in your kingdom.
There, with the whole of creation,
freed from the corruption of sin and death,
may we glorify you through Christ our Lord,
through whom you bestow on the world all that is good.

Through him, and with him, and in him,
O God, almighty Father,
in the unity of the Holy Spirit,
all glory and honor is yours,
for ever and ever.

■ Amen.

COMMUNION RITE
Lord's Prayer

■ At the Savior's command
   and formed by divine teaching,
   we dare to say:

Our Father, who art in heaven,
hallowed be thy name;
thy kingdom come,
thy will be done
on earth as it is in heaven.
Give us this day our daily bread,
and forgive us our trespasses,
as we forgive those who trespass against us;
and lead us not into temptation,
but deliver us from evil.

Pater noster, qui es in caelis:
sanctificetur nomen tuum;
adveniat regnum tuum;
fiat voluntas tua, sicut in caelo, et in terra.
Panem nostrum cotidianum da nobis hodie;
et dimitte nobis debita nostra,
sicut et nos dimittimus debitoribus nostris;
et ne nos inducas in tentationem;
sed libera nos a malo.

■ Deliver us, Lord, we pray, from every evil,
graciously grant peace in our days,
that, by the help of your mercy,
we may be always free from sin
and safe from all distress,
as we await the blessed hope
and the coming of our Savior, Jesus Christ.

■ For the kingdom,
the power and the glory are yours
now and for ever.

Sign of Peace

■ Lord Jesus Christ,
who said to your Apostles:
Peace I leave you, my peace I give you,
look not on our sins,
but on the faith of your Church,

and graciously grant her peace and unity
in accordance with your will.
Who live and reign for ever and ever.

- Amen.
- The peace of the Lord be with you always.
- And with your spirit.

Then, if appropriate, the Deacon, or the Priest, adds:

Let us offer each other the sign of peace.

Breaking of the Bread

*Then he takes the host, breaks it over the paten,
and places a small piece in the chalice, saying quietly:*

- May this mingling of the Body and Blood
of our Lord Jesus Christ
bring eternal life to us who receive it.

Meanwhile the following is sung or said:

- Lamb of God, you take away the sins of the world,
  have mercy on us.
  Lamb of God, you take away the sins of the world,
  have mercy on us.
  Lamb of God, you take away the sins of the world,
  grant us peace.

- Agnus Dei, qui tollis peccata mundi:
  miserere nobis.
  Agnus Dei, qui tollis peccata mundi:
  miserere nobis.
  Agnus Dei, qui tollis peccata mundi:
  dona nobis pacem.

---

*The invocation may even be repeated several times if the fraction is
prolonged. Only the final time, however, is **grant us peace** said.*

Then the Priest, with hands joined, says quietly:

Lord Jesus Christ, Son of the living God,
who, by the will of the Father
and the work of the Holy Spirit,

through your Death gave life to the world,
free me by this, your most holy Body and Blood,
from all my sins and from every evil;
keep me always faithful to your commandments,
and never let me be parted from you.

Or:

May the receiving of your Body and Blood,
Lord Jesus Christ,
not bring me to judgment and condemnation,
but through your loving mercy
be for me protection in mind and body
and a healing remedy.

Communion

The Priest genuflects, takes the host and, holding it slightly raised
above the paten or above the chalice, while facing the people,
says aloud:

■ Behold the Lamb of God,
behold him who takes away the sins of the world.
Blessed are those called to the supper of the Lamb.

And together with the people he adds once:

■ Lord, I am not worthy
that you should enter under my roof,
but only say the word
and my soul shall be healed.

The Priest, facing the altar, says quietly:

May the Body of Christ
keep me safe for eternal life.

And he reverently consumes the Body of Christ.
Then he takes the chalice and says quietly:

May the Blood of Christ
keep me safe for eternal life.

And he reverently consumes the Blood of Christ.

Communion Chant

When the distribution of Communion is over, the Priest
or a Deacon or an acolyte purifies the paten over the chalice
and also the chalice itself.

While he carries out the purification, the Priest says quietly:

What has passed our lips as food, O Lord,
may we possess in purity of heart,
that what has been given to us in time
may be our healing for eternity.

Period of silence or song of praise

Prayer after Communion

Concluding Rites

Brief announcements

- ▪ The Lord be with you.
- ▪ And with your spirit.

Blessing

- ▪ May almighty God bless you,
  the Father, and the Son, ✠ and the Holy Spirit.
- ▪ Amen.

Dismissal

Then the Deacon, or the Priest himself, with hands joined
and facing the people, says:

- ▪ Go forth, the Mass is ended.

Or:

- ▪ Go and announce the Gospel of the Lord.

Or:

- ▪ Go in peace, glorifying the Lord by your life.

Or:

- ▪ Go in peace.
- ▪ Thanks be to God.

EUCHARISTIC EXPOSITION
AND BENEDICTION

The first fruit of Eucharistic contemplation is to fix, to recollect the soul in our Lord, to discover the mystery of his perfections and the love of the ineffable gift of the Eucharist. This view, thoughtful and reflective, of the excessive love of Jesus in preparing, instituting, and perpetuating the Adorable Sacrament, produces in us first adoration, then praise, and lastly, expansion of love. A soul goes out of self in order to unite with Jesus, in order to adhere to the divine object of its contemplation.... Mary before the Eucharist was in contemplation such as neither human nor angelic tongue could express. Jesus Christ alone, the object of it, knew its value..... We love her and confide ourselves to her as to the Mother of Adorers, which is the title most dear to her heart and most glorious to Jesus.

Saint Peter Julian Eymard

EXPOSITION

Once the people have assembled, a song such as the following may be sung while the priest or deacon prepares the Holy Eucharist for adoration.

O Saving Victim/O Salutaris Hostia

Meter: LM

O Saving Victim, op'ning wide
The gate of heav'n to us below!
Our foes press on from ev'ry side:
Your aid supply, your strength bestow.

O salutáris hóstia,
Quae caeli pandis óstium:
Bella premunt hostília,
Da robur fer auxílium.

To your great name be endless praise,
Immortal Godhead, One in Three;

O grant us endless length of days
When our true native land we see.

> *Uni trinóque Dómino*
> *Sit sempitérna glória:*
> *Qui vitam sine término*
> *Nobis donet in pátria.*

ADORATION

The Liturgy of the Hours may be celebrated during the period of exposition, or there may be prayers, songs, readings from Scripture, and a brief homily to direct the attention of the faithful to the worship of the Lord.

**A reading from
the first Letter of Paul to the Corinthians**   11:23-26

FOR I RECEIVED from the Lord what I also handed on to you, that the Lord Jesus, on the night he was handed over, took bread, and after he had given thanks, broke it and said, "This is my body that is for you. Do this in remembrance of me." In the same way also the cup, after supper, saying, "This cup is the new covenant in my blood. Do this, as often as you drink it, in remembrance of me." For as often as you eat this bread and drink the cup, you proclaim the death of the Lord until he comes.

The word of the Lord.

℟ Thanks be to God.

A Eucharistic song such as the following may be sung.

Come Adore/Tantum Ergo Sacramentum
Meter: 87 87 87

Come adore this wondrous presence,
Bow to Christ the source of grace.
Here is kept the ancient promise
Of God's earthly dwelling place.
Sight is blind before God's glory,
Faith alone may see his face.

Tantum ergo Sacraméntum
Venerémur cérnui:
Et antíquum documéntum
Novo cedat rítui:
Praestet fides suppleméntum
Sénsuum deféctui.

Glory be to God the Father,
Praise to his coequal Son,
Adoration to the Spirit,
Bond of love, in Godhead one.
Blest be God by all creation
Joyously while ages run.

Genitóri Genitóque
Laus et jubilátio,
Salus, honor, virtus quoque
Sit et benedíctio:
Procedénti ab utróque
Compar sit laudátio.

BENEDICTION

The priest or deacon may give a blessing. Before the blessing a prayer such as the following may be said.

Minister: You have given them bread from heaven.

℟ Containing in itself all delight.

Minister: Let us pray.

O God, who in this wonderful Sacrament
have left us a memorial of your Passion,
grant us, we pray,
so to revere the sacred mysteries of your Body and Blood
that we may always experience in ourselves
the fruits of your redemption.
Who live and reign with God the Father
in the unity of the Holy Spirit,
one God, for ever and ever.

℟ Amen.

The Divine Praises

Blessed be God.
Blessed be his Holy Name.
Blessed be Jesus Christ, true God and true Man.
Blessed be the Name of Jesus.
Blessed be his most Sacred Heart.
Blessed be his most Precious Blood.
Blessed be Jesus in the most Holy Sacrament of the Altar.
Blessed be the Holy Spirit, the Paraclete.

Blessed be the great Mother of God, Mary most holy.
Blessed be her holy and Immaculate Conception.
Blessed be her glorious Assumption.
Blessed be the name of Mary, Virgin and Mother.
Blessed be Saint Joseph, her most chaste spouse.
Blessed be God in his angels and in his saints.

REPOSITION

After the blessing the minister reposes the Blessed Sacrament in the tabernacle.

A closing song such as the following may be sung.

Holy God, We Praise Thy Name

* Repeat the last two lines.

> Holy God, we praise thy name!
> Lord of all, we bow before thee;
> All on earth thy scepter claim,
> All in heav'n above adore thee;
> Infinite thy vast domain,
> Everlasting is thy reign.*

> Hark! the loud celestial hymn
> Angel choirs above are raising;
> Cherubim and Seraphim
> In unceasing chorus praising,
> Fill the heav'ns with sweet accord:
> Holy, holy, holy Lord!*

Holy Father, Holy Son,
Holy Spirit, Three we name thee,
While in essence only One,
Undivided God we claim thee,
And adoring bend the knee,
While we own the mystery.*

Anima Christi

Anima Christi, sanctifica me.
Corpus Christi, salva me.
Sanguis Christi, inebria me.
Aqua lateris Christi, lava me.
Passio Christi, conforta me.
O Bone Iesu, exaudi me.
Intra tua vulnera absconde me.
Ne permittas me separari a te.
Ab hoste maligno defende me.
In hora mortis meae voca me.
Et iube me venire ad te,
ut cum Sanctis tuis laudem te
in saecula saeculorum. Amen.

Soul of Christ, sanctify me.
Body of Christ, save me.
Blood of Christ, inebriate me.
Water from the side of Christ, wash me.
Passion of Christ, strengthen me.
O good Jesus, hear me.
Within thy wounds hide me.
Suffer me not to be separated from thee.
From the malicious enemy defend me.
In the hour of my death call me
and bid me come unto thee,
that with thy saints I may praise thee
for ever and ever. Amen.

THURSDAY, MAY 16

Prayer for the Morning

Lift up your hearts!
Let us lift them up to the Lord, alleluia!

Glory to the Father, and to the Son,
and to the Holy Spirit, as it was in the beginning,
is now, and will be for ever. Amen. Alleluia!

HYMN
Meter: LM
This hymn can be sung to the tune used for
I Know that My Redeemer Lives

Spirit of God, in love descend,
And make our hearts your place of rest;
In all our need a steadfast friend,
To fill our store with gifts the best;

To cleanse our souls with holy fire
From sordid stains that guilt imparts,
And with your heav'nly pow'r inspire
Our languid zeal, and fainting hearts;

To lift our minds to nobler things
Than earth from all its best can show—
The wealth that flies on speedy wings,
The fleeting joys, like sparks that glow.

PSALM 139
1-6, 9-12, 23-24

I know those whom I have chosen. (Jn 13:18)

To God, the darkest depths of the human heart are as clear as the
page of a book lying open in the sunlight. He knows us through and
through—and loves us as deeply as he knows us! Rather than hide
from him, let us put our life in the hands that fashioned us and

allow him to lead us in the path of life eternal in the wake of Christ our Lord.

O Lord, you search me and you know me,
you know my resting and my rising,
you discern my purpose from afar.
You mark when I walk or lie down,
all my ways lie open to you.

Before ever a word is on my tongue
you know it, O Lord, through and through.
Behind and before you besiege me,
your hand ever laid upon me.
Too wonderful for me, this knowledge,
too high, beyond my reach.

If I take the wings of the dawn
and dwell at the sea's furthest end,
even there your hand would lead me,
your right hand would hold me fast.

If I say: "Let the darkness hide me
and the light around me be night,"
even darkness is not dark for you
and the night is as clear as the day.

O search me, God, and know my heart.
O test me and know my thoughts.
See that I follow not the wrong path
and lead me in the path of life eternal.

Glory to the Father....

Word of God
Isaiah 42:16

I will lead the blind on their journey;/ by paths unknown I will guide them./ I will turn darkness into light before them,/ and make crooked ways straight./ These things I do for them,/ and I will not forsake them.

> *Straight are the paths of the Lord,/*
> *in them the just walk.*
> *(Hos 14:10)*

Canticle of Zechariah   (Text, back cover B)

I am the Lord, your God,/ who grasp your right hand;/ It is I who say to you, "Fear not,/ I will help you." (Is 41:13)

Intercessions

God searches us and knows us. Let us lift up to him our prayers, saying:

℟   In your love, remember us.

Our ways lie open to you, O Lord:
– make your ways our own. ℟

Our words are known to you before we speak, O Lord:
– make each word a work of kindness done in your name. ℟

You will not forsake us, O Lord:
– keep us from forsaking you. ℟

Personal intentions

Our Father....

O God our Father, you sent your only Son, our Lord Jesus Christ, to be our way, our truth, and our life. At this morning hour, we lift our hearts to you in prayer and ask that you guide us through this day according to your will, through the same Christ our Lord. Amen.

Mass

Thursday of the Fourth Week of Easter

"God, according to his promise", has brought to us a Savior, Jesus. He strips us of all our pretension and defiance by washing our feet. And then he assures us that he has chosen us and that he will use us as his missionaries to the world to proclaim his faithfulness. We, who are "not worthy to unfasten the sandals of his feet," proclaim Christ to the world with feet washed by Jesus himself.

ENTRANCE ANTIPHON   Cf. Ps 68 (67):8-9, 20

O God, when you went forth before your people,/ marching with them and living among them,/ the earth trembled, heavens poured down rain, alleluia.

COLLECT

O God, who restore human nature
to yet greater dignity than at its beginnings,
look upon the amazing mystery of your loving
    kindness,
and in those you have chosen to make new
through the wonder of rebirth
may you preserve the gifts
of your enduring grace and blessing.
Through our Lord Jesus Christ, your Son,
who lives and reigns with you in the unity
    of the Holy Spirit,
one God, for ever and ever.

    ● *From this man's descendants God, according to his promise, has brought to Israel a savior, Jesus.* ●

**A reading from
the Acts of the Apostles**   13:13-25

FROM PAPHOS, PAUL and his companions set sail and arrived at Perga in Pamphylia. But John left them and returned to Jerusalem. They continued on from Perga and reached Antioch in Pisidia. On the sabbath they entered into the synagogue and took their seats. After the reading of the law and the prophets, the synagogue officials sent word to them, "My brothers, if one of you has a word of exhortation for the people, please speak."

So Paul got up, motioned with his hand, and said, "Fellow children of Israel and you others who are God-fearing, listen. The God of this people Israel chose our ancestors and exalted the people during their sojourn in the land of Egypt. With uplifted arm he led them out, and for about forty years he put up with them in the desert. When he had destroyed seven nations in the land of Canaan, he gave them their land as an inheritance at the end of about four hundred and fifty years. After these things he provided judges up to Samuel the prophet. Then they asked for a king. God gave them Saul, son of Kish, a man from the tribe of Benjamin, for forty years. Then he removed him and raised up David as their king; of him he testified, *I have found David, son of Jesse, a man after my own heart; he will carry out my every wish.* From this man's descendants God, according to his promise, has brought to Israel a savior, Jesus. John heralded his coming by proclaiming a baptism of repentance to all the people of Israel; and as John was completing his course, he would say, 'What do you suppose that I am? I am not he. Behold, one is coming after me; I am not worthy to unfasten the sandals of his feet.'"

The word of the Lord.

——— • PSALM 89 • ———

℟ (2) **For ever I will sing the goodness of the Lord.**

Or: Alleluia.

The favors of the LORD I will sing forever;
  through all generations my mouth shall proclaim
    your faithfulness.
For you have said, "My kindness is established forever";
  in heaven you have confirmed your faithfulness. ℟

"I have found David, my servant;
  with my holy oil I have anointed him,
That my hand may be always with him,
  and that my arm may make him strong." ℟

"My faithfulness and my mercy shall be with him,
  and through my name shall his horn be exalted.
He shall say of me, 'You are my father,
  my God, the Rock, my savior.'" ℟

Alleluia, alleluia. Jesus Christ, you are the faithful witness,/ the firstborn of the dead,/ you have loved us and freed us from our sins by your Blood. Alleluia, alleluia.

• *Whoever receives the one I send receives me.* •

**A reading from
the holy Gospel according to John** 13:16-20

WHEN JESUS HAD washed the disciples' feet, he said to them: "Amen, amen, I say to you, no slave is greater than his master nor any messenger greater than the one who sent him. If you understand this, blessed are you if you do it. I am not speaking of all of you. I know those whom I have chosen. But so that the Scripture might be fulfilled, *The one who ate my food has raised his heel against me.* From now on I am telling you before it happens, so that when it happens you may believe that I AM. Amen, amen, I say to you, whoever receives the

one I send receives me, and whoever receives me receives the one who sent me."
The Gospel of the Lord.

PRAYER OVER THE OFFERINGS
May our prayers rise up to you, O Lord,
together with the sacrificial offerings,
so that, purified by your graciousness,
we may be conformed to the mysteries of your
    mighty love.
Through Christ our Lord.

PREFACE I-V OF EASTER ——————— pages 218 to 219

COMMUNION ANTIPHON   Mt 28:20
Behold, I am with you always,/ even to the end of the age,
alleluia.

PRAYER AFTER COMMUNION
Almighty ever-living God,
who restore us to eternal life
in the Resurrection of Christ,
increase in us, we pray, the fruits of this paschal
    Sacrament
and pour into our hearts the strength of this saving food.
Through Christ our Lord.

MEDITATION OF THE DAY

"If you understand this, blessed are you"

[The Lord said:] Stay with me, *in* me who never leave you. I have waited so long for you. This is the only reality: *I love you and I take care of you*. And that is for now and for eternity. Everything else must be borne with meekness and patience. They are only fleeting shadows which pass around you. But I remain. I love you and I take care of you. If anyone attacks you, leave it to me; let me have the joy of defending you when I wish and as I please. If you suffer, come nearer to me.

I am always waiting for you. I will tell you my secrets which console and strengthen.

If you give me nothing, I am not able to do the good which I leave to your initiative. Give me the tiny seed of your sacrifices, of your efforts; I will make it fruitful. But give me the seed. Do not lose a moment, not a single occasion of offering to me all that I send you. My grace does not leave you for an instant: welcome it. I want my heaven to fill your soul, your cell, your convent.

SISTER MARY OF THE HOLY TRINITY

Sister Mary of the Holy Trinity († 1942) was a Poor Clare of Jerusalem.

Prayer for the Evening

Let us bless God all our lives!
Let us praise him with joy, alleluia!

Glory to the Father.... Alleluia!

HYMN

Meter: CM
This hymn can be sung to the tune used for
We Walk by Faith

Our road runs through a wilderness,
A realm of wanderings;
Beneath a silent, desert sun
The spirit finds its springs.

Each soul must make the exodus
Through sacred, arid space
And stack the hallelujah stones
That mark the promised place.

We do not pass this way alone
But in profound array;
The wise, the peaceable, the just
Are never far away.

In time we cherish desert roads
The slow, demanding pace;
We are a people turned to God
By thirst as well as grace.

PSALM 12

Food from heaven you gave your people in their hunger,/ water from a rock you sent them in their thirst. (cf. Neh 9:15)

In the desert where the Israelites found salvation, as Saint Paul reminds his hearers today, Christ is the source of the waters of life flowing from his pierced side. He is the bread of life broken on the cross. His love is better than life; his love is life. For him let us hunger and thirst!

Help, O Lord, for good men have vanished:
truth has gone from the sons of men.
Falsehood they speak one to another,
with lying lips, with a false heart.

May the Lord destroy all lying lips,
the tongue that speaks high-sounding words,
those who say, "Our tongue is our strength;
our lips are our own, who is our master?"

"For the poor who are oppressed and the needy
who groan
I myself will arise," says the Lord.
"I will grant them the salvation for which they thirst."

The words of the Lord are words without alloy,
silver from the furnace, seven times refined.

It is you, O Lord, who will take us in your care
and protect us for ever from this generation.
See how the wicked prowl on every side,
while the worthless are prized highly by the sons
of men.

Glory to the Father....

Word of God
1 John 4:10-11

I N THIS IS LOVE: not that we have loved God, but that he loved us and sent his Son as expiation for our sins. Beloved, if God so loved us, we also must love one another.

We love because he first loved us. (1 Jn 4:19)

CANTICLE OF MARY
(Text, back cover A)

I [am] the Alpha and the Omega, the beginning and the end. To the thirsty I will give a gift from the spring of life-giving water. (Rv 21:6)

INTERCESSIONS

Jesus Christ invites us to the banquet of life, where he offers himself as real food and real drink. To him we pray:

℟   For you we long!

You are the spring of life-giving water:
– refresh those who grow weary in their search for you. ℟

You are the bread from heaven:
– feed those who hunger for your love. ℟

You are the life of all the living:
– bring to the joy of everlasting life all those who have died. ℟

Personal intentions

Our Father....

May the God of hope fill us with all joy and peace in believing, so that we may abound in hope by the power of the Holy Spirit. Amen. (cf. Rom 15:13)

MARIAN ANTIPHON
(page 12 or 13)

Saint Who?

Saints Who Were Visionaries

Saint Catherine Labouré
Virgin († 1876)   Feast: December 31

Catherine was the eighth of ten children born to a farm family in Fain-lès-Moutiers, Burgundy, France. After her mother's death, nine-year-old Catherine grasped a statue of the Blessed Virgin, begging Mary to take her mother's place. At twenty-three she went to the Daughters of Charity.

From the first, Catherine's prayer was extraordinary. She saw Jesus and the blazing heart of Daughters of Charity founder, Saint Vincent de Paul. She received foreknowledge of coming war. Then, in July 1830, the Blessed Mother came and spoke with her. On two successive visits, Mary revealed that she wished to have a medal made and distributed. One side was to bear the image of Mary standing on a globe with her hands outstretched, radiating rays of light, with the prayer, "O Mary, conceived without sin, pray for us who have recourse to thee." The other side was to have a cross mounted above an "M," with the hearts of Jesus and Mary. Mary promised her protection to those who wore the medal and made the prayer.

Catherine told her spiritual director, who approached the archbishop. The medal was stamped, and many graces were reported. The medal was dubbed "miraculous." Through it all, Catherine remained anonymous. She spent the next forty-five years of her life serving the poor with her fellow sisters. Her intact remains lie today in a chapel on the rue du Bac in Paris.

Eternal Father, through the intercession of Saint Catherine Labouré, help me to live from the certainty that I am known, loved, and wanted by you.

FRIDAY, MAY 17

Prayer for the Morning

God dwells among us: come, let us adore, alleluia!

*Glory to the Father, and to the Son,
and to the Holy Spirit, as it was in the beginning,
is now, and will be for ever. Amen. Alleluia!*

HYMN

Meter: LM
This hymn can be sung to the tune used for
Jesu Dulcis Memoria

O Heart, the Ark that holds the law—
Not that whence bondage came of old,
But law of pardon and of grace
And law of mercy manifold;

O Heart, for this new covenant
The spotless shrine unto us given;
The Temple holier than of old,
Its veil more useful than that riven.

For love decreed that thou shouldst bear
From lance's thrust the open wound,
That of the love invisible
We might adore the hidden wound.

Beneath this sign of love, behold,
A Victim, bloodied, mystic, lies;
Our Christ as Priest has offered up
In both these ways his sacrifice.

What loved one will not love requite?
What soul redeemed refuses love,
Nor chooses in this Heart to find
His everlasting home above?

Psalm 132 1-5, 7-9, 13-14

In my Father's house there are many dwelling places. If there were not, would I have told you that I am going to prepare a place for you? (Jn 14:2)

In the house of Jesus' Father, the Temple, there were many courts and rooms provided for the use of different groups of people in their desire to enter God's presence and worship him in the place where he dwelt. According to John's Gospel, which we read during Easter, Jesus is the new and eternal Temple where God dwells among us. In his heart, opened to all peoples on the cross, there is a place for everyone who seeks God.

O Lord, remember David
and all the many hardships he endured,
the oath he swore to the Lord,
his vow to the Strong One of Jacob.

"I will not enter the house where I live
nor go to the bed where I rest.
I will give no sleep to my eyes,
to my eyelids I will give no slumber
till I find a place for the Lord,
a dwelling for the Strong One of Jacob."

"Let us go to the place of his dwelling;
let us go to kneel at his footstool."

Go up, Lord, to the place of your rest,
you and the ark of your strength.
Your priests shall be clothed with holiness:
your faithful shall ring out their joy.

For the Lord has chosen Zion;
he has desired it for his dwelling:
"This is my resting-place for ever,
here have I chosen to live."

Glory to the Father....

Word of God
Revelation 21:3

I HEARD A LOUD voice from the throne saying, "Behold, God's dwelling is with the human race. He will dwell with them and they will be his people and God himself will always be with them [as their God]."

The glory of the LORD filled the Dwelling. (Ex 40:34)

CANTICLE OF ZECHARIAH
(Text, back cover B)

In Christ you also are being built together into a dwelling place of God in the Spirit. (cf. Eph 2:22)

INTERCESSIONS

God dwells among us in the Church. Let us turn to him and pray:

℟   Remember your people, Lord.

You are in our midst; your name we bear:
– make us a fit dwelling place for your love. ℟

You have made us temples of your Spirit:
– cleanse our hearts and make of them a house of prayer. ℟

You have chosen us as your resting place for ever:
– grant us peace in your presence. ℟

Personal intentions

Our Father....

God of glory, you dwell in our midst through Jesus Christ, the new and eternal Temple of your Presence. Turn our hearts to worship you in the midst of our daily lives, that we may come one day to dwell with you in light, through the same Christ our Lord. Amen.

Mass

Friday of the Fourth Week of Easter

"To us this word of salvation has been sent": "I am the way and the truth and the life." Paul insists, "We ourselves are proclaiming this good news to you." What God promised, he has brought to fulfillment for us in Christ, "Where I am you also may be." Tragically, some "failed to recognize him." By faith in God and faith in Jesus we recognize the salvation for which we long, and need not let our hearts be troubled.

Entrance Antiphon   Rv 5:9-10

You have redeemed us, Lord, by your Blood,/ from every tribe and tongue and people and nation,/ and have made us into a kingdom, priests for our God, alleluia.

Collect

O God, author of our freedom and of our salvation,
listen to the voice of our pleading
and grant that those you have redeemed
by the shedding of your Son's Blood
may have life through you
and, under your protection,
rejoice for ever unharmed.
Through our Lord Jesus Christ, your Son,
who lives and reigns with you in the unity
    of the Holy Spirit,
one God, for ever and ever.

  • *God has fulfilled his promise by raising Jesus from the dead.* •

A reading from
the Acts of the Apostles   13:26-33

WHEN PAUL CAME to Antioch in Pisidia, he said in the synagogue: "My brothers, children of the family of Abraham, and those others among you who are God-fearing, to us this word of salvation has been sent. The inhabitants of Jerusalem and their leaders failed to recognize him, and by condemning him they fulfilled the oracles of the prophets that are read sabbath after sabbath. For even though they found no grounds for a death sentence, they asked Pilate to have him put to death, and when they had accomplished all that was written about him, they took him down from the tree and placed him in a tomb. But God raised him from the dead, and for many days he appeared to those who had come up with him from Galilee to Jerusalem. These are now his witnesses before the people. We ourselves are proclaiming this good news to you that what God promised our fathers he has brought to fulfillment for us, their children, by raising up Jesus, as it is written in the second psalm, *You are my Son; this day I have begotten you.*"

The word of the Lord.

———• PSALM 2 •———

℟ (7bc) **You are my Son; this day I have begotten you.**

Or: Alleluia.

"I myself have set up my king
    on Zion, my holy mountain."
I will proclaim the decree of the LORD:
    The LORD said to me, "You are my son;
    this day I have begotten you." ℟

"Ask of me and I will give you
    the nations for an inheritance
    and the ends of the earth for your possession.
You shall rule them with an iron rod;
    you shall shatter them like an earthen dish." ℟

And now, O kings, give heed;
    take warning, you rulers of the earth.
Serve the LORD with fear, and rejoice before him;
    with trembling rejoice. ℟

Alleluia, alleluia. I am the way and the truth and the
life, says the Lord;/ no one comes to the Father except
through me. Alleluia, alleluia.

> ● *I am the way and the truth and the life.* ●

A reading from
the holy Gospel according to John   14:1-6

JESUS SAID TO his disciples:
        "Do not let your hearts be
troubled. You have faith in God; have faith also in me.
In my Father's house there are many dwelling places.
If there were not, would I have told you that I am going to prepare a place for you? And if I go and prepare
a place for you, I will come back again and take you
to myself, so that where I am you also may be. Where
I am going you know the way." Thomas said to him,
"Master, we do not know where you are going; how can
we know the way?" Jesus said to him, "I am the way and
the truth and the life. No one comes to the Father except through me."
The Gospel of the Lord.

PRAYER OVER THE OFFERINGS
        Accept in compassion, Lord, we pray,
        the offerings of your family,
        that under your protective care
        they may never lose what they have received,
        but attain the gifts that are eternal.
        Through Christ our Lord.

PREFACE I-V OF EASTER ———————————— pages 218 to 219

COMMUNION ANTIPHON   Rom 4:25
Christ our Lord was handed over for our transgressions/ and
was raised again for our justification, alleluia.

PRAYER AFTER COMMUNION
Keep safe, O Lord, we pray,
those whom you have saved by your kindness,
that, redeemed by the Passion of your Son,
they may rejoice in his Resurrection.
Who lives and reigns for ever and ever.

MEDITATION OF THE DAY

"I am the way and the truth and the life"

These words of our Lord and Master Jesus Christ contain an abridgment of all the motives for our faith, our
hope, and our love. The life of the soul, the true life,
the eternal life, is the only end of the human person
and the dearest desire of his heart. Jesus Christ has declared to us that he is himself this life, and that we can
only be completely and supremely and eternally happy
in the possession of him. Therefore he alone must be
the one sovereign and unchanging object of our love.

The means of attaining to this true life is by knowing and embracing the truth, and by drawing away, in
our mind and heart, from all that is false and untrue.
Now Jesus Christ tells us that he is the Truth, the in-
fallible Truth, the essential Truth; and therefore, everything outside him must be falsehood and untruth. We
ought then to apply ourselves to know Jesus Christ
thoroughly, and we ought to employ all the strength
of our mind and all the honesty of our heart with that
intention; we ought to regulate our judgment of things
upon his, our affections upon his, being certain that

there is nothing really estimable and lovable but what he esteems and loves.

Father Jean-Nicolas Grou, s.j.

Father Grou († 1803) was a French Jesuit priest and a beloved spiritual master.

Prayer for the Evening

Jesus Christ is the source of life:
come, let us adore him, alleluia!

Glory to the Father, and to the Son,
and to the Holy Spirit, as it was in the beginning,
is now, and will be for ever. Amen. Alleluia!

Hymn   Meter: CM
This hymn can be sung to the tune used for
Amazing Grace

Blest be the everlasting God,
The Father of our Lord;
Be his abounding mercy praised,
His majesty adored.

When from the dead he raised his Son,
To dwell with him on high,
He gave our souls a lively hope
That they should never die.

There's an inheritance divine
Reserved against that day,
Which uncorrupted, undefiled,
Can never waste away.

Saints by the pow'r of God are kept,
Till their salvation come:
We walk by faith as strangers here,
But Christ shall call us home.

PSALM 49 6-12, 15b-16

Store up treasures in heaven, where neither moth nor decay destroys, nor thieves break in and steal. For where your treasure is, there also will your heart be. (Mt 6:20-21)

Where we invest our trust and our hope, we invest our lives. Let us choose to invest in the true source of life, Jesus Christ!

Why should I fear in evil days
the malice of the foes who surround me,
men who trust in their wealth,
and boast of the vastness of their riches?

For no man can buy his own ransom,
or pay a price to God for his life.
The ransom of his soul is beyond him.
He cannot buy life without end,
nor avoid coming to the grave.

He knows that wise men and fools must both perish
and leave their wealth to others.
Their graves are their homes for ever,
their dwelling place from age to age,
though their names spread wide through the land.

With the morning their outward show vanishes
and the grave becomes their home.
But God will ransom me from death
and take my soul to himself.

Glory to the Father....

Word of God 1 Peter 1:17-21

Now if you invoke as Father him who judges impartially according to each one's works, conduct yourselves with reverence during the time of your sojourning, realizing that you were ransomed from your futile conduct, handed on by your ancestors, not with perishable things like silver or gold but with the precious blood of Christ as of a spotless unblemished lamb. He was known before the foundation of the world but revealed in the final time for you, who through him believe in God who raised him from the dead and gave him glory, so that your faith and hope are in God.

> *The Son of Man came to give his life*
> *as a ransom for many. (cf. Mk 10:45)*

CANTICLE OF MARY   (Text, back cover A)

I am the way and the truth and the life. No one comes to the Father except through me. (Jn 14:6)

INTERCESSIONS

To Christ who heals our ills and raises us to life, we pray:

℟   Ransom us, O Lord.

When we are tempted to compromise Christian principles out of fear of the rich and powerful: ℟

When we are tempted to drain our time, energy, and love from families and friends for the sake of material gain: ℟

When we are tempted to trust in our own resources rather than in you as the source of life: ℟

Personal intentions

Our Father....

In the foreknowledge of God the Father, through sanctification by the Spirit, for obedience and sprinkling with the blood of Jesus Christ: may grace and peace be ours in abundance. Amen. (cf. 1 Pt 1:2)

MARIAN ANTIPHON   (page 12 or 13)

SAINT WHO?

Saints Who Were Visionaries

Saint Francis Xavier Bianchi
Priest († 1815)   Feast: January 31

Francis' mother served the sick poor in their home, yet little Francis was no spiritual prodigy. He would often steal things from his parents, hoping they would not notice. Slowly, though, a call to the priesthood grew within him. Against his father's objections, Francis went to the Barnabites at Naples.

Francis was ordained at twenty-four and then continued his studies, rising to become a respected professor and a leader in the order. Yet even as he pursued his academic work, the poor were never far from his heart. He prayed with abandon, too, and in 1800 he began to receive mystical gifts. From this time, he doubled his penances and his efforts to help others. He spent many hours in the confessional and was sought by many for his ability to read hearts and his prophetic knowledge of impending events.

Francis' intense penances probably hastened the deterioration of his health; for the last thirteen years of his life he lost the use of his legs. Still he carried on with his daily duties, miraculously standing every day to say Mass. When Mount Vesuvius erupted in 1805, the people carried him to the lava flow. His prayers stopped its progress toward the town. Already popularly proclaimed a saint upon his death, Francis was formally canonized in 1951.

Eternal Father, through the intercession of Saint Francis Xavier Bianchi, help me to give, even when it hurts.

Great Conversion Stories

Ahmet Al-Mansur
(Saint Bernard of Alzira)

John Janaro

Ahmet Al-Mansur was born in 1135, the second son of a noble Muslim family of Alzira, which was then part of the Andalusian taifa (kingdom) of Valencia on the coast of the Mediterranean in southeastern Spain. Though the local title of "emir" ("duke") was destined for his older brother, Ahmed was also educated for the royal service in Valencia. The kingdom was a place of erudition and culture, where Ahmed not only studied the Qu'ran and statecraft, but also was exposed to medieval Islamic Spain's heritage of science and the humanities.

Ahmed undoubtedly also learned some things about Christianity. The recently united Christian kingdoms of Catalonia and Aragon bordered Valencia to the north. Catalonia had built connections with Christian Europe, and had recently established three Cistercian monasteries, where French pioneering monks would soon be joined by native vocations.

At that time, the Iberian Peninsula was a place of frequent conflict, and Valencia needed good diplomats. Ahmed was a true *Andalusian*—a member of the "old Arab" aristocracy in Muslim Spain, a direct descendant of the original Arab colonists who settled there immediately after its conquest in the 8th century. He was educated and cultured, but there could be no doubts about the sincerity of his commitment to his Islamic faith, his family, and his well-rooted traditions. He was the ideal emissary to carry out delicate negotiations between rival kingdoms with different religions.

In 1160, Ahmed was sent to Barcelona, the Catalonian capital, to negotiate the release of some Valencian prisoners. The mission failed, and Ahmed began the journey back to Valencia. Something happened, however, that was not at all unusual for a medieval traveler: he got lost. The accounts of his life don't tell us how or why he got lost (or what happened to the retinue of guards and servants who, no doubt, accompanied him). But he found himself in the woods at the foot of the Prades Mountains. Though he didn't realize it, the Cistercian monastery of Poblet was nearby. The accounts tell us, however, that he heard the chanting of the monks and was fascinated by its beauty and simplicity. This, along with the fact that he needed help, led him to seek shelter at the monastery.

The abbot and the monks welcomed him, and he experienced the extraordinary embrace of Christian charity through the practice of Benedictine hospitality. He saw the profound devotion of the monks, and from his own Islamic tradition of prayer he could not deny that they truly served God. Yet their faith was in Jesus Christ, and their love compelled him—a stranger, even an "enemy"—to feel mysteriously "at home" in a way he had never felt before.

Ahmed prayed to know the will of God, and whether in fact Jesus was God's Only Begotten Son. Clearly his prayers were answered. He was baptized with the name Bernard and joined the monastery. He would spend the next twenty-one years there, before being sent back to Valencia as a missionary. He went to his own family in Alzira, where he converted his sisters Gracia and Maria. However, his older brother, now the local emir, was not convinced, and he put his siblings to death in 1180. Later canonized as martyrs, all three are venerated to this day especially in Valencia and Catalonia.

John Janaro is associate professor emeritus of theology at Christendom College, and author of Never Give Up: My Life and God's Mercy (Servant). He blogs at www.johnjanaro.com.

SATURDAY, MAY 18
Saint John I

Prayer for the Morning

In honor of Mary, the Mother of God,
let us give praise and thanks to the Lord, alleluia!

Glory to the Father.... Alleluia!

Hymn   Meter: 87 87 87
This hymn can be sung to the tune used for
Let All Mortal Flesh Keep Silence

You who own the faith of Jesus,
Sing the wonders that were done
When the love of God the Father
O'er our sin the vict'ry won,
When he made the Virgin Mary
Mother of his only Son.

Blessed were the chosen people
Out of whom the Lord did come,
Blessed was the land of promise
Fashioned for his earthly home;
But more blessed far the mother
She who bore him in her womb.

Wherefore let all faithful people
Tell the honor of her name,
Let the Church in her foreshadowed
Part in her thanksgiving claim;
What Christ's mother sang in gladness
Let Christ's people sing the same.

Psalm 52   10-11

A spreading olive tree, goodly to behold,/ the Lord has named you.
(Jer 11:16b)

One tradition holds that the tree of life in the garden of Eden was the olive tree. In the Mediterranean world of the Bible, its fruit provided food, and oil for light, heat, and healing. Mary bore the One who is the light of the world and the healing of the nations.

I am like a growing olive tree
in the house of God.
I trust in the goodness of God
for ever and ever.

I will thank you for evermore;
for this is your doing.
I will proclaim that your name is good,
in the presence of your friends.

Glory to the Father….

Word of God   Sirach 24:12-14

I HAVE STRUCK ROOT among the glorious people,/ in the portion of the LORD, his heritage.
   Like a cedar on Lebanon I am raised aloft,/ like a cypress on Mount Hermon,/ Like a palm tree in Engedi,/ like a rosebush in Jericho,/ Like a fair olive tree in the field,/ like a plane tree growing beside the water.

Every tree is known by its own fruit.
(Lk 6:44)

CANTICLE OF ZECHARIAH   (Text, back cover B)

Most blessed are you among women, and blessed is the fruit of your womb. (Lk 1:42)

INTERCESSIONS

Brought to life by the fruit of Mary's womb, let us pray:

℟   Give life, O Lord!

The Virgin Mary received your Word in faith and brought forth fruit in love:
– through her intercession, may your Church bear fruit that will last. ℟

The Virgin Mary gave birth to your Son, our Savior:
– through her intercession, bring your Church to full maturity in your Kingdom. ℟

The Virgin Mary is honored as the Mother of God:
– through her intercession, gather children from every land into your family through the proclamation of the Word and the celebration of the sacraments. ℟

Personal intentions

Our Father....

O God, you give life to the world through the life, Death, and Resurrection of your Son, our Lord Jesus Christ. Through the intercession of his Blessed Mother, grant us the light and healing he brings, who lives and reigns with you in the unity of the Holy Spirit, one God, for ever and ever. Amen.

MASS

Saturday of the Fourth Week of Easter

ENTRANCE ANTIPHON　　　　　　　　　　Cf. 1 Pt 2:9
O chosen people, proclaim the mighty works of him/ who called you out of darkness into his wonderful light, alleluia.

COLLECT
　　O God, who in the celebration of Easter
　　graciously give to the world
　　the healing of heavenly remedies,
　　show benevolence to your Church,
　　that our present observance
　　may benefit us for eternal life.

Through our Lord Jesus Christ, your Son,
who lives and reigns with you in the unity
   of the Holy Spirit,
one God, for ever and ever.

● *We now turn to the Gentiles.* ●

A reading from
the Acts of the Apostles   13:44-52

O**N THE FOLLOWING** sabbath almost the whole city gathered to hear the word of the Lord. When the Jews saw the crowds, they were filled with jealousy and with violent abuse contradicted what Paul said. Both Paul and Barnabas spoke out boldly and said, "It was necessary that the word of God be spoken to you first, but since you reject it and condemn yourselves as unworthy of eternal life, we now turn to the Gentiles. For so the Lord has commanded us, *I have made you a light to the Gentiles, that you may be an instrument of salvation to the ends of the earth.*"

The Gentiles were delighted when they heard this and glorified the word of the Lord. All who were destined for eternal life came to believe, and the word of the Lord continued to spread through the whole region. The Jews, however, incited the women of prominence who were worshipers and the leading men of the city, stirred up a persecution against Paul and Barnabas, and expelled them from their territory. So they shook the dust from their feet in protest against them and went to Iconium. The disciples were filled with joy and the Holy Spirit.

The word of the Lord.

── PSALM 98 ──

℟ (3cd) All the ends of the earth have seen the saving power of God.

Or: Alleluia.

Sing to the LORD a new song,
  for he has done wondrous deeds;
His right hand has won victory for him,
  his holy arm. ℟

The LORD has made his salvation known:
  in the sight of the nations he has revealed
    his justice.
He has remembered his kindness and his faithfulness
  toward the house of Israel. ℟

All the ends of the earth have seen
  the salvation by our God.
Sing joyfully to the LORD, all you lands;
  break into song; sing praise. ℟

Alleluia, alleluia. If you remain in my word, you will truly be my disciples,/ and you will know the truth, says the Lord. Alleluia, alleluia.

● *Whoever has seen me has seen the Father.* ●

**A reading from
the holy Gospel according to John** 14:7-14

JESUS SAID TO his disciples: "If you know me, then you will also know my Father. From now on you do know him and have seen him." Philip said to Jesus, "Master, show us the Father, and that will be enough for us." Jesus said to him, "Have I been with you for so long a time and you still do not know me, Philip? Whoever has seen me has seen the Father. How can you say, 'Show us the Father'? Do you not believe that I am in the Father and

the Father is in me? The words that I speak to you I do not speak on my own. The Father who dwells in me is doing his works. Believe me that I am in the Father and the Father is in me, or else, believe because of the works themselves. Amen, amen, I say to you, whoever believes in me will do the works that I do, and will do greater ones than these, because I am going to the Father. And whatever you ask in my name, I will do, so that the Father may be glorified in the Son. If you ask anything of me in my name, I will do it."
The Gospel of the Lord.

Prayer over the Offerings
Graciously sanctify these gifts, O Lord, we pray,
and, accepting the oblation of this spiritual sacrifice,
make of us an eternal offering to you.
Through Christ our Lord.

Preface I-V of Easter ———————— pages 218 to 219

Communion Antiphon   Jn 17:24
Father, I wish that, where I am,/ those you gave me may also be with me,/ that they may see the glory that you gave me, alleluia.

Prayer after Communion
We have partaken of the gifts of this sacred mystery,
humbly imploring, O Lord,
that what your Son commanded us to do
in memory of him
may bring us growth in charity.
Through Christ our Lord.

Saint John I   *Optional memorial*
• *Elected when he was already advanced in years to succeed Saint Hormisdas in the See of Peter, John I suffered in his own body for the sake of peace between the powers of the East and West. At the request of the Ostrogoth King Theodoric the Great, then ruler of*

Rome, John went to Constantinople to end the brutal
persecution of Arians by the Byzantine Emperor Justin I.
John secured charity toward the Arians, but, upon his
return to Italy, was imprisoned by order of Theodoric.
John died on May 18, 526, of starvation and exhaustion.
He was buried in Rome as a "victim for Christ." ●

Entrance Antiphon   Cf. 4 Esdr 2:35
Perpetual light will shine on your Saints, O Lord,/ and life
without end for ever, alleluia.

Collect
    O God, who reward faithful souls
    and who have consecrated this day
    by the martyrdom of Pope Saint John the First,
    graciously hear the prayers of your people
    and grant that we, who venerate his merits,
    may imitate his constancy in the faith.
    Through our Lord Jesus Christ, your Son,
    who lives and reigns with you in the unity
        of the Holy Spirit,
    one God, for ever and ever.

Prayer over the Offerings
    Receive, we pray, O Lord,
    the sacrifice of conciliation and praise
    which we offer to your majesty
    in commemoration of the blessed Martyr John the First,
    that it may lead us to obtain pardon
    and confirm us in perpetual thanksgiving.
    Through Christ our Lord.

Communion Antiphon   Jn 12:24
Unless a grain of wheat falls into the ground and dies,/ it
remains just a grain of wheat;/ but if it dies, it produces much
fruit, alleluia.

Prayer after Communion
    We have received your heavenly gifts,
    rejoicing at this feast day, O Lord;
    grant, we pray, that we, who in this divine banquet

proclaim the Death of your Son,
may merit to be partakers with the holy Martyrs
in his Resurrection and his glory.
Who lives and reigns for ever and ever.

MEDITATION OF THE DAY

"Whoever has seen me"

One must see and experience Jesus such as he is—divine and human—so that we can better comprehend and be more grateful for the humiliation of the Incarnate Word upon becoming man in Mary's virginal womb without ever ceasing to be God, being moved only by love, by his infinite generosity toward us sinners.

In that divinity which we can scarcely glimpse, the Father who is Light is present, the Son, who is Light from Light, is present, and the Holy Spirit, Eternal Center of Eternal Light, is present. Let us not close the eyes of our soul to this uncreated light, to divinity itself, even if it should blind us, should annihilate us. For thus we shall comprehend something of our nothingness and at the same time we shall rejoice in him who is everything....

The Most Holy Humanity of Jesus is like a door, or a path, or a stepping-stone. For us to approach divinity, one must pass through that Most Sacred Humanity to reach it. The divinity of Jesus is life itself. It is the Light of the World. It is the Eternal Truth without shadow.

O Lord, you are my repose, my happiness, my thanksgiving, my portion and my only love. I have no virtues, but you possess them all, and you are mine, divine and human. Having you, I have all I need to pay my debts and to make amends to the divinity offended by my sins, that I may be purified and enter into heaven.

O Mary, obtain for us from God that light that will eclipse the things of earth, that clarity that transcends the visible, so that we may be able to enter into the sanctuary of the Heart of Jesus. We want to be able to take abode in that God-Man. We want to lose ourselves in the unfathomable depths of his love and rejoice even here in this earthly exile, knowing through you what Jesus is like. That he is all love, and is ever seeking our love. Amen.

Blessed Concepción Cabrera de Armida
Blessed Concepción Cabrera de Armida, "Conchita" († 1937), was a wife, mother, and writer in Mexico.

Prayer for the Evening
Vigil of the Fifth Sunday of Easter

The Lord lives in us and we in him:
let us give thanks and praise, alleluia!

Glory to the Father.... Alleluia!

Hymn   Meter: LM
This hymn can be sung to the tune used for
Praise God from Whom All Blessings Flow

Exult, creation round God's throne!
All heaven, rejoice! All angels, sing!
Salvation's trumpet sound aloud
For Jesus Christ, our risen King.

Exult, O earth, in radiant hope;
In Christ's majestic splendor shine!
The Lord is here, the victory won,
The darkness drowned in light divine.

Exult, all Christians, one in praise
With our Jerusalem above!
This roof shall ring with Easter songs
That echo Christ's redeeming love.

Canticle   1 Corinthians 13:1-8a, 13

This is my commandment: love one another as I love you. No one has greater love than this, to lay down one's life for one's friends. (Jn 15:12-13)

Like the Apostles, we are called to proclaim the good news of God's redeeming love not by words alone but by our lives. As we live in love, so we mirror God's love to the world around us, where what is called "love" is so often a counterfeit of the love that impelled Jesus Christ to lay down his life for us all.

If I speak in human and angelic tongues
but do not have love,
I am a resounding gong or a clashing cymbal.

And if I have the gift of prophecy
and comprehend all mysteries and all knowledge;
if I have all faith so as to move mountains,
but do not have love, I am nothing.

If I give away everything I own,
and if I hand my body over so that I may boast
but do not have love, I gain nothing.

Love is patient, love is kind.
It is not jealous, love is not pompous,
it is not inflated, it is not rude,
it does not seek its own interests,
it is not quick-tempered, it does not brood over injury,
it does not rejoice over wrongdoing but rejoices with
   the truth.

It bears all things, believes all things,
hopes all things, endures all things.
Love never fails.

Faith, hope, love remain, these three;
but the greatest of these is love.

Word of God   1 John 2:7-10

Beloved, I am writing no new commandment to you but an old commandment that you had from the beginning. The old commandment is the word that you have heard. And yet I do write a new commandment to you, which holds true in him and among you, for the darkness is passing away, and the true light is already shining. Whoever says he is in the light, yet hates his brother, is still in the darkness. Whoever loves his brother remains in the light, and there is nothing in him to cause a fall.

His commandment is this:
we should believe in the name of his Son, Jesus Christ,
and love one another just as he commanded us.
(1 Jn 3:23)

CANTICLE OF MARY (Text, back cover A)
This I command you: love one another. (Jn 15:17)

INTERCESSIONS

To Christ, the love of God made visible among us, we pray in hope:

℟   Your love endures for ever.

You are patient, you are kind:
– recreate us in your image. ℟

You love without beginning and without end:
– make us your true disciples. ℟

You laid down your life for all humanity, and you took it up again:
– raise all people to glory in your presence. ℟

Personal intentions

Our Father....

May the blessing of almighty God, the Father, Son, and Holy Spirit, descend on us and remain with us for ever. Amen.

MARIAN ANTIPHON (page 12 or 13)

SAINT WHO?

Saints Who Were Visionaries

Saint Edmund of Abingdon
Bishop († 1240)   Feast: November 16

Edmund was born of a merchant and his devout wife in Abingdon, Berkshire, England. At twelve, he was sent to grammar school at Oxford. While there, it is said, he spontaneously offered himself as the spouse of the Virgin Mary, placing a ring on the finger of her statue. On a midsummer day while on a walk near the school, Edmund saw the Christ Child in a vision. "I know the secrets of your heart," our little Lord said, "and I have been your inseparable companion…. From now on I promise you that I and my Mother, your spouse, shall be your helpers and comforters." Then the little Child blessed Edmund.

After his time at Oxford, Edmund went to Paris, where he was one of the first to study Aristotle's philosophy. A five-year stint teaching at Oxford followed, and then Edmund capped his studies with the theology course in Paris. He was ordained a priest at this time and then returned to Oxford as a theology professor. All knew him to be a careful scholar, but also generous in alms-giving and unrelenting in prayer. Pope Gregory IX asked Edmund to preach the sixth Crusade in 1227.

In 1233, Edmund was named Archbishop of Canterbury. He enacted reforms while resisting the interference of King Henry III in Church affairs. He died near Pontigny, France, on his way to Rome, and was canonized a mere six years later.

Loving Father, through the intercession of Saint Edmund of Abingdon, send me little Jesus and his Mother Mary as my helpers and comforters.

Lectio Divina

A Prayerful Reading of Sacred Scripture

The Gospel for the Fifth Sunday of Easter
John 13:31-33a, 34-35

When Judas had left them, Jesus said, "Now is the Son of Man glorified, and God is glorified in him" (13:31).
Today's Gospel takes us back to Holy Thursday, after the washing of the disciples' feet and the announcement of Judas' betrayal. Why, five weeks after Easter, go back to the terrible hours before the crucifixion? Because now we understand the horror of the cross in light of its effect—the destruction of sin and death. Can this give us a new perspective today? Can we view our own life and its crosses through the eyes of faith, with confidence in Jesus? *Judas... left them*: Exposed, Judas flees. In truth, the revelation that Jesus knows our hearts need not cause us to run and hide, but to move deeper into the safety of his company. If only Judas had cried out at that very moment: *Kyrie, eleison! Christe, eleison!* Instead, tragically, he distanced himself from Jesus. We cannot bear the burden of our sins alone. Fortunately, we don't need to—*Now is the Son of Man glorified*: Jesus is in complete control. What will appear to be a disaster will be the greatest event the world has ever known: sin is vanquished, God is glorified.

"If God is glorified in him, God will also glorify him in himself, and God will glorify him at once" (13:32).
Jesus only wants to give us what is his as the Son of God: "I have told you this so that my joy might be in you and your joy might be complete" (Jn 15:11; consider also Jn 17:1-5, 20-26). When we are misunderstood, persecuted, or suffering—and especially at the hour of our death—our union with Jesus means God is glorified in us, too. *At once*:

To what moment does this refer? "While he is yet on the very cross shall his glory appear. For the sun was darkened, rocks were rent, and many bodies of those that slept arose. In this way he restores the drooping spirits of his disciples, and persuades them, instead of sorrowing, to rejoice" (Saint John Chrysostom). Do we believe that we are close to God and loved by him also *at once*, that is, here and now, even in moments of affliction, or in our weaknesses? Or do we imagine that it can only be later, sometime in the future, after we have improved ourselves or gotten rid of our problems? If so, our struggles are easily taken to be obstacles to God's love. Yet, perhaps that is precisely how God is loving us, keeping us close, and therefore glorifying us? "The LORD is close to the brokenhearted,/ saves those whose spirit is crushed (Ps 34:19).

"My children, I will be with you only a little while longer"
(13:33a).
It is not an insult to be called *my children* by the Lord Jesus, but a privilege (1 Jn 3:1). Jesus is a father to us because, receiving everything from the Father (Jn 16:15), he generates within us the new life of grace. We delight in being his children, freed from the burden of having to be independent or self-sufficient. (Recall Judas' awful departure from Jesus, above.) Consider Matthew 18:1-5: While the disciples are concerned about becoming the greatest, Jesus teaches them that the true way to greatness is spiritual childhood, of being shamelessly dependent on him. Do we ever feel that the heights of union with God are not possible for us? That our own life is too ordinary, that we do not have the strength of character we see in the great saints? "Instead of becoming discouraged, I said to myself: God cannot inspire unrealizable desires. I can then in spite of my littleness aspire to holiness…. [Thus] I wanted to find an elevator which would raise me to Jesus, for I am too small to climb the rough stairway of perfection. I searched, then, in the Scriptures for some

sign of this.... The elevator which must raise me to heaven is your arms, O Jesus! And for this I had no need to grow up, but rather I had to remain little and become this more and more" (Saint Thérèse of Lisieux).

"I give you a new commandment: love one another. As I have loved you, so you also should love one another" (13:34).
If the old law (Lev 19:18) already teaches us to love one another, why does Jesus call it a new commandment? Saint Augustine: The new law "is that love which our Lord distinguishes from earthly affection: *As I have loved you....* Not the love with which men love one another, but that of the children of the Most High God, who would be brethren of his Only Begotten Son, and therefore love one another with that love with which he loved them." Consider 1 Jn 4:19: "We love because he first loved us."

"This is how all will know that you are my disciples, if you have love for one another" (13:35).
It is not miracles or mighty deeds that become the mark of being Christ's disciples, but charity—Jesus' own love active within us. This can be true of even the simplest and most unremarkable of lives, even in giving a cup of cold water (Mt 10:42). Dorotheus of Gaza: "Just as in a circle the lines drawn from the circumference to the center become closer to one another, the closer they come to the center (and the farther away they are from the center, the farther they are from each other), so, too, the more someone approaches the love of God and of Christ, the more he approaches the love of neighbor. For God is the center of the world, as well as of our hearts and our love.... In God, therefore, all love of neighbors converges and is united." And where do we continue to find and be filled with the love of God? The *sacramentum caritatis*, the Eucharist (Jn 6:56-58).

Suggested Prayer of the Faithful

(Each local community should compose its own Universal Prayer, but may find inspiration in the texts proposed here.)

God has made his dwelling with us and promises to make all things new. Counting on the Father's boundless mercy we now pray:

That all members of the Church may be strengthened in holiness and truth, and walk in the fear of the Lord.

For children preparing to receive First Holy Communion: that the gift of the Holy Eucharist will draw them into an unending friendship with the Lord.

That divisions will be healed, violence will cease, and the peace and justice of God's Kingdom will reign in every nation on earth.

For the poor, the vulnerable, the lonely, and the forgotten: that they know the security and love of Jesus.

That Christian husbands and wives be strengthened in their loving commitment to one another, modeling the union of Christ and the Church.

For the grace this week to love others as Jesus has loved us.

Loving Father, your Son taught us to ask for what we need. Fill us with confidence, and may your grace always remain in us. Through Christ our Lord. Amen. ■

SUNDAY, MAY 19
Fifth Sunday of Easter

Prayer for the Morning

The Lord is good and upright:
come, let us adore, alleluia!

Glory to the Father…. Alleluia!

Hymn   Meter: 77 77
This hymn can be sung to the tune used for
Savior of the Nations, Come

What will rise with Christ today,
Drinking in the April air?
Scattered forests, gray and bare,
Do these breathe the Easter air?

What will rise with Christ today,
Gathered into blessèd birth?
Fur and feather of the earth,
Do these dream of second birth?

What will rise with Christ today,
Silencing their enemy?
Will the creatures of the sea
Leap beside humanity?

What will rise with Christ today,
Bringing threatened things in tow?
Do we, pausing as we grow,
Rise to guide a world in tow?

Psalm 25   4-9, 12-14

I give you a new commandment: love one another. As I have loved
you, so you also should love one another. (Jn 13:34)

Jesus lives the way of love, which he teaches to his disciples as the great commandment for Christian life.

Lord, make me know your ways.
Lord, teach me your paths.
Make me walk in your truth, and teach me:
for you are God my savior.

In you I hope all day long
because of your goodness, O Lord.
Remember your mercy, Lord,
and the love you have shown from of old.
Do not remember the sins of my youth.
In your love remember me.

The Lord is good and upright.
He shows the path to those who stray,
he guides the humble in the right path;
he teaches his way to the poor.

If anyone fears the Lord
he will show him the path he should choose.
His soul shall live in happiness
and his children shall possess the land.
The Lord's friendship is for those who revere him;
to them he reveals his covenant.

Glory to the Father....

Word of God
Mark 12:28-31

ONE OF THE SCRIBES, when he came forward and heard them disputing and saw how well he had answered them, asked him, "Which is the first of all the commandments?" Jesus replied, "The first is this: 'Hear, O Israel! The Lord our God is Lord alone! You shall love the Lord your God with all your heart, with all your soul, with all your mind, and with all your strength.'

The second is this: 'You shall love your neighbor as yourself.' There is no other commandment greater than these."

If you keep my commandments,
you will remain in my love, just as I have kept
my Father's commandments and remain in his love.
(Jn 15:10)

Canticle of Zechariah   (Text, back cover B)

This is how all will know that you are my disciples, if you have love for one another. (Jn 13:35)

Intercessions

God is love; to Christ we pray:

℟   Show us the path we should choose!

You are the way:
– lead us in your ways today and throughout the coming week. ℟

You are the truth:
– let truth be our guide in every conversation. ℟

You are the life:
– teach us to live according to your love. ℟

Personal intentions

Our Father....

God of mercy and of truth, you sent your only Son to lead us on the way to fullness of life. Through the mystery of his Death and Resurrection, transform our hearts from disobedience to discipleship, and from self-centeredness to love, through the same Christ our Lord. Amen.

MASS

Fifth Sunday of Easter

At the Last Supper, Jesus tells the Eleven: "As I have loved you, so you also should love one another. All will know that you are my disciples if you love one another." The love of Jesus Christ for us is precisely what makes it possible to love like him in turn— he loves us first, and his love changes us. Thus, when we bear his own love for one another, this moves others to believe in Christ, to know that "God's dwelling is with the human race." This is how Paul and Barnabas "made a considerable number of disciples."

ENTRANCE ANTIPHON   Cf. Ps 98 (97):1-2
O sing a new song to the Lord,/ for he has worked wonders;/ in the sight of the nations/ he has shown his deliverance, alleluia.

GLORIA ——————————————————————— page 212

COLLECT
    Almighty ever-living God,
    constantly accomplish the Paschal Mystery within us,
    that those you were pleased to make new in Holy
       Baptism
    may, under your protective care, bear much fruit
    and come to the joys of life eternal.
    Through our Lord Jesus Christ, your Son,
    who lives and reigns with you in the unity
       of the Holy Spirit,
    one God, for ever and ever.

    ● *They called the Church together and reported what God had done with them.* ●

A reading from
the Acts of the Apostles   14:21-27

AFTER PAUL and Barnabas had proclaimed the good news to that city and made a considerable number of disciples, they returned to Lystra and to Iconium and

to Antioch. They strengthened the spirits of the disciples and exhorted them to persevere in the faith, saying, "It is necessary for us to undergo many hardships to enter the kingdom of God." They appointed elders for them in each church and, with prayer and fasting, commended them to the Lord in whom they had put their faith. Then they traveled through Pisidia and reached Pamphylia. After proclaiming the word at Perga they went down to Attalia. From there they sailed to Antioch, where they had been commended to the grace of God for the work they had now accomplished. And when they arrived, they called the church together and reported what God had done with them and how he had opened the door of faith to the Gentiles.
The word of the Lord.

——• PSALM 145 •——

℟ (cf. 1) **I will praise your name for ever, my king and my God.**

Or: Alleluia.

The LORD is gracious and merciful,
　　slow to anger and of great kindness.
The LORD is good to all
　　and compassionate toward all his works. ℟

Let all your works give you thanks, O LORD,
　　and let your faithful ones bless you.
Let them discourse of the glory of your kingdom
　　and speak of your might. ℟

Let them make known your might to the children
　　　of Adam,
　　and the glorious splendor of your kingdom.
Your kingdom is a kingdom for all ages,
　　and your dominion endures through all
　　　generations. ℟

● *God will wipe every tear from their eyes.* ●

A reading from
the Book of Revelation
21:1-5a

THEN I, JOHN, saw a new heaven and a new earth. The former heaven and the former earth had passed away, and the sea was no more. I also saw the holy city, a new Jerusalem, coming down out of heaven from God, prepared as a bride adorned for her husband. I heard a loud voice from the throne saying, "Behold, God's dwelling is with the human race. He will dwell with them and they will be his people and God himself will always be with them as their God. He will wipe every tear from their eyes, and there shall be no more death or mourning, wailing or pain, for the old order has passed away."

The One who sat on the throne said, "Behold, I make all things new."

The word of the Lord.

Alleluia, alleluia. I give you a new commandment, says the Lord:/ love one another as I have loved you. Alleluia, alleluia.

● *I give you a new commandment: love one another.* ●

A reading from
the holy Gospel according to John
13:31-33a, 34-35

WHEN JUDAS HAD left them, Jesus said, "Now is the Son of Man glorified, and God is glorified in him. If God is glorified in him, God will also glorify him in himself, and God will glorify him at once. My children, I will be with you only a little while longer. I give you a new commandment: love one another. As I have loved

you, so you also should love one another. This is how all will know that you are my disciples, if you have love for one another."
The Gospel of the Lord.

CREDO ———————————————————————— page 214

Prayer over the Offerings
O God, who by the wonderful exchange effected in
this sacrifice
have made us partakers of the one supreme Godhead,
grant, we pray,
that, as we have come to know your truth,
we may make it ours by a worthy way of life.
Through Christ our Lord.

Preface I-V of Easter ———————————— pages 218 to 219

Communion Antiphon   Cf. Jn 15:1, 5
I am the true vine and you are the branches, says the Lord./
Whoever remains in me, and I in him, bears fruit in plenty,
alleluia.

Prayer after Communion
Graciously be present to your people, we pray,
O Lord,
and lead those you have imbued with heavenly mysteries
to pass from former ways to newness of life.
Through Christ our Lord.

A formula of Solemn Blessing, pages 78-79, may be used.

• ————————————————————————————————— •
M E D I T A T I O N   O F   T H E   D A Y
• ————————————————————————————————— •

The Commandment of Love

If you don't have love for one another, then how can you love Christ? How can they see Jesus in you? That's why we need a clean heart, to see Jesus. Love one another. That's all Jesus came to teach us. The whole Gospel is very, very simple. Do you love me? Obey my commandments. He's turning and twisting just to get around to one thing: love one another. He wants us to be really, really loving....

Intense love does not measure; it just gives. To be an apostle of the Sacred Heart, one must be burning with love, intense love for your neighbor....

These words of Jesus, *Love one another, even as I have loved you*, should be not only a light to us, but they should also be a flame consuming the selfishness which prevents the growth of holiness. Jesus *loved us to the end*, to the very limit of love: the cross. This love must come from within, from our union with Christ. It must be an outpouring of our love for God, in one family, a family with the common Father, who is in heaven. Loving must be as normal to us as living and breathing, day after day until our death.

SAINT TERESA OF CALCUTTA

Saint Teresa of Calcutta († 1997) founded the Missionaries of Charity and won the Nobel Peace Prize.

Prayer for the Evening

*We adore you, O Lord,
and we praise you, alleluia!*

*Glory to the Father, and to the Son,
and to the Holy Spirit, as it was in the beginning,
is now, and will be for ever. Amen. Alleluia!*

HYMN   Meter: LM
This hymn can be sung to the tune used for
I Know that My Redeemer Lives

Christ is alive! Let Christians sing.
The cross stands empty to the sky.
Let streets and homes with praises ring.
Love, drowned in death, shall never die.

Christ is alive! No longer bound
to distant years in Palestine,
but saving, healing, here and now,
and touching every place and time.

Christ is alive, and comes to bring
good news to this and every age,
till earth and sky and ocean ring
with joy, with justice, love and praise.

PSALM 119 33-40

Children, let us love not in word or speech but in deed and truth.
(1 Jn 3:18)

To recite God's law of love means nothing; to live it is everything.
Only in the risen Christ can we aspire to grow into that life-giving
law which we embraced in our baptism.

Teach me the demands of your precepts
and I will keep them to the end.
Train me to observe your law,
to keep it with my heart.

Guide me in the path of your commands;
for there is my delight.
Bend my heart to your will
and not to love of gain.

Keep my eyes from what is false:
by your word, give me life.
Keep the promise you have made
to the servant who fears you.

Keep me from the scorn I dread,
for your decrees are good.
See, I long for your precepts:
then in your justice, give me life.

Glory to the Father....

Word of God
1 John 5:2-3

I N THIS WAY we know that we love the children of God when we love God and obey his commandments. For the love of God is this, that we keep his commandments. And his commandments are not burdensome.

Whoever says, "I know him," but does not keep his commandments is a liar, and the truth is not in him.
(1 Jn 2:4)

CANTICLE OF MARY
(Text, back cover A)

It is not those who hear the law who are just in the sight of God; rather, those who observe the law will be justified. (Rom 2:13)

INTERCESSIONS

As disciples of the risen Lord, let us pray:

℟   By your word give us life!

By your love,
– keep us faithful to your law: ℟

By your love,
– keep us in communion with one another and with you: ℟

By your love,
– keep us firm in our daily efforts to grow in love: ℟
Personal intentions

Our Father….

Peace be to all, and love with faith, from God the Father and the Lord Jesus Christ. Amen. (cf. Eph 6:23)

MARIAN ANTIPHON
(page 12 or 13)

MONDAY, MAY 20
Saint Bernardine of Siena

Prayer for the Morning

The Lord will reign for ever, alleluia!

Glory to the Father, and to the Son,
and to the Holy Spirit, as it was in the beginning,
is now, and will be for ever. Amen. Alleluia!

HYMN   Meter: 87 87 D

Lord, whose love in humble service
Bore the weight of human need,
Who upon the cross, forsaken,
Worked your mercy's perfect deed:
We, your servants, bring the worship
Not of voice alone, but heart;
Consecrating to your purpose
Every gift which you impart.

Still your children wander homeless;
Still the hungry cry for bread;
Still the captives long for freedom;
Still in grief we mourn our dead.
As you, Lord, in deep compassion
Healed the sick and freed the soul,
By your Spirit send your power
To our world to make it whole.

As we worship, grant us vision,
Till your love's revealing light
In its height and depth and greatness
Dawns upon our quickened sight,
Making known the needs and burdens
Your compassion bids us bear,

Stirring us to ardent service,
Your abundant life to share.

PSALM 146   5-10

Paul called out in a loud voice, "Stand up straight on your feet." He
jumped up and began to walk about. (cf. Acts 14:10)

The apostolic Church began immediately to heal the lame in Jesus'
name, as a sign that the work of deliverance begun by Christ continued in and through the Church.

He is happy who is helped by Jacob's God,
whose hope is in the Lord his God,
who alone made heaven and earth,
the seas and all they contain.

It is he who keeps faith for ever,
who is just to those who are oppressed.
It is he who gives bread to the hungry,
the Lord, who sets prisoners free,

the Lord who gives sight to the blind,
who raises up those who are bowed down,
the Lord, who protects the stranger
and upholds the widow and orphan.

It is the Lord who loves the just
but thwarts the path of the wicked.
The Lord will reign for ever,
Zion's God, from age to age.

Glory to the Father....

Word of God   Acts 3:6-10

PETER SAID, "I have neither
silver nor gold, but what
I do have I give you: in the name of Jesus Christ the
Nazorean, [rise and] walk." Then Peter took him by
the right hand and raised him up, and immediately his

feet and ankles grew strong. He leaped up, stood, and walked around, and went into the temple with them, walking and jumping and praising God. When all the people saw him walking and praising God, they recognized him as the one who used to sit begging at the Beautiful Gate of the temple, and they were filled with amazement and astonishment at what had happened to him.

The crowds were amazed when they saw the mute speaking, the deformed made whole, the lame walking, and the blind able to see, and they glorified the God of Israel. (Mt 15:31)

CANTICLE OF ZECHARIAH (Text, back cover B)

The blind regain their sight, the lame walk, lepers are cleansed, the deaf hear, the dead are raised, and the poor have the good news proclaimed to them. (Mt 11:5)

INTERCESSIONS

With confidence in Christ our Healer, we pray:

℟ You are our saving help, O Lord!

Free those who are paralyzed by sinful ways,
– and teach them to run with joy in the way of your commandments. ℟

Give sight to those who are blinded by self-centeredness,
– and teach them to see the beauty of those around them. ℟

Grant hearing to those who are deaf of heart,
– and teach them to rejoice in your word. ℟

Personal intentions

Our Father....

God our Father, you sent your only Son to bring your healing love into our wounded world. Through the power of his Death and Resurrection, make whole all that is broken in us and between us, that we may sing praise to your name with one voice through Jesus Christ our Lord. Amen.

MASS

Monday of the Fifth Week of Easter

ENTRANCE ANTIPHON
The Good Shepherd has risen,/ who laid down his life for his sheep/ and willingly died for his flock, alleluia.

COLLECT
>May your right hand, O Lord, we pray,
>encompass your family with perpetual help,
>so that, defended from all wickedness
>by the Resurrection of your Only Begotten Son,
>we may make our way by means of your heavenly gifts.
>Through our Lord Jesus Christ, your Son,
>who lives and reigns with you in the unity
>   of the Holy Spirit,
>one God, for ever and ever.

● *We proclaim to you Good News that you should turn from these idols to the living God.* ●

A reading from
the Acts of the Apostles
14:5-18

THERE WAS an attempt in Iconium by both the Gentiles and the Jews, together with their leaders, to attack and stone Paul and Barnabas. They realized it, and fled to the Lycaonian cities of Lystra and Derbe and to the surrounding countryside, where they continued to proclaim the Good News.

At Lystra there was a crippled man, lame from birth, who had never walked. He listened to Paul speaking, who looked intently at him, saw that he had the faith to be healed, and called out in a loud voice, "Stand up straight on your feet." He jumped up and began to walk about. When the crowds saw what Paul had done, they cried out in Lycaonian, "The gods have come down to us in human form." They called Barnabas "Zeus" and Paul "Hermes," because he was the chief speaker. And the priest of Zeus, whose temple was at the entrance to the city, brought oxen and garlands to the gates, for he together with the people intended to offer sacrifice.

The Apostles Barnabas and Paul tore their garments when they heard this and rushed out into the crowd, shouting, "Men, why are you doing this? We are of the same nature as you, human beings. We proclaim to you good news that you should turn from these idols to the living God, *who made heaven and earth and sea and all that is in them.* In past generations he allowed all Gentiles to go their own ways; yet, in bestowing his goodness, he did not leave himself without witness, for he gave you rains from heaven and fruitful seasons, and filled you with nourishment and gladness for your hearts." Even with these words, they scarcely restrained the crowds from offering sacrifice to them.

The word of the Lord.

———• Psalm 115 •———

℟ (1ab) **Not to us, O Lord, but to your name give the glory.**

Or: Alleluia.

Not to us, O Lord, not to us
  but to your name give glory
    because of your mercy, because of your truth.

Why should the pagans say,
  "Where is their God?" ℟

Our God is in heaven;
  whatever he wills, he does.
Their idols are silver and gold,
  the handiwork of men. ℟

May you be blessed by the LORD,
  who made heaven and earth.
Heaven is the heaven of the LORD,
  but the earth he has given to the children of men. ℟

Alleluia, alleluia. The Holy Spirit will teach you everything/ and remind you of all I told you. Alleluia, alleluia.

> ● *The Advocate whom the Father will send will teach you everything.* ●

A reading from
the holy Gospel according to John   14:21-26

JESUS SAID TO his disciples: "Whoever has my commandments and observes them is the one who loves me. Whoever loves me will be loved by my Father, and I will love him and reveal myself to him." Judas, not the Iscariot, said to him, "Master, then what happened that you will reveal yourself to us and not to the world?" Jesus answered and said to him, "Whoever loves me will keep my word, and my Father will love him, and we will come to him and make our dwelling with him. Whoever does not love me does not keep my words; yet the word you hear is not mine but that of the Father who sent me.

"I have told you this while I am with you. The Advocate, the Holy Spirit whom the Father will send

in my name—he will teach you everything and remind you of all that I told you."
The Gospel of the Lord.

PRAYER OVER THE OFFERINGS
May our prayers rise up to you, O Lord,
together with the sacrificial offerings,
so that, purified by your graciousness,
we may be conformed to the mysteries of your
    mighty love.
Through Christ our Lord.

PREFACE I-V OF EASTER ———————— pages 218 to 219

COMMUNION ANTIPHON   Jn 14:27
Peace I leave with you; my peace I give to you./ Not as the world gives do I give it to you,/ says the Lord, alleluia.

PRAYER AFTER COMMUNION
Almighty ever-living God,
who restore us to eternal life
in the Resurrection of Christ,
increase in us, we pray, the fruits of this paschal
    Sacrament
and pour into our hearts the strength of this saving
    food.
Through Christ our Lord.

SAINT BERNARDINE OF SIENA   *Optional memorial*

● *Having entered the Franciscans in 1402, Bernardine achieved fame as a preacher in Milan and throughout Italy. Upwards of 30,000 people were known to come to hear his open-air sermons. Bernardine promoted devotion to the Holy Name of Jesus, and reconciled warring factions. He championed the reforms of the Friars Minor, drawing in numerous vocations. Three times, Bernardine was offered the office of bishop. He refused each time, preferring to remain poor. Bernardine died in 1444, shortly after preaching for fifty straight days in his hometown in the Republic of Siena.* •

ENTRANCE ANTIPHON

O chosen people, proclaim the mighty works of him/ who called you out of darkness into his wonderful light, alleluia.

COLLECT

O God, who gave the Priest Saint Bernardine of Siena
a great love for the holy Name of Jesus,
grant, through his merits and prayers,
that we may ever be set aflame
with the spirit of your love.
Through our Lord Jesus Christ, your Son,
who lives and reigns with you in the unity
of the Holy Spirit,
one God, for ever and ever.

PRAYER OVER THE OFFERINGS

Look upon the sacrificial gifts we offer, almighty God,
on the feast day of blessed Bernardine of Siena,
and grant that we, who celebrate the mysteries
of the Lord's Passion,
may imitate what we now do.
Through Christ our Lord.

COMMUNION ANTIPHON   Ez 34:15

I will pasture my sheep;/ I myself will give them rest, says the Lord, alleluia.

PRAYER AFTER COMMUNION

By the power of this mystery, O Lord,
confirm your servants in the true faith,
that they may everywhere profess in word and deed
the faith for which blessed Bernardine of Siena never
ceased to labor
and for which he spent his whole life.
Through Christ our Lord.

MEDITATION OF THE DAY

Keeping His Word, Slowly but Surely

If you do a good deed, be it ever so simple, and do it out of love and of charity, this is most pleasing to God; for though it may be a little, it is indeed very pleasing to him. But he does wish in truth that you proceed from good to better. I once saw a man who [was always] performing good deeds, and each time he would say: "I wish that I might begin to do a little good." Though he was already doing it, yet for all this he did not seem to himself to be doing good. And I saw his soul attain to such an estate of perfection that it was a wonderful thing.

And therefore I have greater faith in him who proceeds little by little, from good to better, than in him who leaps all of a sudden into every great undertaking. As said a holy father, admonishing and teaching: "If you had a thousand years to live in the service of God, see always that you go from good to better; and in like manner if you had to live but for a day, go always from good to better."

Do you wish to have an example of this? Have you seen great riches come all of a sudden, and as quickly as they come so quickly do they depart? Therefore I say it is better that you should proceed little by little from virtue to virtue.

Lo! Consider water…. If you would heat it, first it rises to such a degree that it becomes lukewarm. And leaving it still longer on the fire it passes from the lukewarm stage to heat…. So doth a soul which is cold, and wishes to attain to the heat of the love of God.

SAINT BERNARDINE OF SIENA

Saint Bernardine of Siena († 1444) was an Italian Franciscan and great preacher who spread devotion to the Holy Name.

Prayer for the Evening

God dwells in our midst: come, let us adore, alleluia!

Glory to the Father, and to the Son,
and to the Holy Spirit, as it was in the beginning,
is now, and will be for ever. Amen. Alleluia!

HYMN   Meter: 87 87 D
This hymn can be sung to the tune used for
There's a Wideness in God's Mercy

God has called you out of darkness
Into his most marvelous light,
Brought his truth to life within you,
Turned your blindness into sight.
Let your light so shine around you
That God's name is glorified,
And all find fresh hope and purpose
In Christ Jesus crucified.

Once you were an alien people,
Strangers to God's heart of love,
But he brought you home in mercy,
Citizens of heaven above.
Let his love flow out to others,
Let them feel the Father's care,
That they too may know his welcome
And his countless blessings share.

PSALM 15

Whoever loves me will keep my word, and my Father will love him, and we will come to him and make our dwelling with him. (Jn 14:23)

To dwell in God's presence, we must be filled with love alone. The word we receive through Jesus Christ cleanses us, heals us, and makes us dwelling places for the God who is love.

Lord, who shall be admitted to your tent
and dwell on your holy mountain?

He who walks without fault;
he who acts with justice
and speaks the truth from his heart;
he who does not slander with his tongue;

he who does no wrong to his brother,
who casts no slur on his neighbor,
who holds the godless in disdain,
but honors those who fear the Lord;

he who keeps his pledge, come what may;
who takes no interest on a loan
and accepts no bribes against the innocent.
Such a man will stand firm for ever.

Glory to the Father....

Word of God   Ephesians 3:14-19

For this reason I kneel before the Father, from whom every family in heaven and on earth is named, that he may grant you in accord with the riches of his glory to be strengthened with power through his Spirit in the inner self, and that Christ may dwell in your hearts through faith; that you, rooted and grounded in love, may have strength to comprehend with all the holy ones what is the breadth and length and height and depth, and to know the love of Christ that surpasses knowledge, so that you may be filled with all the fullness of God.

Let the word of Christ dwell in you richly.
(Col 3:16)

CANTICLE OF MARY

(Text, back cover A)

Do you not know that you are the temple of God, and that the Spirit of God dwells in you? (1 Cor 3:16)

INTERCESSIONS

In Christ our dwelling place, we pray:

℞ Stay with us, Lord!

You build us into a dwelling place in the Spirit:
– fill us with the glory of your presence. ℞

You come to us in word and sacrament:
– drive out before you all that cannot give you glory. ℞

You will dwell with us for ever in heaven:
– bring into your presence all who have died in
loneliness. ℞

Personal intentions

Our Father....

May we come to know the love of Christ that surpasses knowledge, so that we may be filled with all the fullness of God. Amen. (cf. Eph 3:19)

MARIAN ANTIPHON

(page 12 or 13)

SAINT WHO?

Saints Who Were Visionaries

Saint Catherine Thomas
Virgin († 1574)   Feast: April 1

The sunny island of Mallorca, located in the Mediterranean Sea east of Spain, boasts one canonized saint, Catherine Thomas. She was born at Valldemossa in 1533, the youngest of six children. Both of Catherine's peasant parents died while she was young, and an uncle took her in. He fed her and clothed her and made her earn her keep working at his farm as a servant. Yet Catherine found solace in prayer. The locals, aware of her solemn nature, nicknamed her *Viejecita*, "little old woman."

When Catherine was seventeen, her confessor managed to get her a place as a domestic servant with a wealthy family. She learned to read. A few years later, she entered the Canonesses of Saint Augustine at the convent of Saint Mary Magdalen in Palma as a choir sister. Soon Catherine was manifesting extraordinary mystical graces. She fell into ecstasy, usually after receiving Holy Communion. At other times, the devil would appear and physically assault her. Afterward, Saint Cosmas and Saint Damian appeared to salve her wounds. She also was visited by Saint Catherine of Siena and Saint Anthony.

Upon her death, the people of Majorca immediately declared Catherine a saint. She was formally canonized in 1930 by Pope Pius XI and is celebrated in yearly festivals on the island.

*Merciful Father, through the intercession of
Saint Catherine Thomas, bring me friends
who will stand by me when trials come.*

TUESDAY, MAY 21
Saint Christopher Magallanes and Companions

Prayer for the Morning

Our God is a God of peace:
let us give thanks and praise, alleluia!

Glory to the Father.... Alleluia!

HYMN

Meter: 76 76 D
This hymn can be sung to the tune used for
The Church's One Foundation

Behold, how like a monarch
Peace enters in to reign
When all things rightly ordered
Proclaim Christ's true domain.
God crowns each true peacemaker
With blessings from above
To share with friend and neighbor
The treasure of God's love.

The sacrifice of Jesus,
His rising from the dead,
His sending of the Spirit
Turns this world on its head.
The promise of our Savior
Sings, "Heaven is at hand.
Receive the Holy Spirit.
Peace to you and your land."

PSALM 34   12-15, 17-18

The world must know that I love the Father and that I do just as the
Father has commanded me. (Jn 14:31)

Jesus shows us the way to true peace: obedience to the Father's will
rather than to the clamor of self-interest. In living as he lived, we

not only live in peace ourselves; we also make a place of peace for all those around us.

Come, children, and hear me
that I may teach you the fear of the Lord.
Who is he who longs for life
and many days, to enjoy his prosperity?

Then keep your tongue from evil
and your lips from speaking deceit.
Turn aside from evil and do good;
seek and strive after peace.

The Lord turns his eyes to the just
and his ears to their appeal.
They call and the Lord hears
and rescues them in all their distress.

Glory to the Father....

Word of God   Romans 2:5-11

By your stubbornness and impenitent heart, you are storing up wrath for yourself for the day of wrath and revelation of the just judgment of God, who will repay everyone according to his works: eternal life to those who seek glory, honor, and immortality through perseverance in good works, but wrath and fury to those who selfishly disobey the truth and obey wickedness. Yes, affliction and distress will come upon every human being who does evil, Jew first and then Greek. But there will be glory, honor, and peace for everyone who does good, Jew first and then Greek. There is no partiality with God.

God is not the God of disorder but of peace.
(cf. 1 Cor 14:33)

CANTICLE OF ZECHARIAH (Text, back cover B)

The concern of the flesh is death, but the concern of the spirit is life and peace. (Rom 8:6)

INTERCESSIONS

In a world divided, let us pray for the Spirit of peace:

℟ You hear your children's appeal.

God of peace, make peace among those at war: ℟

God of justice, make right what we have made wrong: ℟

God of goodness, make holy what we have turned to our own selfish ends: ℟

Personal intentions

Our Father....

God of peace, you sent among us the Prince of Peace, our Lord Jesus Christ. Through the victory of his cross, put to death all within and around us that is still dedicated to division and death. Who lives and reigns with you in the unity of the Holy Spirit, one God, for ever and ever. Amen.

MASS

Tuesday of the Fifth Week of Easter

ENTRANCE ANTIPHON Rv 19:5; 12:10

Sing praise to our God,/ all you who fear God, both small and great,/ for now salvation and strength have come,/ and the power of his Christ, alleluia.

COLLECT

O God, who restore us to eternal life
in the Resurrection of Christ,
grant your people constancy in faith and hope,
that we may never doubt the promises
of which we have learned from you.

Through our Lord Jesus Christ, your Son,
who lives and reigns with you in the unity
   of the Holy Spirit,
one God, for ever and ever.

● *They called the Church together and reported what
God had done with them.* ●

A reading from
the Acts of the Apostles   14:19-28

IN THOSE DAYS, some Jews from Antioch and Iconium arrived and won over the crowds. They stoned Paul and dragged him out of the city, supposing that he was dead. But when the disciples gathered around him, he got up and entered the city. On the following day he left with Barnabas for Derbe.

After they had proclaimed the good news to that city and made a considerable number of disciples, they returned to Lystra and to Iconium and to Antioch. They strengthened the spirits of the disciples and exhorted them to persevere in the faith, saying, "It is necessary for us to undergo many hardships to enter the Kingdom of God." They appointed presbyters for them in each Church and, with prayer and fasting, commended them to the Lord in whom they had put their faith. Then they traveled through Pisidia and reached Pamphylia. After proclaiming the word at Perga they went down to Attalia. From there they sailed to Antioch, where they had been commended to the grace of God for the work they had now accomplished. And when they arrived, they called the Church together and reported what God had done with them and how he had opened the door of faith to the Gentiles. Then they spent no little time with the disciples.

The word of the Lord.

——• Psalm 145 •——

℟ (see 12) **Your friends make known, O Lord, the glorious splendor of your kingdom.**

Or: Alleluia.

Let all your works give you thanks, O LORD,
  and let your faithful ones bless you.
Let them discourse of the glory of your kingdom
  and speak of your might. ℟

Making known to men your might
  and the glorious splendor of your kingdom.
Your kingdom is a kingdom for all ages,
  and your dominion endures through all
    generations. ℟

May my mouth speak the praise of the LORD,
  and may all flesh bless his holy name forever and
    ever. ℟

Alleluia, alleluia. Christ had to suffer and to rise from the dead,/ and so enter into his glory. Alleluia, alleluia.

• *My peace I give to you.* •

A reading from
the holy Gospel according to John   14:27-31a

JESUS SAID TO his disciples: "Peace I leave with you; my peace I give to you. Not as the world gives do I give it to you. Do not let your hearts be troubled or afraid. You heard me tell you, 'I am going away and I will come back to you.' If you loved me, you would rejoice that I am going to the Father; for the Father is greater than I. And now I have told you this before it happens, so that when it happens you may believe. I will no longer

speak much with you, for the ruler of the world is coming. He has no power over me, but the world must know that I love the Father and that I do just as the Father has commanded me."
The Gospel of the Lord.

Prayer over the Offerings
Receive, O Lord, we pray,
these offerings of your exultant Church,
and, as you have given her cause for such great gladness,
grant also that the gifts we bring
may bear fruit in perpetual happiness.
Through Christ our Lord.

Preface I-V of Easter ———————— pages 218 to 219

Communion Antiphon   Rom 6:8
If we have died with Christ,/ we believe that we shall also live with Christ, alleluia.

Prayer after Communion
Look with kindness upon your people, O Lord,
and grant, we pray,
that those you were pleased to renew by eternal
    mysteries
may attain in their flesh
the incorruptible glory of the resurrection.
Through Christ our Lord.

Saint Christopher Magallanes and Companions   *Optional memorial*

● *Christopher Magallanes and twenty-four others were murdered in Mexico from 1915 to 1937, most during the Cristero uprising. This revolt pitted Catholic peasants against the violently anti-clerical Mexican government. The Cristeros sometimes took up arms, but each of these men, in obedience to the Mexican bishops, refused to fight. To a man, they humbly accepted death, praising God and blessing*

*their executioners. "I am innocent and I die innocent.
I forgive with all my heart those responsible for my
death, and I ask God that the shedding of my blood
may serve to bring peace to divided Mexicans" were
Magallanes' final words.* ●

Entrance Antiphon
Cf. Mt 25:34

Come, you blessed of my Father;/ receive the kingdom
prepared for you/ from the foundation of the world, alleluia.

Collect

Almighty and eternal God,
who made the Priest Saint Christopher Magallanes
 and his companions
faithful to Christ the King even to the point
 of martyrdom,
grant us, through their intercession,
that, persevering in confession of the true faith,
we may always hold fast to the commandments
 of your love.
Through our Lord Jesus Christ, your Son,
who lives and reigns with you in the unity
 of the Holy Spirit,
one God, for ever and ever.

Prayer over the Offerings

In honor of the precious death of your just ones,
 O Lord,
we come to offer that sacrifice
from which all martyrdom draws its origin.
Through Christ our Lord.

Communion Antiphon
Cf. Rv 2:7

To the victor I will give the right to eat from the tree of life,/
which is in the paradise of my God, alleluia.

Prayer after Communion

As we celebrate by this divine banquet
the heavenly victory of the blessed Martyrs
 Christopher Magallanes and his companions,
we beseech you, Lord, to bestow victory

on those who eat here below of the Bread of life
and to allow them to eat as victors from the tree
of life in paradise.
Through Christ our Lord.

MEDITATION OF THE DAY

"Peace be with you"

We are celebrating...*the peace of our Lord and Savior Jesus Christ*—the peace that was announced by the angels at his birth; the peace that he communicated to all who came into contact with him during his earthly life; the peace that he gave to his Apostles when he stood among them after his Resurrection, saying: *Peace be with you* (Jn 20:19).

We are celebrating the peace that Christ won for us by his Paschal Mystery—by his Passion, Death, and Resurrection from the dead. We are able to enjoy peace because God sent his own Son into the world to be our Redeemer.

And the peace that we are celebrating is our redemption from sin, our deliverance from God's anger and from eternal punishment. Without Christ we would have remained, in the words of Saint Paul, *children of wrath* (Eph 2:3). But in truth we have been liberated by Christ; everything is new in our relationship with God. Christ has reconciled us to himself, *making peace by the blood of his cross* (Col 1:20). We have been called out of the darkness of sin into the Kingdom of God's marvelous light, where we have received mercy and grace and peace from Jesus Christ.

Through God's love we have not only received the gift of human life but we have also become adopted children of God. Through Christ's great peacemaking act—his sacrifice on the cross—we have become his brothers and sisters, and, with him, heirs of eternal life. Because of this new relationship of ours with God in

Christ, peace is now possible: peace in our hearts and in our homes, peace in our communities and in our nations, peace throughout the world. Yes, Jesus Christ is the supreme peacemaker of human history, the reconciler of human hearts, the liberator of humanity, the Redeemer of man. *He is our peace* (Eph 2:14).

SAINT JOHN PAUL II

Saint John Paul II († 2005) reigned as pope from 1978 until 2005.

Prayer for the Evening

Let our prayer arise before God like incense,
the raising of our hands in prayer like the evening
sacrifice, alleluia!

Glory to the Father.... Alleluia!

HYMN　　　　　　　　　　　　　　Meter: 78 78 77 with repeats

Holy God, we praise thy name;
Lord of all, we bow before thee!
All on earth thy scepter claim,
All in heaven above adore thee;
Infinite thy vast domain,
Everlasting is thy reign.
Infinite thy vast domain,
Everlasting is thy reign.

Thou art King of glory, Christ:
Son of God, yet born of Mary;
For us sinners sacrificed,
And to death a tributary:
First to break the bars of death,
Thou hast opened heaven to faith.
First to break the bars of death,
Thou hast opened heaven to faith.

Spare thy people, Lord, we pray,
By a thousand snares surrounded:
Keep us without sin today,
Never let us be confounded.
Lo, I put my trust in thee;
Never, Lord, abandon me.
Lo, I put my trust in thee;
Never, Lord, abandon me.

Psalm 141

1-5a, 8

May the spoken words of my mouth,/ the thoughts of my heart,/ win
favor in your sight, O Lord. (Ps 19:15)

In every age, there are those who use the spoken words of the mouth
and the thoughts of the heart to find fault with God's ways, as did the
doubting Israelites in the desert, or the doubting opponents of Jesus
in the Gospel, or as we do ourselves when God's plan does not fit our
own. Honest questions are never offensive to God, but freely chosen
or self-centered disbelief reveal an inner bitterness from which we ask
to be guarded. Let us put our trust in and hand on to others the Good
News of the astonishing gift of life given through the cross.

I have called to you, Lord; hasten to help me!
Hear my voice when I cry to you.
Let my prayer arise before you like incense,
the raising of my hands like an evening oblation.

Set, O Lord, a guard over my mouth;
keep watch at the door of my lips!
Do not turn my heart to things that are wrong,
to evil deeds with men who are sinners.

Never allow me to share in their feasting.
If a good man strikes or reproves me it is kindness;
but let the oil of the wicked not anoint my head.
To you, Lord God, my eyes are turned:
in you I take refuge; spare my soul!

Glory to the Father....

Word of God
Deuteronomy 4:9

TAKE CARE and be earnestly on your guard not to forget the things which your own eyes have seen, nor let them slip from your memory as long as you live, but teach them to your children and to your children's children.

I could strengthen you with talk,/
or shake my head with silent lips. (Jb 16:5)

CANTICLE OF MARY
(Text, back cover A)

Are the consolations of God not enough for you,/ and speech that deals gently with you? (Jb 15:11)

INTERCESSIONS

With earnest words of petition, we turn to God:

℟   Receive our prayer, O Lord.

You have called your people to pray always:
– may we grow in awareness that every thought, word, and deed lies open to you. ℟

You receive all our offerings in love:
– may we offer them more and more faithfully in love. ℟

You desire to bring all people into your glory:
– receive the lives of those who have died. ℟

Personal intentions

Our Father….

May grace, mercy, and peace be with us from God the Father and Christ Jesus our Lord. Amen. (cf. 2 Tm 1:2)

MARIAN ANTIPHON
(page 12 or 13)

Saint Who?

Saints Who Were Visionaries

Saint Drythelm
Married Layman († c. 700)   Feast: September 1

A virtuous layman from Cunningham in England, Drythelm grew ill and then died, or seemed to. The mourners who gathered around his bed were shocked when, after a few hours, he suddenly revived. All fled, but for his wife. "Fear not," he told her, "for I am now truly risen from death...however, I am not to live hereafter as I was wont, but from henceforward after a very different manner." He went at once to pray at the local church and returned to divide his wealth between his wife, his sons, and the poor. He then entered the monastery of Melrose.

In later life, Drythelm freely shared the story of his near-death experience. He told how a guide appeared and led him first to a valley of "consuming flames and cutting cold," the purgatory for sinners who had repented at the end of their lives. Beyond that he saw a fearful stinking pit, the very mouth of hell. His guide then transported him to a light-filled valley, the purgatory of those who had led virtuous lives. And beyond that he glimpsed the wonders of heaven itself. Then, he was escorted back to the living.

Eventually, Drythelm's monastery assigned him a hermitage where he was free to pray and fast with abandon. He did penance by reciting the psalms while plunged up to his neck in the icy water of the River Tweed.

Eternal Father, through the intercession of
Saint Drithelm, confirm me in the conviction
that I am made for eternal life.

WEDNESDAY, MAY 22
Saint Rita of Cascia

Prayer for the Morning

All who are thirsty,
come to the living waters, alleluia!

Glory to the Father.... Alleluia!

HYMN

Meter: 87 87 87
This hymn can be sung to the tune used for
Let All Mortal Flesh Keep Silence

When I heard the Savior calling
Weary, burdened souls to rest—
"'Tis the voice of love that calls me,
I will honor his behest";
And I found repose from sorrow,
Leaning on my Savior's breast.

Seek not rest in worldly promise;
Worldly rest has troubled dreams.
Not so true the world's fulfillment,
As at first the promise seems.
He who tastes the Living Water
Thirsts not after other streams.

PSALM 42
2-4, 8-10, 12

Jesus said: "Let anyone who thirsts come to me and drink." (cf. Jn 7:37)

Branches severed, branches hanging tenuously from Christ the vine, wither. Branches firmly grafted into Christ the vine continue to be refreshed and renewed by the water of life, the Spirit of God, for whom all human beings thirst, knowingly or unknowingly.

Like the deer that yearns
for running streams,

so my soul is yearning
for you, my God.

My soul is thirsting for God,
the God of my life;
when can I enter and see
the face of God?

My tears have become my bread,
by night, by day,
as I hear it said all the day long:
"Where is your God?"

Deep is calling on deep,
in the roar of waters:
your torrents and all your waves
swept over me.

By day the Lord will send
his loving kindness;
by night I will sing to him,
praise the God of my life.

I will say to God, my rock:
"Why have you forgotten me?
Why do I go mourning,
oppressed by the foe?"

Why are you cast down, my soul,
why groan within me?
Hope in God; I will praise him still,
my savior and my God.

Glory to the Father....

Word of God   Isaiah 55:1

ALL YOU WHO are thirsty,/ come to the water!/ You
who have no money,/ come, receive grain and eat;/

Come, without paying and without cost,/ drink wine and milk!

Lord, give us always this water to drink! (cf. Jn 4:15)

CANTICLE OF ZECHARIAH (Text, back cover B)

Whoever drinks the water I shall give will never thirst. (Jn 4:14)

INTERCESSIONS (cf. Saint Ambrose)

Let us pray to the risen Christ, in whom all thirst is slaked:

℟ Give us living water to drink!

You are the vine, and we the branches:
– bear in us the fruit of life. ℟

You are the rock in the desert from which the waters flow, and we the thirsty:
– cool our weary souls with the living waters of your Holy Spirit. ℟

You are the living Word, and we those who hunger to hear:
– bring life to those who grope for a sense of purpose in life. ℟

Personal intentions

Our Father....

Ever-living God, you have given us the water of life to drink through our risen Savior, vine, rock, Word. Make us so thirst for him that we will turn aside from all lesser thirsts, through him who lives and reigns with you in the unity of the Holy Spirit, one God, for ever and ever. Amen.

MASS

Wednesday of the Fifth Week of Easter

ENTRANCE ANTIPHON   Cf. Ps 71 (70):8, 23

Let my mouth be filled with your praise, that I may sing aloud;/ my lips shall shout for joy, when I sing to you, alleluia.

COLLECT

O God, restorer and lover of innocence,
direct the hearts of your servants towards yourself,
that those you have set free from the darkness of
    unbelief
may never stray from the light of your truth.
Through our Lord Jesus Christ, your Son,
who lives and reigns with you in the unity
    of the Holy Spirit,
one God, for ever and ever.

● *They decided to go up to Jerusalem to the Apostles and presbyters about this question.* ●

A reading from
the Acts of the Apostles   15:1-6

SOME WHO HAD come down from Judea were instructing the brothers, "Unless you are circumcised according to the Mosaic practice, you cannot be saved." Because there arose no little dissension and debate by Paul and Barnabas with them, it was decided that Paul, Barnabas, and some of the others should go up to Jerusalem to the Apostles and presbyters about this question. They were sent on their journey by the Church, and passed through Phoenicia and Samaria telling of the conversion of the Gentiles, and brought great joy to all the brethren. When they arrived in Jerusalem, they were welcomed by the Church, as well as by the Apostles and the presbyters, and they reported what God had done with them. But some from the party of the Pharisees who had become believers stood up and said, "It is necessary to circumcise them and direct them to observe the Mosaic law."

The Apostles and the presbyters met together to see about this matter.

The word of the Lord.

•PSALM 122•

℟ (see 1) Let us go rejoicing to the house of the Lord.

Or: Alleluia.

I rejoiced because they said to me,
  "We will go up to the house of the LORD."
And now we have set foot
  within your gates, O Jerusalem. ℟

Jerusalem, built as a city
  with compact unity.
To it the tribes go up,
  the tribes of the LORD. ℟

According to the decree for Israel,
  to give thanks to the name of the LORD.
In it are set up judgment seats,
  seats for the house of David. ℟

Alleluia, alleluia. Remain in me, as I remain in you, says the Lord;/ whoever remains in me will bear much fruit. Alleluia, alleluia.

  • *Whoever remains in me and I in him will bear much fruit.* •

A reading from
the holy Gospel according to John   15:1-8

JESUS SAID to his disciples:
"I am the true vine, and my

Father is the vine grower. He takes away every branch in me that does not bear fruit, and everyone that does he prunes so that it bears more fruit. You are already pruned because of the word that I spoke to you. Remain in me, as I remain in you. Just as a branch cannot bear fruit on its own unless it remains on the vine, so neither can you unless you remain in me. I am the vine, you are the branches. Whoever remains in me and I in him will bear much fruit, because without me you can do nothing. Anyone who does not remain in me will be thrown out like a branch and wither; people will gather them and throw them into a fire and they will be burned. If you remain in me and my words remain in you, ask for whatever you want and it will be done for you. By this is my Father glorified, that you bear much fruit and become my disciples."
The Gospel of the Lord.

Prayer over the Offerings
Grant, we pray, O Lord,
that we may always find delight in these paschal
mysteries,
so that the renewal constantly at work within us
may be the cause of our unending joy.
Through Christ our Lord.

Preface I-V of Easter ──────────── pages 218 to 219

Communion Antiphon
The Lord has risen and shone his light upon us,/ whom he has redeemed by his Blood, alleluia.

Prayer after Communion
Hear, O Lord, our prayers,
that this most holy exchange,
by which you have redeemed us,
may bring your help in this present life
and ensure for us eternal gladness.
Through Christ our Lord.

SAINT RITA OF CASCIA
Optional memorial

- *Born of peasant stock in Roccaporena, Italy, Rita desired to remain a virgin from her youth, but her parents chose marriage for her. Fourteen years later, Rita's husband was murdered. Her prayers were answered when her two sons died rather than avenge the crime. Rita later joined the Augustinians at Cascia, where for forty years she cultivated a devotion to Christ crucified. Her emblem in art is the rose that miraculously bloomed in the winter of her death. Speaking on the centenary of her canonization, Saint John Paul II said, "Rita offers her rose to each of you: in receiving it, spiritually strive to live as witnesses to a hope that never disappoints and as missionaries of a life that conquers death."* ●

ENTRANCE ANTIPHON
Cf. Hos 2:21-22

The Lord has taken her as his bride for ever/ in faithfulness and mercy, alleluia.

COLLECT

Bestow on us, we pray, O Lord,
the wisdom and strength of the Cross,
with which you were pleased to endow Saint Rita,
so that, suffering in every tribulation with Christ,
we may participate ever more deeply in his
    Paschal Mystery.
Who lives and reigns with you in the unity
    of the Holy Spirit,
one God, for ever and ever.

PRAYER OVER THE OFFERINGS

Most merciful God,
who were pleased to create in blessed Rita
the New Man in your image, the old having passed away,
graciously grant, we pray,
that, renewed like her,
we may offer you the acceptable sacrifice of conciliation.
Through Christ our Lord.

COMMUNION ANTIPHON   Cf. Lam 3:24-25
The Lord is my portion:/ he is good to the soul that seeks
him, alleluia.

PRAYER AFTER COMMUNION
    By the power of this Sacrament, Lord, we pray,
    lead us always in your love,
    through the example of blessed Rita,
    and bring to fulfillment the good work
        you have begun in us
    until the day of Christ Jesus.
    Who lives and reigns for ever and ever.

MEDITATION OF THE DAY

Without Him, Nothing. With Him, Everything.

We may ask ourselves in what way, or in how many
ways, was our blessed Lord and Savior the cause of
our grace and our salvation. In every way! That is the
true answer.

For it is only "through Jesus Christ our Lord," as the
Church so often reminds us, that we dare to hope for
grace and that salvation which is its fruit. It was he who
blotted out the handwriting that was against us, and he
did this, in the graphic words of the Apostle, by nailing
it to the cross on which he died. He it was who loved us
so dearly that he washed us from our sins in his own
blood (Rev 1:5). So, Saint Thomas summing up a series
of most beautiful articles on the Passion of our Savior
[explains] that God is the cause of our salvation, and
Jesus Christ is God. And because his most sacred humanity was the instrument of the divinity, all his actions
and sufferings were the instrumental means by which
the great work was brought about. He is also the cause
of all our graces, because these actions and sufferings
were meritorious, inasmuch as they were freely accepted and most lovingly endured by his human will. And

if we look at these same sufferings as endured in his adorable body, we shall see how the work was done.

Because of the greatness of his love, and the unspeakable dignity of his divine Person, as well as because of the multitude of his sufferings, an atonement that was in every way most superabundant was offered to God's justice. Because his blood as shed in death was the price of this atonement, and he paid it with such lavish generosity, he, and he alone, is our Redeemer; and lastly, inasmuch as the voluntary sacrifice of his life was the most perfect act of worship that could be given to God, it is by his death—the death of the Son of God—that the world is reconciled to its Creator. What a significance is given by thoughts like these to that eloquent cry of Saint Paul: *Blessed be God, the Father of our Lord Jesus Christ, who has blessed us with all spiritual blessings in Christ* (Eph. 1:8).

FATHER RAPHAEL MOSS, O.P.

Father Moss (†1940) was an English Dominican priest, theologian, and missionary.

Prayer for the Evening

The Lord lives in us and we in him:
let us give thanks and praise, alleluia!

Glory to the Father.... Alleluia!

HYMN

Meter: CMD
This hymn can be sung to the tune used for
I Heard the Voice of Jesus Say

Abide in me, the Master said,
the true and living vine;
my life shall be, the Master said,
poured out for you as wine.
His body to the cross he gave,
his blood he freely shed,

who came in love to seek and save,
for so the Master said.

Believe in me, the Master said,
for I have called you friends,
and yours shall be, the Master said,
the life that never ends.
And so, with sin and sorrow past,
when death itself is dead,
the Lord shall raise us up at last,
for so the Master said.

CANTICLE   Hosea 14:2-3a, 5-6a, 8b, 10
I am the true vine, and my Father is the vine grower. (Jn 15:1)

The vineyard is a symbol of God's beloved people, planted and tended with care. Jesus, the Son of Man, heir to all creation, was sent into the vineyard to restore it from the ruin made of it by sin and death.

Return, O Israel, to the Lord, your God;
you have collapsed through your guilt.
Take with you words,
and return to the Lord;
Say to him, "Forgive all iniquity."

I will heal their defection,
I will love them freely;
for my wrath is turned away from them.

I will be like the dew for Israel:
he shall blossom like the lily.
They shall blossom like the vine,
and his fame shall be like the wine of Lebanon.

Let him who is wise understand these things;
let him who is prudent know them.
Straight are the paths of the Lord,
in them the just walk,
but sinners stumble in them.

Glory to the Father….

Word of God
Isaiah 27:2a-3

T HE PLEASANT vineyard, sing about it!/ I, the LORD, am its keeper,/ I water it every moment;/ Lest anyone harm it,/ night and day I guard it.

Your mother was like a vine/ planted by the water;/ Fruitful and branchy was she/ because of the abundant water. (Ez 19:10)

CANTICLE OF MARY
(Text, back cover A)

I am the vine, you are the branches. Whoever remains in me and I in him will bear much fruit, because without me you can do nothing. (Jn 15:5)

INTERCESSIONS

To Christ the living vine, we pray:

℟   O Lord, come to our help!

You are the vine and we the branches:
– may we always be one in you. ℟

You have watered your vine with the living water that flows from the cross:
– may we always live in you. ℟

You have nourished and guarded your vine in faithful love:
– may we always bear fruit for your glory. ℟

Personal intentions

Our Father….

May mercy, peace, and love be ours in abundance. Amen. (cf. Jude 2)

MARIAN ANTIPHON
(page 12 or 13)

Saint Who?

Saints Who Were Visionaries

Saint Pachomius
Founder († 348)

Feast: May 9

Two men stand at the beginning of monasticism in the East: Saint Anthony the Great and Saint Pachomius. Anthony was the first man to "go out into the desert" to live poverty, chastity, and obedience in solitude as a hermit, thereby founding "eremitical" monasticism. Pachomius, who was born three decades after Anthony, was the first man to establish a community of vowed religious following a "rule," the heart of "cenobitic" monasticism.

A pagan from Egypt, Pachomius was twenty-four when Roman soldiers came through his town and forcibly conscripted all the young men into the army. For a time, he and the others were held in a prison where Christians came to minister. They showed him such kindness, that, after his stint in the army, Pachomius wanted nothing more than to give his life to Christ. He was baptized and then studied under an aged hermit. After he moved to a deserted place called Tabennisi, Pachomius received a vision in which God commanded him to found a monastery.

Gradually, other young men joined him, and he gathered them into a community, giving them a *Rule* for life. According to one account, Pachomius had such power to unite men "because of his goodness." At the time of Pachomius' death nine monasteries for men and two for women were following his *Rule*.

Loving Father, through the intercession of Saint Pachomius, remove all that is in me that prevents me from reaching out to others.

THURSDAY, MAY 23

Prayer for the Morning

God is our stronghold, the God who shows us love:
let us give thanks and praise, alleluia!

Glory to the Father…. Alleluia!

HYMN

Meter: LM
This hymn can be sung to the tune used for
Jesu Dulcis Memoria

I sing as I arise today!
I call on my Creator's might:
The will of God to be my guide,
The eye of God to be my sight,

The word of God to be my speech,
The hand of God to be my stay,
The shield of God to be my strength,
The path of God to be my way.

PSALM 59

2-3, 17-18

As the Father loves me, so I also love you. Remain in my love. (Jn 15:9)

In a culture that values autonomy and self-reliance, we sometimes imagine that we can call only on our own personal strength to shoulder the burdens of those we care for and to face our own difficulties. The Gospel reminds us again and again that God's love is our true source of strength. On him the strongest person can lean without apology. The proof lies in the empty cross.

Rescue me, God, from my foes;
protect me from those who attack me.
O rescue me from those who do evil
and save me from bloodthirsty men.

As for me, I will sing of your strength
and each morning acclaim your love
for you have been my stronghold,
a refuge in the day of my distress.

O my Strength, it is you to whom I turn,
for you, O God, are my stronghold,
the God who shows me love.

Glory to the Father....

Word of God   1 Corinthians 10:13

NO TRIAL has come to you but what is human. God is faithful and will not let you be tried beyond your strength; but with the trial he will also provide a way out, so that you may be able to bear it.

*Draw your strength from the Lord
and from his mighty power. (Eph 6:10)*

CANTICLE OF ZECHARIAH   (Text, back cover B)

I have the strength for everything through him who empowers me.
(Phil 4:13)

INTERCESSIONS

To God our strength we cry out:

℟   To you we turn! Hear us!

You are our stronghold in time of trouble:
– grant us the wisdom and the courage to place our
trust in you. ℟

You are our defender against all evil:
– teach us always to call upon you in prayer. ℟

You have delivered your people from death by the power of the cross:
– strengthen us to bear one another's burdens in love. ℟

Personal intentions

Our Father....

Lord God of power and might, you have revealed to us in the Death and Resurrection of Jesus Christ that true strength lies in self-surrendering love. Make us his faithful disciples in every trial, and make us a genuine source of strength to one another, through the same Christ our Lord. Amen.

Mass

Thursday of the Fifth Week of Easter

Jesus reveals an awesome reality: He loves us the very way that the Father loves him. What "God first concerned himself with" remains his main desire: "acquiring a people for his name." Thus, Christ begs: "Remain in my love." We do so by keeping his commandments, for they save us "from the destructive force of egoism and falsehood. To keep the commandments is to be faithful to our deepest aspirations" (Saint John Paul II). The commandments are God's way of teaching us how to live within reality, the only sure way we will have complete and lasting joy.

ENTRANCE ANTIPHON   Cf. Ex 15:1-2
Let us sing to the Lord, for he has gloriously triumphed./ The Lord is my strength and my might;/ he has become my salvation, alleluia.

COLLECT
     O God, by whose grace,
     though sinners, we are made just
     and, though pitiable, made blessed,
     stand, we pray, by your works,
     stand by your gifts,

that those justified by faith
may not lack the courage of perseverance.
Through our Lord Jesus Christ, your Son,
who lives and reigns with you in the unity
   of the Holy Spirit,
one God, for ever and ever.

● *It is my judgment, therefore, that we ought to stop
troubling the Gentiles who turn to God.* ●

A reading from
the Acts of the Apostles
15:7-21

AFTER MUCH DEBATE had taken place, Peter got up and said to the Apostles and the presbyters, "My brothers, you are well aware that from early days God made his choice among you that through my mouth the Gentiles would hear the word of the Gospel and believe. And God, who knows the heart, bore witness by granting them the Holy Spirit just as he did us. He made no distinction between us and them, for by faith he purified their hearts. Why, then, are you now putting God to the test by placing on the shoulders of the disciples a yoke that neither our ancestors nor we have been able to bear? On the contrary, we believe that we are saved through the grace of the Lord Jesus, in the same way as they." The whole assembly fell silent, and they listened while Paul and Barnabas described the signs and wonders God had worked among the Gentiles through them.

After they had fallen silent, James responded, "My brothers, listen to me. Symeon has described how God first concerned himself with acquiring from among the Gentiles a people for his name. The words of the prophets agree with this, as is written:

*After this I shall return/ and rebuild the fallen hut
of David;/ from its ruins I shall rebuild it/ and raise it*

up again,/ so that the rest of humanity may seek out the Lord,/ even all the Gentiles on whom my name is invoked./ Thus says the Lord who accomplishes these things,/ known from of old.

It is my judgment, therefore, that we ought to stop troubling the Gentiles who turn to God, but tell them by letter to avoid pollution from idols, unlawful marriage, the meat of strangled animals, and blood. For Moses, for generations now, has had those who proclaim him in every town, as he has been read in the synagogues every sabbath."

The word of the Lord.

⟶ Psalm 96 ⟶

℟ (3) **Proclaim God's marvelous deeds to all the nations.**

Or: Alleluia.

Sing to the Lord a new song;
  sing to the Lord, all you lands.
Sing to the Lord; bless his name. ℟

Announce his salvation, day after day.
Tell his glory among the nations;
  among all peoples, his wondrous deeds. ℟

Say among the nations: The Lord is king.
He has made the world firm, not to be moved;
  he governs the peoples with equity. ℟

Alleluia, alleluia. My sheep hear my voice, says the Lord;/ I know them, and they follow me. Alleluia, alleluia.

  • *Remain in my love, that your joy might be complete.* •

A reading from
the holy Gospel according to John   15:9-11

JESUS SAID TO his disciples: "As
the Father loves me, so I also
love you. Remain in my love. If you keep my commandments, you will remain in my love, just as I have kept my
Father's commandments and remain in his love.

"I have told you this so that my joy might be in you
and your joy might be complete."
The Gospel of the Lord.

PRAYER OVER THE OFFERINGS
    O God, who by the wonderful exchange effected in
        this sacrifice
    have made us partakers of the one supreme Godhead,
    grant, we pray,
    that, as we have come to know your truth,
    we may make it ours by a worthy way of life.
    Through Christ our Lord.

PREFACE I-V OF EASTER ———————— pages 218 to 219

COMMUNION ANTIPHON   2 Cor 5:15
Christ died for all, that those who live/ may live no longer
for themselves,/ but for him who died for them and is risen,
alleluia.

PRAYER AFTER COMMUNION
    Graciously be present to your people, we pray, O Lord,
    and lead those you have imbued with heavenly mysteries
    to pass from former ways to newness of life.
    Through Christ our Lord.

• ————————————————————————— •
  M E D I T A T I O N   O F   T H E   D A Y
• ————————————————————————— •

Remaining in God's Love

That God is love is the firm belief of many people.
In a vague general way they affirm this, yet they do

not expect him to manifest his love in any dynamic or intimate way. And they seem to have no great desire to want to know him more, to speak to him, or to make him a real part of their life experience. Imagine a young man who thinks he loves a girl, but fails to visit her and never even wants to; who never speaks *to* her or even *about* her.

Such a mixture of affirmation and negation also often underlies these questions so frequently addressed to religious people: "I do believe in God, but why do I have to believe that Christ was God?" "Why must I go to services in a building called a church? Can't I just talk to God when I feel like it and live my own life, trying to be as good as possible?"…

I have often thought that questions involving doubt about Christ and the Church are very much related to questions about love. Therefore, one of the best approaches to them is to delve into the nature of love and to show that many aspects of Catholicism…which a person may think are unnecessary encumbrances or even distortions, really follow directly from the one premise that God is love.

RONDA CHERVIN

Ronda Chervin is a convert from Judaism, professor of philosophy and theology, and author of over fifty books.

Prayer for the Evening

The Lord will never forsake his friends:
come, let us give thanks and praise, alleluia!

Glory to the Father…. Alleluia!

HYMN

Meter: 77 77
This hymn can be sung to the tune used for
Forty Days and Forty Nights

Cast your burden on the Lord,
Only lean upon his word;

You will soon have cause to bless
His eternal faithfulness.

He sustains you by his hand,
He enables you to stand;
Those whom Jesus once has loved
From his grace are never moved.

Jesus, Guardian of your flock,
Be yourself our constant rock;
Make us, by your powerful hand,
Strong as Zion's mountain stand.

Psalm 37   23-28

I was always in your presence;/ you were holding me by my right
hand. (Ps 73:23)

A child who feels lost or afraid often reaches out for a parent's hand.
It is reassuring to picture the Lord holding us by the hand to guide
us, protect us, and keep us from falling whenever we feel alone,
bewildered, and in need of help. That is his gift to those who live
in his love.

The Lord guides the steps of a man
and makes safe the path of one he loves.
Though he stumble he shall never fall
for the Lord holds him by the hand.

I was young and now I am old,
but I have never seen the just man forsaken
nor his children begging for bread.
All the day he is generous and lends
and his children become a blessing.

Then turn away from evil and do good
and you shall have a home for ever;
for the Lord loves justice
and will never forsake his friends.

Glory to the Father....

Word of God

Deuteronomy 7:8

I T WAS BECAUSE the LORD loved you and because of his fidelity to the oath he had sworn to your fathers, that he brought you out with his strong hand from the place of slavery, and ransomed you from the hand of Pharaoh, king of Egypt.

All his holy ones were in his hand;/ they followed at his feet/ and he bore them up on his pinions. (Dt 33:3)

CANTICLE OF MARY

(Text, back cover A)

My soul clings to you;/ your right hand holds me fast. (Ps 63:9)

INTERCESSIONS

The Lord guides us and keeps us; with confidence, we pray:

℟   Make safe the paths of those you love!

For all to whom you have entrusted the task of guiding others in your ways:
– strengthen them in wisdom, courage, and faith. ℟

For all who feel alone, abandoned, frightened, or lost:
– hold them by the hand and guide them to safety. ℟

For all children who have no one to trust:
– keep them in your care and show them your love. ℟

Personal intentions

Our Father....

May the Lord bless and protect us all the days of our life. Amen.

MARIAN ANTIPHON

(page 12 or 13)

SAINT WHO?

Saints Who Were Visionaries

Saints Tharsilla and Emiliana
Virgins († c. 550)   Feasts: December 24 and January 5

Saint Gregory the Great had three aunts, Tharsilla, Emiliana, and Gordiana—all sisters of his father, Gordian, the senator. All three women took private vows of virginity, choosing to remain on their father's estate on the Clivus Scauri in Rome, where they gave themselves over to fasting, prayer, and works of mercy. Of the three, Gordiana alone felt unable to continue in this strict lifestyle. Despite her sisters' encouragement, she left her home for life in the world. But Tharsilla and Emiliana persevered.

After many years of holy works, Tharsilla received one night a heavenly visitor, her ancestor, Pope Saint Felix III. Felix showed Tharsilla the throne that had been prepared for her in heaven. "Come!" he said to her. "I will receive you into this habitation of light." The next day Tharsilla became ill with fever. Her sickness became grave and her pain intense, until, in the throes of her passion, she cried out, "Behold! Jesus is coming!" She died that very night, the eve of Christmas.

A few days later, Tharsilla came in a vision to Emiliana and offered her sister the opportunity to celebrate Epiphany with her in heaven. Emiliana then fell sick herself. She died on January 5.

Loving Father, through the intercession of Saints Tharsilla and Emiliana, grant me perseverance, that I might one day meet you face to face.

FRIDAY, MAY 24

Prayer for the Morning

God is in our midst, a mighty savior:
come, let us adore, alleluia!

Glory to the Father, and to the Son,
and to the Holy Spirit, as it was in the beginning,
is now, and will be for ever. Amen. Alleluia!

HYMN

Meter: 87 87 D
This hymn can be sung to the tune used for
Come, Thou Fount of Every Blessing

O my soul, bless God the Father;
All within me bless his name:
Bless the Father, and forget not
All his mercies to proclaim,
Who forgiveth thy transgressions,
Thy diseases all who heals;
Who redeems thee from destruction,
Who with thee so kindly deals.

Far as east from west is distant,
He hath put away our sin;
Like the pity of a father
Hath the Lord's compassion been.
As it was without beginning,
So it lasts without an end;
To their children's children ever
Shall his righteousness extend.

Psalm 39   9-14

At the time, all discipline seems a cause not for joy but for pain, yet later it brings the peaceful fruit of righteousness to those who are trained by it. (Hb 12:11)

When seen in the light of Easter joy, our sins can weigh us down with discouragement. Yet God's love does not deal in punishment as human vengeance does. God's love disciplines and prunes us in order to free and purify us—sometimes a painful process—so that we may not die like a withered branch but live and bear much fruit in the risen Christ.

Set me free from all my sins,
do not make me the taunt of the fool.
I was silent, not opening my lips,
because this was all your doing.

Take away your scourge from me.
I am crushed by the blows of your hand.
You punish man's sins and correct him;
like the moth you devour all he treasures.
Mortal man is no more than a breath;
O Lord, hear my prayer.

O Lord, turn your ear to my cry.
Do not be deaf to my tears.
In your house I am a passing guest,
a pilgrim, like all my fathers.
Look away that I may breathe again
before I depart to be no more.

Glory to the Father....

Word of God   Zephaniah 3:16-18

O N THAT DAY, it shall be said to Jerusalem:/ Fear not, O Zion, be not discouraged!/ The LORD, your God, is in your midst,/ a mighty savior;/ He will rejoice over you with gladness,/ and renew you in his love,/ He will sing joyfully because of you,/ as one sings at festivals./ I will remove disaster from among you,/ so that none may recount your disgrace.

Take courage, it is I; do not be afraid. (Mt 14:27)

CANTICLE OF ZECHARIAH (Text, back cover B)

It was not you who chose me, but I who chose you and appointed you to go and bear fruit that will remain, so that whatever you ask the Father in my name he may give you. (Jn 15:16)

INTERCESSIONS

Mindful of God's saving love for us, we pray:

℟   Have mercy on your people, Lord.

You are the potter and we the clay:
– shape us in your image according to your will. ℟

You are the shepherd and we the flock:
– seek out those who have strayed from your ways. ℟

You are the host and we the guests at your table:
– feed the hungry of spirit with the bread of your loving forgiveness. ℟

Personal intentions

Our Father....

God of mercy and compassion, you brought about the salvation of the world through the Death and Resurrection of Jesus Christ. Have mercy on us when we fail to live the new life you have given us; raise us up when our sinfulness sinks us into discouragement; grant us courage to renew our desire to live according to your will, through the same Christ our Lord. Amen.

Mass

Friday of the Fifth Week of Easter

The Psalmist exhorts us, "Awake, O my soul." We can fall into the doldrums of self-doubt, of reduced and nihilistic lives. Then we hear Christ say, "It was not you who chose me, but I who chose you"—Jesus does not suggest or propose that we bear fruit, he "appoints" us to do so. As Christians, we have confidence in the name and call of Jesus…and in a Father who hears our prayers.

Entrance Antiphon   Rv 5:12
Worthy is the Lamb who was slain,/ to receive power and divinity,/ and wisdom and strength and honor, alleluia.

Collect
> Grant us, Lord, we pray,
> that, being rightly conformed to the paschal
>   mysteries,
> what we celebrate in joy
> may protect and save us with perpetual power.
> Through our Lord Jesus Christ, your Son,
> who lives and reigns with you in the unity
>   of the Holy Spirit,
> one God, for ever and ever.

> ● *It is the decision of the Holy Spirit and of us not to place on you any burden beyond these necessities.* ●

A reading from
the Acts of the Apostles   15:22-31

THE Apostles and presbyters, in agreement with the whole Church, decided to choose representatives and to send them to Antioch with Paul and Barnabas. The ones chosen were Judas, who was called Barsabbas, and Silas, leaders among the brothers. This is the letter delivered by them: "The Apostles and the presbyters, your brothers, to the brothers in Antioch, Syria, and Cilicia of Gentile origin: greetings. Since we have heard that some of our number who went out without any mandate from us have upset you with their teachings and disturbed your peace of mind, we have with one accord decided to choose representatives and to send them to you along with our beloved Barnabas and Paul, who have dedicated their lives to the name of our Lord Jesus Christ. So we are sending Judas and Silas who will also convey this same message by word of mouth: 'It is the decision of the Holy Spirit and of us not to place on you any burden beyond these necessities, namely, to abstain from meat sacrificed to idols, from blood, from meats of strangled animals, and from unlawful marriage. If you keep free of these, you will be doing what is right. Farewell.'"

And so they were sent on their journey. Upon their arrival in Antioch they called the assembly together and delivered the letter. When the people read it, they were delighted with the exhortation.

The word of the Lord.

——• PSALM 57 •——

℟ (10a) I will give you thanks among the peoples, O Lord.

Or: Alleluia.

My heart is steadfast, O God; my heart is steadfast;
  I will sing and chant praise.
Awake, O my soul; awake, lyre and harp!
  I will wake the dawn. ℟

I will give thanks to you among the peoples, O LORD,
  I will chant your praise among the nations.
For your mercy towers to the heavens,
  and your faithfulness to the skies.

Be exalted above the heavens, O God;
  above all the earth be your glory! ℟

Alleluia, alleluia. I call you my friends, says the Lord,/
for I have made known to you all that the Father has
told me. Alleluia, alleluia.

  • *This is my commandment: love one another.* •

A reading from
the holy Gospel according to John   15:12-17

JESUS SAID TO his disciples:
  "This is my commandment:
love one another as I love you. No one has greater love
than this, to lay down one's life for one's friends. You are
my friends if you do what I command you. I no longer
call you slaves, because a slave does not know what his
master is doing. I have called you friends, because I have
told you everything I have heard from my Father. It was
not you who chose me, but I who chose you and appointed you to go and bear fruit that will remain, so that
whatever you ask the Father in my name he may give
you. This I command you: love one another."
The Gospel of the Lord.

PRAYER OVER THE OFFERINGS
  Graciously sanctify these gifts, O Lord, we pray,
  and, accepting the oblation of this spiritual sacrifice,
  make of us an eternal offering to you.
  Through Christ our Lord.

PREFACE I-V OF EASTER ————————— pages 218 to 219

COMMUNION ANTIPHON
The Crucified is risen from the dead/ and has redeemed us,
alleluia.

Prayer after Communion

We have partaken of the gifts of this sacred mystery,
humbly imploring, O Lord,
that what your Son commanded us to do
in memory of him
may bring us growth in charity.
Through Christ our Lord.

MEDITATION OF THE DAY

Loving as He Loves

When I am so convinced about some negative aspect of my life, I sometimes sink into despair. I must put my trust in your love and abandon myself to you.

When I am so convinced about some negative aspect of another's life, I am sometimes inclined to detest them and to stay away from them.

Then I must stop to contemplate your love for me. Why do you love me, Lord, when I feel disdain and disgust for my brothers and sisters?

Give me the courage to see things as you see them, Lord, and to love unconditionally. Only then will true communion be realized.

Often, behind a facade of courtesy and attentiveness there exists a hidden dissension, which weakens communion and renders it insincere.

Lord, you are infinite patience.
You are limitless understanding.
Your love is eternal.

VENERABLE FRANCIS XAVIER NGUYỄN VĂN THUẬN

Cardinal Nguyễn Văn Thuận († 2002) was imprisoned by the Vietnamese government for thirteen years.

Prayer for the Evening

Christ suffered that we might rejoice:
come, let us give thanks and praise, alleluia!

Glory to the Father, and to the Son,
and to the Holy Spirit, as it was in the beginning,
is now, and will be for ever. Amen. Alleluia!

Hymn   Meter: 77 77 77
This hymn can be sung to the tune used for
For the Beauty of the Earth

Rock of ages, cleft for me,
Let me hide myself in thee;
Let the water and the blood
From thy wounded side which flowed,
Be of sin the double cure,
Save from wrath and make me pure.

Could my tears for ever flow,
Could my zeal no languish know,
These for sin could not atone—
Thou must save, and thou alone:
In my hand no price I bring,
Simply to thy cross I cling.

Psalm 69   2-4, 14-16

The way we came to know love was that he laid down his life for us;
so we ought to lay down our lives for our brothers. (1 Jn 3:16)

Love demands a high price but pays an immeasurable dividend.
Jesus wept the tears of suffering humanity and, weeping, transformed them into the waters of life. These waters, flowing from
his wounded side, wash away all the tears that stain the face of a
sorrowing world.

Save me, O God,
for the waters have risen to my neck.

I have sunk into the mud of the deep
and there is no foothold.
I have entered the waters of the deep
and the waves overwhelm me.

I am wearied with all my crying,
my throat is parched.
My eyes are wasted away
from looking for my God.

This is my prayer to you,
my prayer for your favor.
In your great love, answer me, O God,
with your help that never fails:
rescue me from sinking in the mud;
save me from my foes.

Save me from the waters of the deep
lest the waves overwhelm me.
Do not let the deep engulf me
nor death close its mouth on me.

Glory to the Father....

Word of God   Ezekiel 47:1b, 8-9a

I SAW WATER flowing out from beneath the threshold of the temple toward the east, for the façade of the temple was toward the east. He said to me, "This water flows into the eastern district down upon the Arabah, and empties into the sea, the salt waters, which it makes fresh. Wherever the river flows, every sort of living creature that can multiply shall live."

One soldier thrust his lance into his side,
and immediately blood and water flowed out.
(Jn 19:34)

Canticle of Mary (Text, back cover A)

Then the angel showed me the river of life-giving water, sparkling like crystal, flowing from the throne of God and of the Lamb. (Rv 22:1)

Intercessions

Let us pray to Jesus Christ, our compassionate high priest, who was tempted in every way that we are but did not sin. (cf. Hb 4:15)

℟ Listen to your people's plea!

Lord Jesus, you wept over Jerusalem:
– grant conversion of heart to all those who have rejected you. ℟

Lord Jesus, you wept over the death of Lazarus:
– comfort those who mourn. ℟

Lord Jesus, you suffered sorrow and distress in the garden of Gethsemane:
– abide with those who watch alone tonight in pain and fear. ℟

Lord Jesus, you have risen into the fullness of joy:
– raise up all our beloved dead. ℟

Personal intentions

Our Father....

May the God of all grace who called us to his eternal glory through Christ Jesus restore, confirm, strengthen, and establish us after we have suffered a little. Amen. (cf. 1 Pt 5:10)

Marian Antiphon (page 12 or 13)

SAINT WHO?

Saints Who Were Visionaries

Seven Founders of the Servite Order
Founders (✝ 13th century)   Feast: February 17

Florence of the early 13th century was a city torn by ongoing family feuds and the chaos and moral confusion that is the bitter fruit of such internecine strife. Yet, Christ had not abandoned these people. A number of well-off men had been drawn into a communion of prayer in the confraternity of the Blessed Virgin Mary under the spiritual direction of Father James of Poggibonsi. They were known as *Laudesi*, or "ones who praise."

On the feast of the Assumption, seven of these men who had gathered for prayer were blessed with a vision of the Virgin herself. At once, they changed the manner of their lives. After the four men who had families (two of them were widowers) arranged for the care of wives and children, all seven retired to a dingy house outside of the city for penance and prayer. Visitors besieged them, and so they left to seek solitude in a wild place, Monte Sennario. After a time, the Bishop of Florence visited them to encourage them to soften their harsh penances and to consider accepting followers. Mary then came again to them. She gave them the *Rule* of Saint Augustine, a habit of black, and a name: "Servants of Mary."

From this time, the Servites, as they came to be known, grew quickly. In 1304, they received approval from the Holy See. They continue to serve today throughout the world.

Father in heaven, through the intercession of the Seven Founders of the Servites, help me to respond promptly to your call.

In the Sacraments
We Encounter Christ the Savior

–Pope Francis

Mothers, Songs, and Sacraments

———————— Father Richard Veras ————————

God's desire to accompany our earthly pilgrimage with tangible signs of his presence is evidenced in the visit of the young Virgin Mary to her older cousin Elizabeth.

Why did Mary go in such haste? Elizabeth was the one name the angel gave her of someone she knew, someone else whose life God had changed forever. The most human response for Mary was to visit her cousin, to desire to see her, and to see the miracle of her motherhood in the flesh.

When did Elizabeth's child first leap in her womb? When she heard the voice of Mary, a physical sign of the presence of the Mother of the Lord and, thus, of the Lord himself. It is at the sound of Mary's greeting that Elizabeth is filled with the Holy Spirit.

What caused Mary to burst forth with her joyful proclamation of the Lord's greatness? It seems that it was the sight of Elizabeth. She saw her cousin, who was beyond child-bearing years, big with child. Mary had believed the angel's announcement, but seeing Elizabeth, expectant and radiant, was a confirmation of God's promise that brought forth the song of Mary that the Church sings to this very day.

And to this very day, our sacraments are accompanied by psalms and songs which express our joy and gratitude to God who gives his Son, Jesus Christ, to be with us—always, and to be made tangibly present through the Holy Spirit in those very sacraments we celebrate.

Father Richard Veras is director of pastoral formation at Saint Joseph's Seminary in New York. He is author of three books, his latest being The Word Made Flesh: Foreshadowed, Fulfilled, Forever (Magnificat).

SATURDAY, MAY 25
Saint Bede the Venerable; Saint Gregory VII;
Saint Mary Magdalene de'Pazzi

Prayer for the Morning

Give ear, listen humbly,/ for the LORD speaks:
come, let us worship, alleluia! (cf. Jer 13:15)

Glory to the Father, and to the Son,
and to the Holy Spirit, as it was in the beginning,
is now, and will be for ever. Amen. Alleluia!

HYMN   Meter: 84 847

Be joyful, Mary, heav'nly queen, alleluia:
Your Son who died was living seen,
Alleluia, rejoice, rejoice, O Mary.

The Son you bore by heaven's grace, alleluia:
Did all our guilt and sin efface,
Alleluia, rejoice, rejoice, O Mary.

The Lord has risen from the dead, alleluia:
He rose in glory as he said,
Alleluia, rejoice, rejoice, O Mary.

O pray to God, O Virgin fair, alleluia:
That he our souls to heaven bear,
Alleluia, rejoice, rejoice, O Mary.

PSALM 119   9-16

His mother kept all these things in her heart. (Lk 2:51)

Mary "kept" the word of God in two ways: by reflecting on it often
and by living it with utmost fidelity. Her obedience brought her to
the dark afternoon of Calvary and to the bright joy of Easter.

How shall the young remain sinless?
By obeying your word.
I have sought you with all my heart:
let me not stray from your commands.

I treasure your promise in my heart
lest I sin against you.
Blessed are you, O Lord;
teach me your statutes.

With my tongue I have recounted
the decrees of your lips.
I rejoiced to do your will
as though all riches were mine.

I will ponder all your precepts
and consider your paths.
I take delight in your statutes;
I will not forget your word.

Glory to the Father....

Word of God
Luke 8:11b, 15

THE SEED is the word of God. [...] As for the seed that fell on rich soil, they are the ones who, when they have heard the word, embrace it with a generous and good heart, and bear fruit through perseverance.

Mary kept all these things,
reflecting on them in her heart. (Lk 2:19)

CANTICLE OF ZECHARIAH
(Text, back cover B)

A good person out of the store of goodness in his heart produces good; for from the fullness of the heart the mouth speaks. (cf. Lk 6:45)

INTERCESSIONS

The Blessed Virgin Mary received the Word of God in humility and love. Through her intercession, let us pray:

℟   Be it done according to your word.

God our Father, you sent your Son, the Word made flesh, into the world:
– open the hearts of all peoples to hear the good news of salvation. ℟

God our Father, you allowed your Son to fall into the ground and die:
– make your Church fruitful for the whole world. ℟

God our Father, your word falls upon thorny, rocky soil:
– remove all obstacles to our hearing and obeying. ℟

God our Father, you desire that your word produce a great harvest:
– send workers into the fields. ℟

Personal intentions

Our Father....

O God, sow your word once more in our hearts today; till patiently the soil of our souls; bring forth a rich harvest, so that all may find nourishment for body and spirit through the lives of your people. Through Christ our Lord. Amen.

MASS

Saturday of the Fifth Week of Easter

ENTRANCE ANTIPHON   Col 2:12
You have been buried with Christ in Baptism,/ through which you also rose again/ by faith in the working of God,/ who raised him from the dead, alleluia.

COLLECT

> Almighty and eternal God,
> who through the regenerating power of Baptism
> have been pleased to confer on us heavenly life,
> grant, we pray,
> that those you render capable of immortality
> by justifying them
> may by your guidance
> attain the fullness of glory.
> Through our Lord Jesus Christ, your Son,
> who lives and reigns with you in the unity
> of the Holy Spirit,
> one God, for ever and ever.

● *Come over to Macedonia and help us.* ●

A reading from
the Acts of the Apostles

16:1-10

PAUL REACHED also Derbe and Lystra where there was a disciple named Timothy, the son of a Jewish woman who was a believer, but his father was a Greek. The brothers in Lystra and Iconium spoke highly of him, and Paul wanted him to come along with him. On account of the Jews of that region, Paul had him circumcised, for they all knew that his father was a Greek. As they traveled from city to city, they handed on to the people for observance the decisions reached by the Apostles and presbyters in Jerusalem. Day after day the churches grew stronger in faith and increased in number.

They traveled through the Phrygian and Galatian territory because they had been prevented by the Holy Spirit from preaching the message in the province of Asia. When they came to Mysia, they tried to go on into Bithynia, but the Spirit of Jesus did not allow them, so they crossed through Mysia and came down to Troas. During the night Paul had a vision. A Macedonian stood before him and implored him with these words, "Come over to Macedonia and help us." When he had seen the vision, we sought passage to Macedonia at once, concluding that God had called us to proclaim the Good News to them.

The word of the Lord.

———• PSALM 100 •———

℟ (2a) Let all the earth cry out to God with joy.

Or: Alleluia.

Sing joyfully to the LORD, all you lands;
serve the LORD with gladness;
come before him with joyful song. ℟

Know that the LORD is God;
he made us, his we are;
his people, the flock he tends. ℟

The LORD is good:
his kindness endures forever,
and his faithfulness, to all generations. ℟

Alleluia, alleluia. If then you were raised with Christ,/ seek what is above,/ where Christ is seated at the right hand of God. Alleluia, alleluia.

> • *You do not belong to the world, and I have chosen you out of the world.* •

A reading from
the holy Gospel according to John   15:18-21

JESUS SAID TO his disciples: "If the world hates you, realize

that it hated me first. If you belonged to the world, the world would love its own; but because you do not belong to the world, and I have chosen you out of the world, the world hates you. Remember the word I spoke to you, 'No slave is greater than his master.' If they persecuted me, they will also persecute you. If they kept my word, they will also keep yours. And they will do all these things to you on account of my name, because they do not know the one who sent me."
The Gospel of the Lord.

Prayer over the Offerings

Accept in compassion, Lord, we pray,
the offerings of your family,
that under your protective care
they may never lose what they have received,
but attain the gifts that are eternal.
Through Christ our Lord.

Preface I-V of Easter ——————— pages 218 to 219

Communion Antiphon   Jn 17:20-21

Father, I pray for them, that they may be one in us,/ so that the world may believe it was you who sent me,/ says the Lord, alleluia.

Prayer after Communion

Keep safe, O Lord, we pray,
those whom you have saved by your kindness,
that, redeemed by the Passion of your Son,
they may rejoice in his Resurrection.
Who lives and reigns for ever and ever.

Saint Bede the Venerable   *Optional memorial*

● *The 8th-century monk and scholar Bede was raised from his youth at Wearmouth Abbey in Northumbria, England. Grounded in the liturgical rhythms of monastic life, Bede produced astute*

commentaries on Scripture and the famous chronicle
of the early English Church. For Bede, Christ is the
center of history; he popularized our familiar way of
marking time "in the year of the Lord" or "A.D." Bede
had a keen pastoral sense. He recommended that
lay persons pray always, "reproducing in life what
they celebrate in the liturgy." Upon Bede's death in
735, his contemporary and fellow Anglo-Saxon, the
missionary Saint Boniface, declared, "The candle of
the Church, lit by the Holy Spirit, is extinguished." •

ENTRANCE ANTIPHON   Cf. Sir 15:5

In the midst of the Church he opened his mouth,/ and the
Lord filled him with the spirit of wisdom and understanding/
and clothed him in a robe of glory, alleluia.

COLLECT

O God, who bring light to your Church
through the learning of the Priest Saint Bede,
mercifully grant that your servants
may always be enlightened by his wisdom and helped
    by his merits.
Through our Lord Jesus Christ, your Son,
who lives and reigns with you in the unity
    of the Holy Spirit,
one God, for ever and ever.

PRAYER OVER THE OFFERINGS

May the sacrifice which we gladly present
    on the feast day of blessed Bede,
be pleasing to you, O God,
for, taught by him, we, too, give ourselves entirely
    to you in praise.
Through Christ our Lord.

COMMUNION ANTIPHON   Cf. Lk 12:42

Behold a faithful and prudent steward/ to give them their
allowance of food at the proper time, alleluia.

Prayer after Communion

Through Christ the teacher, O Lord,
instruct those you feed with Christ, the living Bread,
that on the feast day of blessed Bede they may
  learn your truth
and express it in works of charity.
Through Christ our Lord.

MEDITATION OF THE DAY

Knowing Jesus and the One Who Sent Him

Since the Son is in the Father and the Father is in the
Son, and the one who sees the Son sees the Father too, it
is evident that all who resist belief in the Son with stub-
born mind are proven not to know the Father. Hence
the same John, teaching the truth of divine unity, says,
No one who denies the Son has the Father; and again,
Everyone who loves the parent loves the child.

But because the disciples, who knew the Father and
the Son well, were going to suffer many things for defending and speaking of their knowledge, the Lord added with prudent counsel: *But I have said these things,
that when their hour comes you may remember that
I told you of them.* His saying *I told you of them* we
must ponder very seriously—"I who am going to die
for the sake of your life and salvation, I who am going
to redeem you with my blood, I who am going to aid
you always in your tribulations, I who am going to give
you eternal rewards after your tribulations."...

He who warned them ahead of time that the hour
of persecution would come is the one who, a little later, pledged his help to his faithful in the persecution,
saying, *You will have distress in the world; but have
confidence; I have overcome the world.* He elsewhere
promised the crown of life to those who are sincerely
engaged in strife, saying, *Blessed are those who suffer*

persecution for the sake of justice, for theirs is the Kingdom of heaven.

SAINT BEDE THE VENERABLE

Saint Bede the Venerable († 735) was an English Benedictine monk, a biblical scholar, and the first English historian.

Prayer for the Evening

Vigil of the Sixth Sunday of Easter

*Let all nations come and worship
in God's presence, alleluia!*

*Glory to the Father, and to the Son,
and to the Holy Spirit, as it was in the beginning,
is now, and will be for ever. Amen. Alleluia!*

HYMN   Meter: 77 77 77
This hymn can be sung to the tune used for
For the Beauty of the Earth

God of mercy, God of grace,
Show the brightness of thy face;
Shine upon us, Savior, shine,
Fill thy Church with light divine.
And thy saving health extend
Unto earth's remotest end.

Let the people praise thee, Lord;
Be by all that live adored;
Let the nations shout and sing,
Glory to their Savior King;
At thy feet their tribute pay,
And thy holy will obey.

CANTICLE Revelation 15:3-4

The Advocate, the holy Spirit that the Father will send in my name—he will teach you everything and remind you of all that [I] told you. (Jn 14:26)

The Spirit of God fills the Church with joy at the memory of the great work of our salvation wrought through the Death and Resurrection of Jesus Christ, the Holy One of God.

Mighty and wonderful are your works,
Lord God Almighty!
Righteous and true are your ways,
O King of the nations!

Who would dare refuse you honor,
or the glory due your name, O Lord?

Since you alone are holy,
all nations shall come
and worship in your presence.
Your mighty deeds are clearly seen.

Word of God 1 Samuel 12:22-24

For the sake of his own great name the LORD will not abandon his people, since the LORD himself chose to make you his people. As for me, far be it from me to sin against the LORD by ceasing to pray for you and to teach you the good and right way. But you must fear the LORD and worship him faithfully with your whole heart; keep in mind the great things he has done among you.

*I will teach you the manner of God's dealings,/
and the way of the Almighty I will not conceal.*
(Jb 27:11)

CANTICLE OF MARY   (Text, back cover A)

Thus says the LORD, your redeemer,/ the Holy One of Israel:/ I, the LORD, your God,/ teach you what is for your good,/ and lead you on the way you should go. (Is 48:17)

INTERCESSIONS

Let us pray to Christ, our Teacher:

℟   Mighty and wonderful are your works!

You are the Word of God:
– teach your people the ways of justice and love. ℟

You are the Truth of God:
– teach your people to walk in your light. ℟

You are the Love of God made flesh among us:
– teach your people to observe your commandments. ℟

You are the Life:
– teach your people to follow you to life everlasting. ℟

Personal intentions

Our Father....

Grace be with all who love our Lord Jesus Christ in immortality. Amen. (Eph 6:24)

MARIAN ANTIPHON   (page 12 or 13)

❧ ❧ ❧

SAINT WHO?

Saints Who Were Visionaries

Saint Waningus of Fécamp
Abbot († c. 683)   Feast: January 9

Waningus was born in Rouen, France, of a noble family. He became a courtier under King Clotaire III, who made him governor of Pays de Caux, today in the region of Normandy. A great fan of the hunt, Waningus was nevertheless devout. He considered the virgin-martyr Eulalia, who had suffered torture for Christ at the age of thirteen, his patroness. One night, Eulalia came to Waningus in a dream and repeated to him the words of Christ: *It is easier for a camel to pass through the eye of a needle than for one who is rich to enter the kingdom of God* (Mt 19:24). From this time, Waningus withdrew more and more from the world. At last he decided to follow Christ as a monk.

In 658, Waningus founded the monastery of Fontenelle with another courtier-turned-monk, Wandregesilus. He entrusted his son Desideratus to be educated as a monk there. At Fécamp, he founded a church and a monastery for women. Before long, 360 women had entered. Waningus appointed Saint Childemarcha as abbess, and she oversaw the perpetual singing of the office within the abbey chapel. When Saint Leger was fleeing the clutches of the devious Master of the Palace, Ebroin, the nuns at Fécamp gave him refuge.

Waningus died around 683 and is venerated in Normandy.

Compassionate Father, through the intercession of Saint Waningus of Fécamp, help me to give with the awareness of all that I have received.

Suggested Prayer of the Faithful

(Each local community should compose its own Universal Prayer, but may find inspiration in the texts proposed here.)

God is greater than our fears and knows our needs. Counting on the Father's boundless mercy, we now pray:

That the Church will stand before the world without stain or blemish, holy and obedient to God's Word.

That divisions in the world will be healed, violence will cease, and the peace of God's Kingdom will bless the earth.

For blessings on police, firefighters, emergency medical technicians, and all those who protect us at the risk of their own lives.

That God will strengthen and preserve our parish in his holy service.

That those suffering from addictions may come to have liberation and peace.

For the grace this week to rejoice in the firm belief that Jesus will never abandon us.

Heavenly Father, we know that you hear our prayers and attend to our needs. Increase in us the virtues of faith, hope, and love. Through Christ our Lord. Amen. ∎

SUNDAY, MAY 26
Sixth Sunday of Easter

Prayer for the Morning

Sing a new song to the Lord
for he has worked wonders, alleluia!

Glory to the Father, and to the Son,
and to the Holy Spirit, as it was in the beginning,
is now, and will be for ever. Amen. Alleluia!

HYMN   Meter: LM
This hymn can be sung to the tune used for
I Know that My Redeemer Lives

This day our risen Savior reigns,
Creation's undefeated King,
While angels in resplendent light
With mighty voice his triumph sing.

This day the Lord has made his own,
Who broke from his confining grave.
His living presence fills the world
That by his Cross he came to save.

To God the Father glory give
For Jesus Christ his deathless Son,
Who with the Holy Spirit lives
Immortal, and for ever One.

PSALM 98

This is the plan proposed for the whole earth,/ and this the hand outstretched over all nations. (Is 14:26)

God's plan of salvation, accomplished through the Death and Resurrection of Jesus Christ, embraces all peoples. In the hope of the Spirit, we rejoice in the fulfillment of his promises.

Sing a new song to the Lord
for he has worked wonders.
His right hand and his holy arm
have brought salvation.

The Lord has made known his salvation;
has shown his justice to the nations.
He has remembered his truth and love
for the house of Israel.

All the ends of the earth have seen
the salvation of our God.
Shout to the Lord, all the earth,
ring out your joy.

Sing psalms to the Lord with the harp
with the sound of music.
With trumpets and the sound of the horn
acclaim the King, the Lord.

Let the sea and all within it thunder;
the world, and all its peoples.
Let the rivers clap their hands
and the hills ring out their joy.

Rejoice at the presence of the Lord,
for he comes to rule the earth.
He will rule the world with justice
and the peoples with fairness.

Glory to the Father....

Word of God Romans 15:7-9

Welcome one another, then, as Christ welcomed you, for the glory of God. For I say that Christ became a minister of the circumcised to show God's truthfulness, to confirm the promises to the patriarchs, but so that the Gentiles might glorify God for his mercy.

I proclaim you, O Lord, among the nations,/
and I will sing praise to your name.
(cf. 2 Sm 22:50)

Canticle of Zechariah
(Text, back cover B)

Let all the nations gather together,/ let the peoples assemble! (Is 43:9)

Intercessions

The Lord comes to rule the whole earth; to him we pray:

℟ You bring us salvation!

You came in human flesh through the Virgin Mary:
– teach us to love all humanity, redeemed by your love. ℟

You died for the people of every place and time:
– teach us to respect people of every age, of every race, of every nation. ℟

You arose to rule in fairness over all peoples:
– teach us to pursue justice and peace among nations. ℟

Personal intentions

Our Father....

God of all the earth, you sent your only Son to redeem all peoples from sin and death. May his saving presence tear down the walls we have built between us, that he may rule the whole world in peace and love, who lives and reigns with you in the unity of the Holy Spirit, one God, for ever and ever. Amen.

MASS

Sixth Sunday of Easter

When the Ascension of the Lord is celebrated the following Sunday, the second reading (Rv 22:12-14, 16-17, 20) and Gospel (Jn 17:20-26) from the Seventh Sunday of Easter may be read on the Sixth Sunday of Easter.

Christ's promise at the Last Supper—"Whoever loves me will keep my word, and my Father and I will make our dwelling with him"—is all that we need to be happy in life. Barnabas and Paul "dedicate their lives to the name of our Lord Jesus Christ" in order to keep and to identify with Christ's Word in every dimension of their lives. God acknowledges such dedication by ordaining that the names of the twelve Apostles be inscribed on the wall of the heavenly Jerusalem. The same is offered to us who refuse to let our hearts be troubled, but who cling to the name of Christ instead.

ENTRANCE ANTIPHON   Cf. Is 48:20
Proclaim a joyful sound and let it be heard;/ proclaim to the ends of the earth:/ The Lord has freed his people, alleluia.

GLORIA ———————————————————— page 212

COLLECT
  Grant, almighty God,
  that we may celebrate with heartfelt devotion these
      days of joy,
  which we keep in honor of the risen Lord,
  and that what we relive in remembrance
  we may always hold to in what we do.
  Through our Lord Jesus Christ, your Son,
  who lives and reigns with you in the unity
      of the Holy Spirit,
  one God, for ever and ever.

  ● *It is the decision of the Holy Spirit and of us not to place on you any burden beyond these necessities.* ●

A reading from
the Acts of the Apostles   15:1-2, 22-29

S OME WHO HAD come down
from Judea were instructing
the brothers, "Unless you are circumcised according
to the Mosaic practice, you cannot be saved." Because
there arose no little dissension and debate by Paul and
Barnabas with them, it was decided that Paul, Barnabas,
and some of the others should go up to Jerusalem to the
apostles and elders about this question.

The apostles and elders, in agreement with the whole
church, decided to choose representatives and to send
them to Antioch with Paul and Barnabas. The ones
chosen were Judas, who was called Barsabbas, and Silas,
leaders among the brothers. This is the letter delivered
by them:

"The apostles and the elders, your brothers, to the
brothers in Antioch, Syria, and Cilicia of Gentile origin:
greetings. Since we have heard that some of our number
who went out without any mandate from us have upset
you with their teachings and disturbed your peace of
mind, we have with one accord decided to choose representatives and to send them to you along with our beloved Barnabas and Paul, who have dedicated their lives
to the name of our Lord Jesus Christ. So we are sending
Judas and Silas who will also convey this same message
by word of mouth: 'It is the decision of the Holy Spirit
and of us not to place on you any burden beyond these
necessities, namely, to abstain from meat sacrificed to
idols, from blood, from meats of strangled animals, and
from unlawful marriage. If you keep free of these, you
will be doing what is right. Farewell.'"
The word of the Lord.

————• PSALM 67 •————

℟ (4) **O God, let all the nations praise you!**

Or: Alleluia.

May God have pity on us and bless us;
  may he let his face shine upon us.
So may your way be known upon earth;
  among all nations, your salvation. ℟

May the nations be glad and exult
  because you rule the peoples in equity;
  the nations on the earth you guide. ℟

May the peoples praise you, O God;
  may all the peoples praise you!
May God bless us,
  and may all the ends of the earth fear him! ℟

• *The angel showed me the holy city coming down out of heaven.* •

**A reading from
the Book of Revelation**   21:10-14, 22-23

T HE ANGEL TOOK me in spirit to a great, high mountain
and showed me the holy city Jerusalem coming down
out of heaven from God. It gleamed with the splendor
of God. Its radiance was like that of a precious stone,
like jasper, clear as crystal. It had a massive, high wall,
with twelve gates where twelve angels were stationed
and on which names were inscribed, the names of the
twelve tribes of the Israelites. There were three gates
facing east, three north, three south, and three west.
The wall of the city had twelve courses of stones as its
foundation, on which were inscribed the twelve names
of the twelve apostles of the Lamb.

I saw no temple in the city for its temple is the Lord God almighty and the Lamb. The city had no need of sun or moon to shine on it, for the glory of God gave it light, and its lamp was the Lamb.
The word of the Lord.

Alleluia, alleluia. Whoever loves me will keep my word, says the Lord,/ and my Father will love him and we will come to him. Alleluia, alleluia.

> ● *The Holy Spirit will teach you everything and remind you of all that I told you.* ●

A reading from
the holy Gospel according to John   14:23-29

Jesus said to his disciples: "Whoever loves me will keep my word, and my Father will love him, and we will come to him and make our dwelling with him. Whoever does not love me does not keep my words; yet the word you hear is not mine but that of the Father who sent me.

"I have told you this while I am with you. The Advocate, the Holy Spirit, whom the Father will send in my name, will teach you everything and remind you of all that I told you. Peace I leave with you; my peace I give to you. Not as the world gives do I give it to you. Do not let your hearts be troubled or afraid. You heard me tell you, 'I am going away and I will come back to you.' If you loved me, you would rejoice that I am going to the Father; for the Father is greater than I. And now I have told you this before it happens, so that when it happens you may believe."
The Gospel of the Lord.

Credo ———————————————————— page 214

Prayer over the Offerings

May our prayers rise up to you, O Lord,
together with the sacrificial offerings,
so that, purified by your graciousness,
we may be conformed to the mysteries of your
mighty love.
Through Christ our Lord.

Preface I-V of Easter ———————— pages 218 to 219

Communion Antiphon   Jn 14:15-16

If you love me, keep my commandments, says the Lord,/ and
I will ask the Father and he will send you another Paraclete,/
to abide with you for ever, alleluia.

Prayer after Communion

Almighty ever-living God,
who restore us to eternal life in the Resurrection of
Christ,
increase in us, we pray, the fruits of this paschal
Sacrament
and pour into our hearts the strength of this saving
food.
Through Christ our Lord.

A formula of Solemn Blessing, pages 78-79, may be used.

MEDITATION OF THE DAY

"My peace I give to you"

It is not rare in the spiritual life to see souls who are
trying generously to advance in virtue fall—by reason
of their desire to cultivate a delicate conscience and to
avoid all deliberate venial sin—into the extremity of inquietude and perturbation, get involved in a thousand
perplexities and scruples, and eventually grow cold in
their trust in our Lord. All of these occurrences spell
the death of devotion....

I do not tire of repeating to all generous souls: Be as delicate as you can with our Lord. Watch your conduct most carefully to avoid all venial sins. But, for the love of God, let this be done without losing confidence and peace....

Let us give an example.... A fervent soul has the misfortune to commit a venial sin, an occurrence that is not rare, considering our innate frailty. Just as soon as this soul has fallen, he recalls everything that he has read and reflected on concerning venial sin, and forthwith he becomes disturbed, overwhelmed with sorrow and suffering. Confidence in God grows cold. The soul withdraws from him. He leaves off prayer, or makes it badly. All his exercises of piety no longer are made with their customary regularity. After many hours of inquietude, he recovers peace of mind, but only by dint of much effort and many consultations....

Let us not act in this manner. Rather, let us consider how we can perfectly reconcile the grief caused by our sins with confidence in God and peace of soul.

Saint Thérèse of the Child Jesus expresses this reconciliation very well when she says: "This I know very well: although I should have on my soul all the crimes that could be committed, I would lose none of my confidence; rather, I would hasten, with my heart broken into pieces by sorrow, to cast myself into the arms of my Savior. I know how greatly he loved the prodigal son; I have marked his words to Mary Magdalen, to the adulterous woman, to the Samaritan. No, no one could make me afraid, because I know to whom to cling by reason of his love and his mercy. I know that all this multitude of offenses would disappear in the twinkling of an eye, as a drop of water cast into a roaring furnace."

Let us note this well: a heart broken into pieces by sorrow, and yet undiminished confidence—these two go together in such a way that, although Saint Thérèse might have been laden with all the sins of the world, she would have flung herself into the arms of Jesus with complete confidence.

SERVANT OF GOD LUIS MARÍA MARTÍNEZ

Archbishop Martínez († 1956) was a spiritual author, and the first official Primate of Mexico.

Prayer for the Evening

Christ dwells among us:
let us give thanks and praise, alleluia!

Glory to the Father, and to the Son,
and to the Holy Spirit, as it was in the beginning,
is now, and will be for ever. Amen. Alleluia!

HYMN

Meter: 77 77
This hymn can be sung to the tune used for
Savior of the Nations, Come

On this day, the first of days,
God the Father's name we praise;
Who, creation's Lord and Spring
Did the world from darkness bring.

On this day the eternal Son
Over death his triumph won;
On this day the Spirit came
With his gifts of living flame.

O that fervent love today
May in every heart have sway,
Teaching us to praise aright
God, the Source of life and light.

God, the blessèd Three in One,
Dwell within my heart alone;
Thou dost give thyself to me;
May I give myself to thee.

PSALM 15

Whoever loves me will keep my word, and my Father will love him, and we will come to him and make our dwelling with him. (Jn 14:23)

God dwells in those who prepare a place for him. The word of Christ heard, loved, and lived by the power of the Holy Spirit is the broom that sweeps all faults, injustices, untruths, slanders, and greed out of the heart that would welcome him.

Lord, who shall be admitted to your tent
and dwell on your holy mountain?

He who walks without fault;
he who acts with justice
and speaks the truth from his heart;
he who does not slander with his tongue;

he who does no wrong to his brother,
who casts no slur on his neighbor,
who holds the godless in disdain,
but honors those who fear the Lord;

he who keeps his pledge, come what may;
who takes no interest on a loan
and accepts no bribes against the innocent.
Such a man will stand firm for ever.

Glory to the Father....

Word of God   Revelation 3:20-21

BEHOLD, I STAND at the door and knock. If anyone hears my voice and opens the door, [then] I will enter his house and dine with him, and he with me. I will give the victor the right to sit with me on my throne, as I myself first won the victory and sit with my Father on his throne.

*I will dwell in the midst of the Israelites
and will be their God. (Ex 29:45)*

CANTICLE OF MARY (Text, back cover A)

They shall make a sanctuary for me, that I may dwell in their midst. (Ex 25:8)

INTERCESSIONS

The Holy Trinity dwells within the baptized. With faith in God's Presence in us and among us, we pray:

℟ Make us holy, O Lord.

You love those who make a home for your word in their hearts:
– dwell within us in love and in power. ℟

You love those who keep truth alight in their hearts:
– purify us of all falsehood. ℟

You love those who seek to live according to the Gospel:
– dwell within us and direct us in your ways. ℟

Personal intentions

Our Father….

May the Lord strengthen our hearts, to be blameless in holiness before our God and Father at the coming of our Lord Jesus with all his holy ones. Amen. (cf. 1 Thes 3:13)

MARIAN ANTIPHON (page 12 or 13)

❧ ❧ ❧

MONDAY, MAY 27
Saint Augustine of Canterbury

Prayer for the Morning

Let us praise the Lord for his goodness,
and bless the King of the ages, alleluia!

Glory to the Father.... Alleluia!

HYMN   Meter: LM

This hymn can be sung to the tune used for
Praise God, from Whom All Blessings Flow

Our justice, Christ, resplendent sun,
From prison tomb bursts forth in light;
Within us joy and gladness dance
For Christ is risen in his might.

From death to life we have been raised,
From earth to heaven we are led:
For Christ our resurrection joy
Is truly risen as he said.

Let all the heavens burst with joy,
Let all the earth with song resound!
Let all creation join the dance
For Christ is risen, death is bound!

CANTICLE OF TOBIT   13:10-11

I will make you a light to the nations,/ that my salvation may reach
to the ends of the earth. (Is 49:6)

The bright light of the Risen Sun, Jesus Christ, burst from the tomb
in glory, and shines to all parts of the earth through the witness of
the Church, illumined by the Spirit to bear witness to his glory. Let
us walk in his light and follow in his way, that, reflecting his brightness, we may enlighten the eyes of the blind with faith and hope.

Praise the Lord for his goodness,
and bless the King of the ages,
so that his tent may be rebuilt in you with joy.

May he gladden within you all who were captives;
all who were ravaged may he cherish within you
for all generations to come.

A bright light will shine to all parts of the earth;
many nations shall come to you from afar,
and the inhabitants of all the limits of the earth,
drawn to you by the name of the Lord God,
bearing in their hands their gifts for the King of heaven.

Every generation shall give joyful praise in you,
and shall call you the chosen one,
through all ages forever.

Glory to the Father....

Word of God
Isaiah 42:6-7

I, THE LORD, have called you for the victory of justice,/ I have grasped you by the hand;/ I formed you, and set you/ as a covenant of the people,/ a light for the nations,/ To open the eyes of the blind,/ to bring out prisoners from confinement,/ and from the dungeon, those who live in darkness.

No one who lights a lamp conceals it with a vessel or sets it under a bed; rather, he places it on a lampstand so that those who enter may see the light. (Lk 8:16)

CANTICLE OF ZECHARIAH
(Text, back cover B)

My eyes have seen your salvation,/ which you prepared in sight of all the peoples,/ a light for revelation to the Gentiles,/ and glory for your people Israel. (Lk 2:30-32)

INTERCESSIONS

In joy we pray:

℟   Lord, draw all people to yourself!

Where there is hatred,
– let us sow love. ℟

Where there is darkness,
– let us bring light. ℟

Where there is sadness,
– let us bring joy. ℟

Personal intentions

Our Father....

Lord God of light, you have shone upon our darkness
and set us free through the Death and Resurrection of
Jesus Christ. Grant us the grace to live in the freedom
of the children of God, that where we walk this day,
we may bring light, through the same Christ our Lord.
Amen.

MASS

Monday of the Sixth Week of Easter

ENTRANCE ANTIPHON   Rom 6:9
Christ, having risen from the dead, dies now no more;/ death
will no longer have dominion over him, alleluia.

COLLECT
Grant, O merciful God,
that we may experience at all times
the fruit produced by the paschal observances.
Through our Lord Jesus Christ, your Son,
who lives and reigns with you in the unity
of the Holy Spirit,
one God, for ever and ever.

● *The Lord opened her heart to pay attention to what Paul taught.* ●

A reading from
the Acts of the Apostles

16:11-15

WE SET SAIL from Troas, making a straight run for Samothrace, and on the next day to Neapolis, and from there to Philippi, a leading city in that district of Macedonia and a Roman colony. We spent some time in that city. On the sabbath we went outside the city gate along the river where we thought there would be a place of prayer. We sat and spoke with the women who had gathered there. One of them, a woman named Lydia, a dealer in purple cloth, from the city of Thyatira, a worshiper of God, listened, and the Lord opened her heart to pay attention to what Paul was saying. After she and her household had been baptized, she offered us an invitation, "If you consider me a believer in the Lord, come and stay at my home," and she prevailed on us. The word of the Lord.

──── ● PSALM 149 ● ────

℟ (see 4a) **The Lord takes delight in his people.**

Or: **Alleluia.**

Sing to the LORD a new song
  of praise in the assembly of the faithful.
Let Israel be glad in their maker,
  let the children of Zion rejoice in their king. ℟

Let them praise his name in the festive dance,
  let them sing praise to him with timbrel and harp.
For the LORD loves his people,
  and he adorns the lowly with victory. ℟

Let the faithful exult in glory;
    let them sing for joy upon their couches.
Let the high praises of God be in their throats.
    This is the glory of all his faithful. Alleluia. ℟

Alleluia, alleluia. The Spirit of truth will testify to me, says the Lord,/ and you also will testify. Alleluia, alleluia.

• *The Spirit of truth will testify to me.* •

A reading from
the holy Gospel according to John   15:26–16:4a

JESUS SAID to his disciples:
    "When the Advocate comes whom I will send you from the Father, the Spirit of truth who proceeds from the Father, he will testify to me. And you also testify, because you have been with me from the beginning.

"I have told you this so that you may not fall away. They will expel you from the synagogues; in fact, the hour is coming when everyone who kills you will think he is offering worship to God. They will do this because they have not known either the Father or me. I have told you this so that when their hour comes you may remember that I told you."
The Gospel of the Lord.

PRAYER OVER THE OFFERINGS
    Receive, O Lord, we pray,
    these offerings of your exultant Church,
    and, as you have given her cause for such great gladness,
    grant also that the gifts we bring
    may bear fruit in perpetual happiness.
    Through Christ our Lord.

PREFACE I–V OF EASTER ———————— pages 218 to 219

COMMUNION ANTIPHON
Jn 20:19

Jesus stood in the midst of his disciples/ and said to them:
Peace be with you, alleluia.

PRAYER AFTER COMMUNION

Look with kindness upon your people, O Lord,
and grant, we pray,
that those you were pleased to renew by eternal mysteries
may attain in their flesh
the incorruptible glory of the resurrection.
Through Christ our Lord.

SAINT AUGUSTINE OF CANTERBURY   *Optional memorial*

• *Augustine was a native of Rome, where he served
as prior of the Monastery of Saint Andrew. Saint
Gregory the Great sent him with thirty companions
from Rome to the Anglo-Saxon kingdom based in
Kent. The mission faltered at first, and Augustine
returned to Rome. But Gregory, confident in
Augustine's leadership, consecrated him abbot of
the fledgling community and sent him back on the
road to England. Reaching Kent, Augustine and his
companions were successful in converting the king,
Ethelbert. Thousands of his subjects followed him into
the Church. Gregory appointed Augustine Archbishop
of Canterbury. He died around the year 604 and is
considered the apostle to England.* •

ENTRANCE ANTIPHON

O chosen people, proclaim the mighty works of him/ who
called you out of darkness into his wonderful light, alleluia.

COLLECT

O God, who by the preaching
of the Bishop Saint Augustine of Canterbury
led the English peoples to the Gospel,
grant, we pray, that the fruits of his labors
may remain ever abundant in your Church.
Through our Lord Jesus Christ, your Son,

who lives and reigns with you in the unity
of the Holy Spirit,
one God, for ever and ever.

Prayer over the Offerings
Look upon the sacrificial gifts we offer, almighty God,
on the feast day of blessed Augustine of Canterbury,
and grant that we, who celebrate the mysteries
of the Lord's Passion,
may imitate what we now do.
Through Christ our Lord.

Communion Antiphon   Ez 34:15
I will pasture my sheep;/ I myself will give them rest, says the
Lord, alleluia.

Prayer after Communion
By the power of this mystery, O Lord,
confirm your servants in the true faith,
that they may everywhere profess in word and deed
the faith for which blessed Augustine of Canterbury
never ceased to labor
and for which he spent his whole life.
Through Christ our Lord.

MEDITATION OF THE DAY

That We May Not Fall Away

But let us now do what is necessary to guard ourselves against [the enemy].

And thus it is greatly necessary for us that we think
about ourselves and eagerly deal with God. And let us
do what is necessary for us and submit to righteousness
and forsake unrighteousness…and eagerly atone for
what we earlier broke. And let us love God and follow
God's laws and do very eagerly what we have promised when we received baptism or when our sponsors
were at baptism for us. And let us put word and deed
rightly together and eagerly cleanse our conscience and
carefully keep our oath and pledge and have a truth

between us without deceit. And let us often understand the great judgment at which we all must appear and protect ourselves eagerly against the…torments of hell and earn for ourselves those glories and joys that God has prepared for those who do his will in the world. May God help us. Amen.

ARCHBISHOP WULFSTAN

Wulfstan (†1023) was an English bishop and distinguished writer and preacher in the Anglo-Saxon period.

Prayer for the Evening

God sends his truth and his love:
let us give thanks and praise, alleluia!

Glory to the Father…. Alleluia!

HYMN

Meter: CM
This hymn can be sung to the tune used for
O God, Our Help in Ages Past

Lo! What a cloud of witnesses
Encompass us around!
They, once like us with suffering tried,
Are now with glory crowned.

Let us, with zeal like theirs inspired,
Strive in the Christian race;
And, freed from every weight of sin,
Their holy footsteps trace.

Behold a Witness nobler still,
Who trod affliction's path:
Jesus, the author, finisher,
Rewarder of our faith.

He, for the joy before him set,
And moved by pitying love,
Endured the cross, despised the shame,
And now he reigns above.

Thither, forgetting things behind,
Press we to God's right hand;
There, with the Savior and his saints,
Triumphantly to stand.

Psalm 57   2-6

They will expel you from the synagogues; in fact, the hour is coming when everyone who kills you will think he is offering worship
to God. (Jn 16:2)

The servants are not greater than the Master. As we are reminded
these days by frequent news reports of the murder of servants of the
Gospel around the world, neither the Resurrection nor the sending
of the promised Spirit of truth and love spares us the privilege of the
consequences of bearing witness to Christ.

Have mercy on me, God, have mercy
for in you my soul has taken refuge.
In the shadow of your wings I take refuge
till the storms of destruction pass by.

I call to God the Most High,
to God who has always been my help.
May he send from heaven and save me
and shame those who assail me.

May God send his truth and his love.

My soul lies down among lions,
who would devour the sons of men.
Their teeth are spears and arrows,
their tongue a sharpened sword.

O God, arise above the heavens;
may your glory shine on earth!

Glory to the Father....

Word of God   Hebrews 12:1-4

S INCE WE ARE surrounded by
so great a cloud of witnesses,

let us rid ourselves of every burden and sin that clings to us and persevere in running the race that lies before us while keeping our eyes fixed on Jesus, the leader and perfecter of faith. For the sake of the joy that lay before him he endured the cross, despising its shame, and has taken his seat at the right of the throne of God. Consider how he endured such opposition from sinners, in order that you may not grow weary and lose heart. In your struggle against sin you have not yet resisted to the point of shedding blood.

We are witnesses of these things, as is the holy Spirit that God has given to those who obey him. (Acts 5:32)

CANTICLE OF MARY (Text, back cover A)

God raised this Jesus; of this we are all witnesses. (Acts 2:32)

INTERCESSIONS

In the power of God's Spirit, let us pray:

℟ May your glory shine on earth!

In lands and homes and hearts darkened by the refusal of faith: ℟

Through those whose witness to the Resurrection threatens their personal safety and the safety of their loved ones: ℟

For those who are afraid to accept the task of bearing witness to Christ: ℟

Personal intentions

Our Father....

May we receive a blessing from the LORD, the God of Israel, under whose wings we have come for refuge. Amen. (cf. Ru 2:12)

MARIAN ANTIPHON (page 12 or 13)

Saint Who?

Saints Who Were Visionaries

Saint Marie of the Incarnation
Religious († 1672)   Feast: April 30

The daughter of a baker from Tours, France, Marie encountered the Christ Child in a dream at age seven. "Do you want to be with me?" he asked. "Yes" was her simple answer. She was married by her parents at seventeen to Claude Martin. Claude died two years later, leaving Marie in precarious financial circumstances, with a six-month-old son, Claude, to care for. Marie moved in with her sister, worked in the family business, and raised her son. Her prayer began to reach great heights, with repeated visions of the Trinity. But she also suffered periods of dryness.

When Claude was twelve, Marie left him with her sister—a deeply painful decision—and went to the Ursulines. She began to perceive an inner call to the natives of the New World. Her desire was fulfilled when she went to New France in 1639, charged with creating a school for the children of Native American converts. From this time to her death, Marie combined an active life building up the fledgling frontier Church with her never-ending prayer. She wrote frequently to her son, who had entered religious life. "[Christ] has never led me by feelings of fear," Marie told him, "but always by a spirit of love and trust."

When Marie died on April 30, 1672, she was already hailed as a saint, the mother of the Church in Canada.

All-compassionate Father, through the intercession of Saint Marie of the Incarnation, root all my actions in prayer.

TUESDAY, MAY 28

Prayer for the Morning

Christ lives as ruler over life and death:
come, let us adore, alleluia!

Glory to the Father, and to the Son,
and to the Holy Spirit, as it was in the beginning,
is now, and will be for ever. Amen. Alleluia!

HYMN   Meter: 888 with alleluias

℟   Alleluia, alleluia, alleluia.

The strife is o'er, the battle done;
Now is the Victor's triumph won;
O let the song of praise be sung:
Alleluia. ℟

Death's mightiest powers have done their worst,
And Jesus hath his foes dispersed;
Let shouts of praise and joy outburst:
Alleluia. ℟

PSALM 2   1-8

Now is the time of judgment on this world; now the ruler of this
world will be driven out. (Jn 12:31)

No matter how powerful the rulers of this world appear to be—
whether political rulers or those unruly forces that seem to control
our own day-to-day behavior at times—all the ends of the earth are
in the possession of the risen Christ, as the Easter story shows us. If
even death could not prevail over him, how can any other opposition hope to succeed?

Why this tumult among nations,
among peoples this useless murmuring?

They arise, the kings of the earth,
princes plot against the Lord and his Anointed.
"Come, let us break their fetters,
come, let us cast off their yoke."

He who sits in the heavens laughs;
the Lord is laughing them to scorn.
Then he will speak in his anger,
his rage will strike them with terror.
"It is I who have set up my king
on Zion, my holy mountain."

I will announce the decree of the Lord:

The Lord said to me: "You are my Son.
It is I who have begotten you this day.
Ask and I shall bequeath you the nations,
put the ends of the earth in your possession."

Glory to the Father....

Word of God   Acts 4:25-30

Y OU SAID by the holy Spirit through the mouth of our
father David, your servant:
   "Why did the Gentiles rage/ and the peoples enter-
tain folly?/ The kings of the earth took their stand/ and
the princes gathered together/ against the Lord and
against his anointed."
Indeed they gathered in this city against your holy servant Jesus whom you anointed, Herod and Pontius
Pilate, together with the Gentiles and the peoples of
Israel, to do what your hand and [your] will had long
ago planned to take place. And now, Lord, take note of
their threats, and enable your servants to speak your
word with all boldness, as you stretch forth [your] hand

to heal, and signs and wonders are done through the name of your holy servant Jesus.

> *We drew courage through our God to speak to you the gospel of God with much struggle. (1 Thes 2:2)*

CANTICLE OF ZECHARIAH
(Text, back cover B)

Now the Lord is the Spirit, and where the Spirit of the Lord is, there is freedom. (2 Cor 3:17)

INTERCESSIONS

Let us pray for the courage of the early Christians, to announce and to live the decrees of the Lord in freedom under every circumstance:

℞ Yours is the kingdom, the power, and the glory.

God of power and might,
– deliver your servants from domination by any other power than yours. ℞

God of mercy and love,
– heal those who have been harmed by those who oppose the Gospel. ℞

God of life and death,
– give life in abundance to all who seek to serve you. ℞

Personal intentions

Our Father....

God of glory and majesty, you pour forth the Spirit of life through the Death and Resurrection of Jesus Christ our Lord. Animate us with your truth, sustain us with your love, and send us forth armed with conviction to proclaim the Good News of your dominion over death, through the same Christ our Lord. Amen.

Mass

Tuesday of the Sixth Week of Easter

The Holy Spirit comes to "convict the world in regard to sin and righteousness and condemnation." That sounds very harsh, but what it means is wonderful: sin can be rooted out, for the Holy Spirit overcomes disbelief; we can still be made righteous, even after Jesus ascends to the Father; and it is not we who have been condemned, but "the ruler of this world." The jailer experiences this righteousness at the earthquake, when Paul and Silas refuse to escape. He begs to be saved, and "his household rejoiced at having come to faith in God." God's name and promise prevail.

Entrance Antiphon   Rv 19:7, 6
Let us rejoice and be glad and give glory to God,/ for the Lord our God the Almighty reigns, alleluia.

Collect
Grant, almighty and merciful God,
that we may in truth receive a share
in the Resurrection of Christ your Son.
Who lives and reigns with you in the unity
    of the Holy Spirit,
one God, for ever and ever.

●   *Believe in the Lord Jesus and you and your household will be saved.* ●

A reading from
the Acts of the Apostles   16:22-34

The crowd in Philippi joined in the attack on Paul and Silas, and the magistrates had them stripped and ordered them to be beaten with rods. After inflicting many blows on them, they threw them into prison and instructed the jailer to guard them securely. When he received these instructions, he put them in the innermost cell and secured their feet to a stake.

About midnight, while Paul and Silas were praying and singing hymns to God as the prisoners listened, there was suddenly such a severe earthquake that the foundations of the jail shook; all the doors flew open, and the chains of all were pulled loose. When the jailer woke up and saw the prison doors wide open, he drew his sword and was about to kill himself, thinking that the prisoners had escaped. But Paul shouted out in a loud voice, "Do no harm to yourself; we are all here." He asked for a light and rushed in and, trembling with fear, he fell down before Paul and Silas. Then he brought them out and said, "Sirs, what must I do to be saved?" And they said, "Believe in the Lord Jesus and you and your household will be saved." So they spoke the word of the Lord to him and to everyone in his house. He took them in at that hour of the night and bathed their wounds; then he and all his family were baptized at once. He brought them up into his house and provided a meal and with his household rejoiced at having come to faith in God.

The word of the Lord.

──• PSALM 138 •──

℟ (7c) **Your right hand saves me, O Lord.**

Or: Alleluia.

I will give thanks to you, O LORD, with all my heart,
  for you have heard the words of my mouth;
    in the presence of the angels I will sing your praise;
I will worship at your holy temple,
  and give thanks to your name. ℟

Because of your kindness and your truth,
  you have made great above all things
    your name and your promise.

When I called, you answered me;
   you built up strength within me. ℟

Your right hand saves me.
The Lord will complete what he has done for me;
   your kindness, O Lord, endures forever;
   forsake not the work of your hands. ℟

Alleluia, alleluia. I will send to you the Spirit of truth,
says the Lord;/ he will guide you to all truth. Alleluia,
alleluia.

   ● *For if I do not go, the Advocate will not come to*
   you. ●

A reading from
the holy Gospel according to John   16:5-11

JESUS SAID to his disciples:
"Now I am going to the one
who sent me, and not one of you asks me, 'Where are
you going?' But because I told you this, grief has filled
your hearts. But I tell you the truth, it is better for you
that I go. For if I do not go, the Advocate will not come
to you. But if I go, I will send him to you. And when
he comes he will convict the world in regard to sin and
righteousness and condemnation: sin, because they do
not believe in me; righteousness, because I am going
to the Father and you will no longer see me; condemnation, because the ruler of this world has been condemned."
The Gospel of the Lord.

PRAYER OVER THE OFFERINGS
   Grant, we pray, O Lord,
      that we may always find delight in these paschal
         mysteries,
      so that the renewal constantly at work within us

may be the cause of our unending joy.
Through Christ our Lord.

PREFACE I-V OF EASTER ——————————— pages 218 to 219

COMMUNION ANTIPHON   Cf. Lk 24:46, 26
The Christ had to suffer and rise from the dead,/ and so enter
into his glory, alleluia.

PRAYER AFTER COMMUNION
Hear, O Lord, our prayers,
that this most holy exchange,
by which you have redeemed us,
may bring your help in this present life
and ensure for us eternal gladness.
Through Christ our Lord.

• ——————————————————— •
MEDITATION OF THE DAY
• ——————————————————— •

What the Advocate Does

We see and will continue to see problems both within
and without. They will always be there. But…it is important to shed the light of the risen Lord upon our
problems, and in a certain sense, to "evangelize" them.
To evangelize our problems. Let us not allow darkness
and fear to distract us and control us; we must cry out
to them: the Lord *is not here, but has risen!* He is our
greatest joy; he is always at our side and will never let
us down.

This is the foundation of our hope, which is not mere
optimism, nor a psychological attitude or desire to be
courageous. Christian hope is a gift that God gives us if
we come out of ourselves and open our hearts to him.
This hope does not disappoint us because the Holy
Spirit has been poured into our hearts (cf. Rom 5:5).

The Paraclete does not make everything look ap-
pealing. He does not remove evil with a magic wand.
But he pours into us the vitality of life, which is not

the absence of problems, but the certainty of being loved and always forgiven by Christ, who for us has conquered sin, conquered death and conquered fear. [The Resurrection] is the celebration of our hope, the celebration of this truth: nothing and no one will ever be able to separate us from his love (cf. Rom 8:39).

Pope Francis

His Holiness Pope Francis was elected to the See of Saint Peter in 2013.

Prayer for the Evening

What marvels the Lord has worked for us!
Let us give thanks and praise, alleluia!

Glory to the Father, and to the Son,
and to the Holy Spirit, as it was in the beginning,
is now, and will be for ever. Amen. Alleluia!

Hymn　　　　　　　　　　　　　　　　　Meter: 87 87 D
This hymn can be sung to the tune used for
Alleluia! Alleluia! Let the Holy Anthem Rise

When from bondage we are summoned
Out of darkness into light,
We must go by hope and patience,
Walk by faith and not by sight.

℟　Let us throw off all that hinders;
Let us run the race to win!
Let us hasten to our homeland
And, rejoicing, enter in.

When our God names us his people,
Then he leads us by the hand
Through a lonely, barren desert,
To a great and glorious land. ℟

PSALM 126

There was suddenly such a severe earthquake that the foundations of the jail shook; all the doors flew open, and the chains of all were pulled loose. (Acts 16:26)

Just as the disciples were delivered from prison, so were all of us delivered from the prison of sin and death by the Resurrection of Christ and the gift of the Spirit. In moments of discouragement, let us remember the hope that lights our way to a goal far more wonderful than we can imagine even now.

When the Lord delivered Zion from bondage,
it seemed like a dream.
Then was our mouth filled with laughter,
on our lips there were songs.

The heathens themselves said: "What marvels
the Lord worked for them!"
What marvels the Lord worked for us!
Indeed we were glad.

Deliver us, O Lord, from our bondage
as streams in dry land.
Those who are sowing in tears
will sing when they reap.

They go out, they go out, full of tears,
carrying seed for the sowing:
they come back, they come back, full of song,
carrying their sheaves.

Glory to the Father....

Word of God
Baruch 4:22-23

I HAVE TRUSTED in the Eternal God for your welfare,/ and joy has come to me from the Holy One/ Because of the mercy that will swiftly reach you/ from your eternal savior./ With mourning and lament I sent you forth,/

but God will give you back to me/ with enduring gladness and joy.

My word shall not return to me void/ but shall do my will,/ achieving the end for which I sent it.
(cf. Is 55:11)

CANTICLE OF MARY
(Text, back cover A)

The LORD sent me to comfort all who mourn. (cf. Is 61:1-2)

INTERCESSIONS

Let us pray to the victorious Christ especially for those who have grown discouraged in bearing the heat and burden of the day:

℟   Deliver your people, O Lord, from bondage.

For all those whose faith has led them into places of exile and sorrow:
– be their deliverance and their joy. ℟

For all those who labor in hopelessness:
– be their hope and their courage. ℟

For all those who have abandoned pastoral ministry in discouragement:
– be their reconciliation and guide. ℟

Personal intentions

Our Father....

May the LORD guard our going and coming/ both now and for ever. Amen. (cf. Ps 121:8)

MARIAN ANTIPHON
(page 12 or 13)

SAINT WHO?

Saints Who Were Visionaries

Saint Aurea of San Millán

Virgin († c. 1070)   Feast: March 11

Aurea was born of well-to-do parents in Villavelayo, Spain, during the Moorish occupation. From childhood, she was inclined to prayer and penance. As a young woman, Aurea accompanied her parents on a pilgrimage to the monastery of San Millán de Cogolla in La Rioja. She told the prior, Saint Dominic de Silos, that she felt she must stay.

After some deliberation, Dominic decided to comply with Aurea's request. A walled cell was prepared for her adjacent to the upper monastery church (San Millán de Suso). Once she was enclosed in the cell, Aurea remained there day and night. She spent her time praying, doing spiritual reading, and mending the priests' vestments. A small window that looked out on the high altar permitted her to join in the liturgy and to receive the persons who sought her counsel.

Aurea received a number of mystical graces, and was believed to be a worker of miracles. She had a vision of her patron saints, the virgin martyrs Eulalia, Cecilia, and Agatha. Eventually, Aurea's harsh discipline took a toll on her health. She became sick and died in 1070 at the age of twenty-seven. Aurea's mother, Amunia, who joined the monastery after her, is also revered as a saint.

Father in heaven, through the intercession of
Saint Aurea of San Millán,
help me to seek silence and solitude.

WEDNESDAY, MAY 29

Prayer for the Morning

Let us praise the name of the Lord,
for he alone is exalted, alleluia!

Glory to the Father, and to the Son,
and to the Holy Spirit, as it was in the beginning,
is now, and will be for ever. Amen. Alleluia!

Hymn

Meter: 87 87 D
This hymn can be sung to the tune used for
Joyful, Joyful, We Adore Thee

Praise the Lord! ye heavens, adore him;
Praise him, angels in the height.
Sun and moon, rejoice before him;
Praise him, all ye stars of light.
Praise the Lord, for he has spoken;
Worlds his mighty voice obeyed.
Laws which never shall be broken
For their guidance he has made.

Worship, honor, glory, blessing,
Lord, we offer unto thee.
Young and old, thy praise expressing,
In glad homage bend the knee.
All the saints in heaven adore thee;
We would bow before thy throne.
As thine angels serve before thee,
So on earth thy will be done.

Psalm 148

1-10

The God who made the world and all that is in it, the Lord of heaven
and earth, does not dwell in sanctuaries made by human hands, nor

is he served by human hands because he needs anything. Rather it is he who gives to everyone life and breath and everything. (Acts 17:24-25)

All creation sings praise to God simply by being fully what the Creator intended. In the risen Christ, through the life-breath of the Spirit, all creation is brought to fullness in the great song of praise sung by a world made new.

Praise the Lord from the heavens,
praise him in the heights.
Praise him, all his angels,
praise him, all his host.

Praise him, sun and moon,
praise him, shining stars.
Praise him, highest heavens
and the waters above the heavens.

Let them praise the name of the Lord.
He commanded: they were made.
He fixed them for ever,
gave a law which shall not pass away.

Praise the Lord from the earth,
sea creatures and all oceans,
fire and hail, snow and mist,
stormy winds that obey his word;

all mountains and hills,
all fruit trees and cedars,
beasts, wild and tame,
reptiles and birds on the wing.

Glory to the Father....

Word of God
Romans 8:19-21

CREATION AWAITS with eager expectation the revelation of the children of God; for creation was made subject to futility, not of its own accord but because of the one who subjected it, in hope that creation itself would be set free from slavery to corruption and share in the glorious freedom of the children of God.

> *Sing to the LORD a new song,/*
> *his praise from the end of the earth.*
> *(Is 42:10)*

CANTICLE OF ZECHARIAH   (Text, back cover B)

In him we live and move and have our being, for we too are his offspring. (cf. Acts 17:28)

INTERCESSIONS

Created and redeemed by the overflowing love of God, let us offer our praise and thanks:

℟   Blessed are you, O Lord our God, maker and ruler of the universe.

You have filled the universe with wonders:
– fill us with reverence and delight. ℟

You have called into being life of every kind:
– fill us with a desire to cherish life in all its forms. ℟

You have made us in your own image to be your praise:
– fill us with thanksgiving. ℟

Personal intentions

Our Father….

O God, Creator and Redeemer, you are the author of being and life. Inspire in us a spirit of praise, that we may give you glory in everything we think and say and do, through Jesus Christ our Lord. Amen.

Mass

Wednesday of the Sixth Week of Easter

At the Morning Mass

In regions where the Solemnity of the Ascension occurs on the following Sunday, this Mass is also used in the evening.

To the Athenians, Paul appeals to the human conviction that we are made in the image of God. No one can deny that "heaven and earth are full of God's glory." Yet the fallen, rebellious human spirit needs the Spirit of truth to guide us. He unites us to the Father and the Son so that we may glorify God until the end.

Entrance Antiphon   Cf. Ps 18 (17):50; 22 (21):23
I will praise you, Lord, among the nations;/ I will tell of your name to my kin, alleluia.

Collect
> Grant, we pray, O Lord,
> that, as we celebrate in mystery
> the solemnities of your Son's Resurrection,
> so, too, we may be worthy
> to rejoice at his coming with all the Saints.
> Through our Lord Jesus Christ, your Son,
> who lives and reigns with you in the unity
>   of the Holy Spirit,
> one God, for ever and ever.

> • *What therefore you unknowingly worship, I proclaim to you.* •

A reading from the Acts of the Apostles

17:15, 22–18:1

After Paul's escorts had taken him to Athens, they came away with instructions for Silas and Timothy to join him as soon as possible.

Then Paul stood up at the Areopagus and said: "You Athenians, I see that in every respect you are very religious. For as I walked around looking carefully at your shrines, I even discovered an altar inscribed, 'To an Unknown God.' What therefore you unknowingly worship, I proclaim to you. The God who made the world and all that is in it, the Lord of heaven and earth, does not dwell in sanctuaries made by human hands, nor is he served by human hands because he needs anything. Rather it is he who gives to everyone life and breath and everything. He made from one the whole human race to dwell on the entire surface of the earth, and he fixed the ordered seasons and the boundaries of their regions, so that people might seek God, even perhaps grope for him and find him, though indeed he is not far from any one of us. For 'In him we live and move and have our being,' as even some of your poets have said, 'For we too are his offspring.' Since therefore we are the offspring of God, we ought not to think that the divinity is like an image fashioned from gold, silver, or stone by human art and imagination. God has overlooked the times of ignorance, but now he demands that all people everywhere repent because he has established a day on which he will 'judge the world with justice' through a man he has appointed, and he has provided confirmation for all by raising him from the dead."

When they heard about resurrection of the dead, some began to scoff, but others said, "We should like to hear you on this some other time." And so Paul left them. But some did join him, and became believers. Among them were Dionysius, a member of the Court of the Areopagus, a woman named Damaris, and others with them.

After this he left Athens and went to Corinth.
The word of the Lord.

——• Psalm 148 •——

℟ Heaven and earth are full of your glory.

Or: Alleluia.

Praise the LORD from the heavens;
  praise him in the heights.
Praise him, all you his angels;
  praise him, all you his hosts. ℟

Let the kings of the earth and all peoples,
  the princes and all the judges of the earth,
Young men too, and maidens,
  old men and boys. ℟

Praise the name of the LORD,
  for his name alone is exalted;
His majesty is above earth and heaven. ℟

He has lifted up the horn of his people;
Be this his praise from all his faithful ones,
  from the children of Israel, the people close to him.
  Alleluia. ℟

Alleluia, alleluia. I will ask the Father/ and he will give
you another Advocate/ to be with you always. Alleluia,
alleluia.

  • *When the Spirit of truth comes, he will guide you
  to all truth.* •

A reading from
the holy Gospel according to John   16:12-15

JESUS SAID TO his disciples:
  "I have much more to tell
you, but you cannot bear it now. But when he comes,
the Spirit of truth, he will guide you to all truth. He will
not speak on his own, but he will speak what he hears,

and will declare to you the things that are coming. He will glorify me, because he will take from what is mine and declare it to you. Everything that the Father has is mine; for this reason I told you that he will take from what is mine and declare it to you."
The Gospel of the Lord.

Prayer over the Offerings

O God, who by the wonderful exchange effected in
  this sacrifice
have made us partakers of the one supreme Godhead,
grant, we pray,
that, as we have come to know your truth,
we may make it ours by a worthy way of life.
Through Christ our Lord.

Preface I-V of Easter ———————— pages 218 to 219

Communion Antiphon   Cf. Jn 15:16, 19
I have chosen you from the world, says the Lord,/ and have appointed you to go out and bear fruit,/ fruit that will last, alleluia.

Prayer after Communion

Graciously be present to your people, we pray, O Lord,
and lead those you have imbued with heavenly
  mysteries
to pass from former ways to newness of life.
Through Christ our Lord.

MEDITATION OF THE DAY

"He will speak what he hears"

Just as God [the Father] has revealed to us the things that are his, so, too, the Son and so also the Spirit has revealed the things that are God's.... Where, then, there is the manifestation of the Spirit, there is the power of God....

Therefore, the Son of God also has said of the Spirit: *For he shall not speak of himself,* that is, not without the mutual participation of myself and the Father…. He does not speak without me, because he will speak the truth, he breathes wisdom. He does not speak without the Father, because he is the Spirit of God; he hears not from himself, because all things are of God….

All things of the Father the Son has, for again he says: *All things whatsoever the Father has, are mine.* And the things that he himself received…the Spirit also received from him…: *Therefore I said, that he shall receive of mine, and will declare it to you….*

The Spirit is said both to hear from the Father and to glorify the Son…because the Holy Spirit taught us that the Son of God is the image of the invisible God, and the splendor of his glory, and the figure of his substance, for the Spirit spoke also in the Patriarchs and the Prophets, and finally the Apostles…. Thus there is no separation of the divine power and grace, for, although *there are diversities of graces, yet it is the same Spirit; and there are diversities of ministries, yet the same Lord; and there are diversities of operations, yet the same God who works all in all* (1 Cor 12:4-6).

SAINT AMBROSE

Saint Ambrose († 397), known as the Pastoral Doctor, was a model bishop and an eloquent preacher. He was instrumental in the conversion of Saint Augustine.

Prayer for the Evening

Vigil of the Ascension of the Lord

*The Lord goes up with majesty:
come, let us adore, alleluia!*

*Glory to the Father, and to the Son,
and to the Holy Spirit, as it was in the beginning,
is now, and will be for ever. Amen. Alleluia!*

HYMN   Meter: 77 77 with alleluias
                   This hymn can be sung to the tune used for
                          Jesus Christ Is Risen Today

Praise him as he mounts the skies, alleluia!
Christ, the Lord of paradise! Alleluia!
Cry hosanna in the height, alleluia!
As he rises out of sight! Alleluia!

Now at last he takes his throne, alleluia!
From all ages his alone! Alleluia!
With his praise creation rings: alleluia!
"Lord of lords and King of kings!" Alleluia!

Hands and feet and side reveal, alleluia!
Wounds of love, high priesthood's seal! Alleluia!
Advocate, for us he pleads; alleluia!
Heavenly Priest, he intercedes! Alleluia!

Christians, raise your eyes above! Alleluia!
He will come again in love, alleluia!
On that great and wondrous day, alleluia!
When this world will pass away! Alleluia!

At his word new heavens and earth, alleluia!
Will in glory spring to birth! Alleluia!
Risen Lord, our great Amen, alleluia!
Come, Lord Jesus, come again! Alleluia!

PSALM 113

He has sent me to proclaim liberty to captives,/ to let the oppressed
go free. (cf. Lk 4:18)

Ascending into heaven, Jesus takes with him into glory the humanity which he assumed and redeemed. Let us give joyful thanks!

Praise, O servants of the Lord,
praise the name of the Lord!
May the name of the Lord be blessed
both now and for evermore!

From the rising of the sun to its setting
praised be the name of the Lord!

High above all nations is the Lord,
above the heavens his glory.
Who is like the Lord, our God,
who has risen on high to his throne
yet stoops from the heights to look down,
to look down upon heaven and earth?

From the dust he lifts up the lowly,
from his misery he raises the poor
to set him in the company of princes,
yes, with the princes of his people.
To the childless wife he gives a home
and gladdens her heart with children.

Glory to the Father....

Word of God
Ephesians 4:8-10

THEREFORE, IT SAYS:/ "He
ascended on high and took
prisoners captive;/ he gave gifts to men."
What does "he ascended" mean except that he also descended into the lower [regions] of the earth? The one
who descended is also the one who ascended far above
all the heavens, that he might fill all things.

Hosanna in the highest! (Order of Mass)

TE DEUM
(Text, back cover C)

God goes up amid trumpet blasts! Alleluia! (cf. Ps 47:6)

INTERCESSIONS

Let us acclaim our Lord Jesus Christ, who is enthroned
at the right hand of the Father:

℟   O Christ, you are the king of glory!

Jesus, our brother and our king, you have lifted our human condition up to the glory of heaven:
– restore in us the dignity of your first creation. ℟

Jesus, by the power of the Spirit, you left the Father's side and came into this world:
– by the power of that same Spirit, make us pass with you from this world to the Father. ℟

Jesus, you promised to draw all peoples to yourself:
– keep in your Church all those whom the Father has given you. ℟

Jesus, you will judge the world on the last day:
– grant our departed brothers and sisters the joy of seeing in you the Lord of mercy. ℟

Personal intentions

Our Father....

May we be blessed by the LORD,/ the maker of heaven and earth. Amen. (cf. Ps 115:15)

MARIAN ANTIPHON   (page 12 or 13)

❧ ❧ ❧

SAINT WHO?

Saints Who Were Visionaries

Saint Stephen
Protomartyr († 1st century)

Feast: December 26

In chapter 6 of the Acts of the Apostles we learn that Stephen was one of the *seven reputable men, filled with the Spirit and wisdom,* whom the Apostles chose as first deacons of the Church. Distinguished even among these men, Stephen was working *great wonders and signs among the people.*

When challenged to a dispute by the leaders of the Synagogue of Freedmen, Stephen spoke so convincingly of Christ, that his interlocutors, unable to defeat him, resorted to having him accused of blasphemy. Like Jesus, he was taken before the Sanhedrin. Acts 7 presents Stephen's stirring defense, a recounting of God's merciful initiatives toward his people. In the end, Stephen could not help calling out the men with whom he debated. They were, like their ancestors, *a stiff-necked people, uncircumcised in heart and ears.*

This final statement sent Stephen's accusers into an uproar, and, even as they raged, a vision came to Stephen. *Behold,* he cried, *I see the heavens opened and the Son of Man standing at the right hand of God.* At this, his accusers rushed upon him and dragged him outside the city, where they stoned him. With his final breaths, Stephen offered forgiveness. *Lord, do not hold this sin against them.* Then, *he fell asleep.*

Eternal Father, through the intercession of Saint Stephen, help me to forgive my accusers.

Suggested Prayer of the Faithful

(Each local community should compose its own Universal Prayer, but may find inspiration in the texts proposed here.)

Christ ascends into heaven, not to abandon us but to be our hope. Filled with certainty by this glorious event, we pray:

For the Church: that the People of God will live with an ardent hope for heaven.

That the authority of heaven will guide the actions of those who govern on earth.

For an increase in vocations to the priesthood and the consecrated life.

That all believers will witness to the presence of Christ in our midst through generous acts of friendship.

For all who have died in service to our nation, and for all who continue to risk their lives in military service.

That through the grace of the Ascension we will be blessed to keep our minds and hearts fixed on the things of heaven.

Loving Father, because of the Ascension of your Son our human nature is now at home with you in heaven. May this truth be our lasting encouragement and hope. Through Christ our Lord. Amen. ■

THURSDAY, MAY 30
The Ascension of the Lord

Prayer for the Morning

Shout to God with cries of gladness, alleluia!

Glory to the Father, and to the Son,
and to the Holy Spirit, as it was in the beginning,
is now, and will be for ever. Amen. Alleluia!

HYMN
Meter: 87 87 D
This hymn can be sung to the tune used for
There's a Wideness in God's Mercy

See, the Conqueror mounts in triumph;
See the King in royal state,
Riding on the clouds, his chariot,
To his heavenly palace gate.
Hark! the choirs of angel voices
Joyful alleluias sing,
And the portals high are lifted
To receive their heavenly King.

He has raised our human nature
In the clouds to God's right hand;
There we sit in heavenly places,
There with him in glory stand:
Jesus reigns, adored by angels;
Man with God is on the throne;
Mighty Lord, in thine ascension
We by faith behold our own.

So at last, when he appeareth,
We from out our graves may spring,
With our youth renewed like eagles,
Flocking round our heavenly King.
Caught up on the clouds of heaven,

And may meet him in the air,
Rise to realms where he is reigning,
And may reign for ever there.

Psalm 47

Men of Galilee, why are you standing there looking at the sky? This Jesus who has been taken up from you into heaven will return in the same way as you have seen him going into heaven. (Acts 1:11)

Let us live in joyful expectation of his return in glory!

All peoples, clap your hands,
cry to God with shouts of joy!
For the Lord, the Most High, we must fear,
great king over all the earth.

He subdues peoples under us
and nations under our feet.
Our inheritance, our glory, is from him,
given to Jacob out of love.

God goes up with shouts of joy;
the Lord goes up with trumpet blast.
Sing praise for God, sing praise,
sing praise to our king, sing praise.

God is king of all the earth.
Sing praise with all your skill.
God is king over the nations;
God reigns on his holy throne.

The princes of the peoples are assembled
with the people of Abraham's God.
The rulers of the earth belong to God,
to God who reigns over all.

Glory to the Father....

Word of God

WHEN CHRIST came as high priest of the good things that have come to be, passing through the greater and more perfect tabernacle not made by hands, that is, not belonging to this creation, he entered once for all into the sanctuary, not with the blood of goats and calves but with his own blood, thus obtaining eternal redemption.

Glory to God in the highest!
(Order of Mass)

CANTICLE OF ZECHARIAH

(Text, back cover B)

As the disciples were looking on, he was lifted up, and a cloud took him from their sight. (cf. Acts 1:9)

INTERCESSIONS

Let us acclaim and praise the Lord, lifted up beyond our sight.

℟ All praise be yours, O Lord, enthroned in glory!

Lord Jesus Christ, today you have been taken up victorious to the right hand of the Father:
– bring to completion the deliverance of all peoples. ℟

You showed yourself to your disciples for forty days:
– strengthen our faith. ℟

You entered into the Holy of Holies as the eternal priest of the new covenant:
– intercede for us. ℟

Before you took leave of your disciples, you promised
to send the Holy Spirit, that they might preach the
Gospel to the ends of the earth:
– enliven our witness. ℟

Personal intentions

Our Father....

O God, you descended in the cloud to the Mount of
Olives, as once you descended in the cloud upon Mount
Sinai. On Sinai you gave the law of the covenant to
Moses. On the Mount of Olives you took to yourself in
glory the One who is the law of the new and eternal covenant. Let us who are the members of his Body live in
joyful expectation of his return, keeping faith with the
covenant sealed in his blood, until that day when we
can sing your praises face-to-face. Who lives and reigns
with the Father in the unity of the Holy Spirit, one God,
for ever and ever. Amen.

MASS

The Ascension of the Lord

Regarding the Ascension of the Lord, the ecclesiastical provinces
of Boston, Hartford, New York, Newark, Omaha, and Philadelphia
have retained its celebration on the proper Thursday, while all
other provinces have transferred this Solemnity to the Seventh
Sunday of Easter, June 2nd. If transferred, Thursday, May 30th, is
observed as an Easter Weekday (see pages 423 to 426).

"The Ascension of Jesus into heaven," Pope Francis said, *"ac-
quaints us with this deeply consoling reality on our journey: in
Christ, true God and true man, our humanity was taken to God.
Christ opened the path to us.... If we entrust our life to him, if we
let ourselves be guided by him, we are certain to be in safe hands,
in the hands of our Savior."* Thus, as Benedict XVI wrote, it
would be a mistake to interpret the Ascension as *"the temporary
absence of Christ from the world."* Rather, *"we go to heaven to the
extent that we go to Jesus Christ and enter into him."* Heaven is a
person: *"Jesus himself is what we call 'heaven.'"*

ENTRANCE ANTIPHON — Acts 1:11

Men of Galilee, why gaze in wonder at the heavens?/ This Jesus whom you saw ascending into heaven/ will return as you saw him go, alleluia.

GLORIA ———————————————— page 212

COLLECT

Gladden us with holy joys, almighty God,
and make us rejoice with devout thanksgiving,
for the Ascension of Christ your Son
is our exaltation,
and, where the Head has gone before in glory,
the Body is called to follow in hope.
Through our Lord Jesus Christ, your Son,
who lives and reigns with you in the unity
of the Holy Spirit,
one God, for ever and ever.

Or:

Grant, we pray, almighty God,
that we, who believe that your Only Begotten Son,
our Redeemer,
ascended this day to the heavens,
may in spirit dwell already in heavenly realms.
Who lives and reigns with you in the unity
of the Holy Spirit,
one God, for ever and ever.

● *As the Apostles were looking on, Jesus was taken up.* ●

A reading from
the Acts of the Apostles
1:1-11

IN THE FIRST book, Theophilus, I dealt with all that Jesus did and taught until the day he was taken up, after giving instructions through the Holy Spirit to the apostles whom he had chosen. He presented himself alive to them by many proofs after he had suffered, appearing to them during forty days and speaking about the kingdom of God. While meeting with them, he enjoined them not to depart from Jerusalem, but to wait for "the promise of the Father about which you have heard me speak; for John baptized with water, but in a few days you will be baptized with the Holy Spirit."

When they had gathered together they asked him, "Lord, are you at this time going to restore the kingdom to Israel?" He answered them, "It is not for you to know the times or seasons that the Father has established by his own authority. But you will receive power when the Holy Spirit comes upon you, and you will be my witnesses in Jerusalem, throughout Judea and Samaria, and to the ends of the earth." When he had said this, as they were looking on, he was lifted up, and a cloud took him from their sight. While they were looking intently at the sky as he was going, suddenly two men dressed in white garments stood beside them. They said, "Men of Galilee, why are you standing there looking at the sky? This Jesus who has been taken up from you into heaven will return in the same way as you have seen him going into heaven."

The word of the Lord.

———• PSALM 47 •———

℟ (6) **God mounts his throne to shouts of joy: a blare of trumpets for the Lord.**

Or: Alleluia.

All you peoples, clap your hands,
  shout to God with cries of gladness,
For the LORD, the Most High, the awesome,
  is the great king over all the earth. ℟

God mounts his throne amid shouts of joy;
  the LORD, amid trumpet blasts.
Sing praise to God, sing praise;
  sing praise to our king, sing praise. ℟

For king of all the earth is God;
  sing hymns of praise.
God reigns over the nations,
  God sits upon his holy throne. ℟

● *Christ has entered into heaven itself.* ●

**A reading from
the Letter of Saint Paul to the Ephesians**   1:17-23

BROTHERS AND SISTERS: May the God of our Lord Jesus Christ, the Father of glory, give you a Spirit of wisdom and revelation resulting in knowledge of him. May the eyes of your hearts be enlightened, that you may know what is the hope that belongs to his call, what are the riches of glory in his inheritance among the holy ones, and what is the surpassing greatness of his power for us who believe, in accord with the exercise of his great might: which he worked in Christ, raising him from the dead and seating him at his right hand in the heavens, far above every principality, authority, power, and dominion, and every name that is named not only in this age but also in the one to come. And he put all things beneath his feet and gave him as head over all things to the church, which is his body, the fullness of the one who fills all things in every way.
The word of the Lord.

Or:

● *Christ has entered into heaven itself.* ●

A reading from
the Letter to the Hebrews   9:24-28; 10:19-23

CHRIST DID NOT enter into a sanctuary made by hands, a copy of the true one, but heaven itself, that he might now appear before God on our behalf. Not that he might offer himself repeatedly, as the high priest enters each year into the sanctuary with blood that is not his own; if that were so, he would have had to suffer repeatedly from the foundation of the world. But now once for all he has appeared at the end of the ages to take away sin by his sacrifice. Just as it is appointed that men and women die once, and after this the judgment, so also Christ, offered once to take away the sins of many, will appear a second time, not to take away sin but to bring salvation to those who eagerly await him.

Therefore, brothers and sisters, since through the blood of Jesus we have confidence of entrance into the sanctuary by the new and living way he opened for us through the veil, that is, his flesh, and since we have "a great priest over the house of God," let us approach with a sincere heart and in absolute trust, with our hearts sprinkled clean from an evil conscience and our bodies washed in pure water. Let us hold unwaveringly to our confession that gives us hope, for he who made the promise is trustworthy.
The word of the Lord.

Alleluia, alleluia. Go and teach all nations, says the Lord;/ I am with you always, until the end of the world. Alleluia, alleluia.

● *As he blessed them, he was taken up to heaven.* ●

A reading from the conclusion of
the holy Gospel according to Luke

24:46-53

JESUS SAID TO his disciples:
"Thus it is written that the
Christ would suffer and rise from the dead on the third
day and that repentance, for the forgiveness of sins,
would be preached in his name to all the nations, beginning from Jerusalem. You are witnesses of these things.
And behold I am sending the promise of my Father
upon you; but stay in the city until you are clothed with
power from on high."

Then he led them out as far as Bethany, raised his
hands, and blessed them. As he blessed them he parted
from them and was taken up to heaven. They did him
homage and then returned to Jerusalem with great joy,
and they were continually in the temple praising God.
The Gospel of the Lord.

CREDO ——————————————— page 214

PRAYER OVER THE OFFERINGS
We offer sacrifice now in supplication, O Lord,
to honor the wondrous Ascension of your Son:
grant, we pray,
that through this most holy exchange
we, too, may rise up to the heavenly realms.
Through Christ our Lord.

PREFACE I OR II
OF THE ASCENSION OF THE LORD ——————— pages 220 to 221

When the Roman Canon is used, the proper form of the
Communicantes (In communion with those) is said.

COMMUNION ANTIPHON   Mt 28:20

Behold, I am with you always,/ even to the end of the age,
alleluia.

PRAYER AFTER COMMUNION
    Almighty ever-living God,
    who allow those on earth to celebrate divine mysteries,
    grant, we pray,
    that Christian hope may draw us onward
    to where our nature is united with you.
    Through Christ our Lord.

SOLEMN BLESSING (optional)
    May almighty God bless you,
    for on this very day his Only Begotten Son
    pierced the heights of heaven
    and unlocked for you the way
    to ascend to where he is.
    ℟ Amen.

    May he grant that,
    as Christ after his Resurrection
    was seen plainly by his disciples,
    so when he comes as Judge
    he may show himself merciful to you for all eternity.
    ℟ Amen.

    And may you, who believe he is seated
    with the Father in his majesty,
    know with joy the fulfillment of his promise
    to stay with you until the end of time.
    ℟ Amen.

    And may the blessing of almighty God,
    the Father, and the Son, ✠ and the Holy Spirit,
    come down on you and remain with you for ever.
    ℟ Amen.

Or:

Thursday of the Sixth Week of Easter

In regions where the Solemnity of the Ascension occurs on the following Sunday.

ENTRANCE ANTIPHON   Cf. Ps 68 (67):8-9, 20

O God, when you went forth before your people,/ marching with them and living among them,/ the earth trembled, heavens poured down rain, alleluia.

COLLECT

O God, who made your people
partakers in your redemption,
grant, we pray,
that we may perpetually render thanks
for the Resurrection of the Lord.
Who lives and reigns with you in the unity
   of the Holy Spirit,
one God, for ever and ever.

● *Paul stayed with them and worked and entered into
discussions in the synagogue.* ●

A reading from
the Acts of the Apostles   18:1-8

P AUL LEFT ATHENS and went
to Corinth. There he met
a Jew named Aquila, a native of Pontus, who had recently come from Italy with his wife Priscilla because
Claudius had ordered all the Jews to leave Rome. He
went to visit them and, because he practiced the same
trade, stayed with them and worked, for they were tent-
makers by trade. Every sabbath, he entered into discussions in the synagogue, attempting to convince both
Jews and Greeks.

When Silas and Timothy came down from Macedonia,
Paul began to occupy himself totally with preaching the

word, testifying to the Jews that the Christ was Jesus. When they opposed him and reviled him, he shook out his garments and said to them, "Your blood be on your heads! I am clear of responsibility. From now on I will go to the Gentiles." So he left there and went to a house belonging to a man named Titus Justus, a worshiper of God; his house was next to a synagogue. Crispus, the synagogue official, came to believe in the Lord along with his entire household, and many of the Corinthians who heard believed and were baptized.

The word of the Lord.

—— • PSALM 98 • ——

℟ (see 2b) **The Lord has revealed to the nations his saving power.**

Or: Alleluia.

Sing to the LORD a new song,
  for he has done wondrous deeds;
His right hand has won victory for him,
  his holy arm. ℟

The LORD has made his salvation known:
  in the sight of the nations he has revealed his justice.
He has remembered his kindness and his faithfulness
  toward the house of Israel. ℟

All the ends of the earth have seen
  the salvation by our God.
Sing joyfully to the LORD, all you lands;
  break into song; sing praise. ℟

Alleluia, alleluia. I will not leave you orphans, says the Lord;/ I will come back to you, and your hearts will rejoice. Alleluia, alleluia.

● *You will grieve, but your grief will become joy.* ●

A reading from
the holy Gospel according to John
16:16-20

JESUS SAID TO his disciples: "A little while and you will no longer see me, and again a little while later and you will see me." So some of his disciples said to one another, "What does this mean that he is saying to us, 'A little while and you will not see me, and again a little while and you will see me,' and 'Because I am going to the Father'?" So they said, "What is this 'little while' of which he speaks? We do not know what he means." Jesus knew that they wanted to ask him, so he said to them, "Are you discussing with one another what I said, 'A little while and you will not see me, and again a little while and you will see me'? Amen, amen, I say to you, you will weep and mourn, while the world rejoices; you will grieve, but your grief will become joy." The Gospel of the Lord.

PRAYER OVER THE OFFERINGS
May our prayers rise up to you, O Lord,
together with the sacrificial offerings,
so that, purified by your graciousness,
we may be conformed to the mysteries of your
mighty love.
Through Christ our Lord.

PREFACE I-V OF EASTER ———————— pages 218 to 219

COMMUNION ANTIPHON   Mt 28:20
Behold, I am with you always,/ even to the end of the age,
alleluia.

PRAYER AFTER COMMUNION
Almighty ever-living God,
who restore us to eternal life

in the Resurrection of Christ,
increase in us, we pray, the fruits of this paschal
    Sacrament
and pour into our hearts the strength of this saving
    food.
Through Christ our Lord.

MEDITATION OF THE DAY

The Promise of the Ascension

The Savior promises the disciples the descent of the Holy Spirit, which God had announced of old by Joel (cf. Jl 2:28), and power from above, that they might be strong and invincible, and without all fear preach to men everywhere the divine mystery....

Having blessed them...he was carried up unto heaven, that he might share the Father's throne even with the flesh that was united unto him. And this new pathway the Word made for us when he appeared in human form; and hereafter in due time he will come again in the glory of his Father with the angels, and will take us up to be with him.

Let us glorify, therefore, him who being God the Word became man for our sakes; who suffered willingly in the flesh, and arose from the dead, and abolished corruption; who was taken up, and hereafter shall come with great glory to judge the living and the dead, and to give to every one according to his deeds; by whom and with whom to God the Father be glory and power with the Spirit, unto ages of ages. Amen.

Saint Cyril of Alexandria

Saint Cyril of Alexandria († 444) was an eminent figure of ancient Christian literature and a valiant defender of the Faith.

Prayer for the Evening

Christ is the Lord of glory:
come, let us adore, alleluia!

Glory to the Father, and to the Son,
and to the Holy Spirit, as it was in the beginning,
is now, and will be for ever. Amen. Alleluia!

HYMN

[As the Church begins nine days of prayer in preparation for the celebration of Pentecost, let us sing each evening a portion of the ancient hymn of longing for the Holy Spirit, known in English through the familiar hymn "Come, Holy Ghost," which para-phrases the Latin.]

Veni, *Creator Spiritus,*
Mentes tuorum visita:
Imple superna gratia,
Quae tu creasti pectora.

Or: Meter: LM with repeats

Come, Holy Ghost, Creator blest,
And in our hearts take up thy rest;
Come with thy grace and heav'nly aid
To fill the hearts which thou hast made,
To fill the hearts which thou hast made.

PSALM 111

Jesus said, "I am going to my Father and your Father, to my God and your God." (cf. Jn 20:17)

As we give thanks for the great work of the Death and Resurrection of Jesus Christ and rejoice at his Ascension into glory at God's right hand, let us look forward to the fulfillment of his promise not to leave his people orphans but to send the gift of the Holy Spirit, for he is compassion and love.

I will thank the Lord with all my heart
in the meeting of the just and their assembly.
Great are the works of the Lord;
to be pondered by all who love them.

Majestic and glorious his work,
his justice stands firm for ever.
He makes us remember his wonders.
The Lord is compassion and love.

He gives food to those who fear him;
keeps his covenant ever in mind.
He has shown his might to his people
by giving them the lands of the nations.

His works are justice and truth:
his precepts are all of them sure,
standing firm for ever and ever:
they are made in uprightness and truth.

He has sent deliverance to his people
and established his covenant for ever.
Holy his name, to be feared.

To fear the Lord is the first stage of wisdom;
all who do so prove themselves wise.
His praise shall last for ever!

Glory to the Father....

Word of God John 14:27-28

PEACE I LEAVE with you; my
peace I give to you. Not as
the world gives do I give it to you. Do not let your hearts
be troubled or afraid. You heard me tell you, "I am going away and I will come back to you." If you loved me,

you would rejoice that I am going to the Father; for the Father is greater than I.

Come, Lord Jesus! (Rv 22:20)

TE DEUM (Text, back cover C)

I came from the Father and have come into the world. Now I am leaving the world and going back to the Father. (Jn 16:28)

INTERCESSIONS

As we look forward in hope to the celebration of the coming of the promised Spirit, let us pray:

℞   Send forth your Spirit, O Lord.

You have promised to breathe into your Church
the life-giving breath of the Spirit:
– may we live in your peace. ℞

You have promised to pour out upon your Church
the reconciling love of the Spirit:
– may we live in your love. ℞

You have promised to inflame your Church with
the fiery charity of the Spirit:
– may we burn with zeal to preach the Gospel to all creatures. ℞

Personal intentions

Our Father....

May the LORD send forth the Spirit,/ and renew the face of the earth! Amen. (cf. Ps 104:30)

MARIAN ANTIPHON (page 12 or 13)

FRIDAY, MAY 31
The Visitation of the Blessed Virgin Mary

Prayer for the Morning

*Blessed is she who believed that the Lord's word
to her would be fulfilled:
come, let us praise God, alleluia!*

Glory to the Father.... Alleluia!

HYMN
Meter: 87 87 87
This hymn can be sung to the tune used for
Praise, My Soul, the King of Heaven

Portal of the world's salvation,
Lo, a virgin pure and mild,
Humble-hearted, high in station,
Form of beauty undefiled,
Crown of earth's anticipation,
Come the mother-maid with Child.

Virgin sweet, with love o'erflowing,
To the hills in haste she fares;
On a kindred heart bestowing
Blessing from the joy she bears;
Waiting while with mystic showing
Time the sacred birth prepares.

What fair joy o'ershone that dwelling,
Called so great a guest to greet;
What her joy whose love compelling
Found a rest for Mary's feet,
When, the bliss of time foretelling,
Lo, the Voice and Word did meet!

CANTICLE OF SIRACH
39:13-16a

Be glad and exult with all your heart,/ O daughter Jerusalem! (Zep 3:14)

When, in the wombs of their mothers, John the Voice and Jesus the Word met, the women raised their own voices in praise. Elizabeth praised Mary and her Child; Mary turned the joy of them both into a hymn of praise to God.

Listen, my faithful children: open up your petals,
like roses planted near running waters;
Send up the sweet odor of incense,
break forth in blossoms like the lily.
Send up the sweet odor of your hymn of praise;
bless the Lord for all he has done!

Proclaim the greatness of his name,
loudly sing his praises,
With music on the harp and all stringed instruments;
sing out with joy as you proclaim:
The works of God are all of them good.

Glory to the Father....

Word of God   Tobit 12:6b-7b

THANK GOD! Give him the praise and the glory. Before all the living, acknowledge the many good things he has done for you, by blessing and extolling his name in song. Before all men, honor and proclaim God's deeds, and do not be slack in praising him. A king's secret it is prudent to keep, but the works of God are to be declared and made known. Praise them with due honor.

Shout for joy, O daughter Zion!/
sing joyfully, O Israel! (Zep 3:14)

CANTICLE OF ZECHARIAH   (Text, back cover B)

Here he comes/ springing across the mountains,/ leaping across the hills. (Song 2:8)

INTERCESSIONS

The dawn from on high has broken upon us through the faith-filled consent of the Blessed Virgin Mary. Through her intercession, let us pray:

℟ Visit your people, O Lord.

For all those who live in hope of new life:
– reward their patience. ℟

For all those who encourage the faith of others:
– reward their good work. ℟

For those who provide others with means to give praise:
– reward their joy. ℟

For those who bring glad tidings to others:
– reward their generosity. ℟

Personal intentions

Our Father....

O God, you sent the Blessed Virgin Mary to visit her cousin Elizabeth and to share with her the joy of your Son's coming. Give us the will to do your will, that we may glorify you with her for all eternity, through Christ our Lord. Amen.

MASS

Feast of the Visitation of the Blessed Virgin Mary

Mary's first instinct after the Annunciation was to attend to her older cousin, Elizabeth. But what makes a visitation different from a simple visit? A visitation carries with it a special meaning, a purpose of bestowing something exceptional. In the Visitation of the Blessed Virgin Mary, that meaning is not a message but rather the exceptional presence of the Son—the Savior—she carries within her womb. We can be certain that the mystery of the Visitation is effective in our lives, too, for Mary continues to take the initiative to come to us, to introduce us to her Son.

Entrance Antiphon   Cf. Ps 66 (65):16
Come and hear, all who fear God;/ I will tell what the Lord
did for my soul, alleluia.

Gloria ————————————————————— page 212

Collect
  Almighty ever-living God,
  who, while the Blessed Virgin Mary was carrying your
      Son in her womb,
  inspired her to visit Elizabeth,
  grant us, we pray,
  that, faithful to the promptings of the Spirit,
  we may magnify your greatness
  with the Virgin Mary at all times.
  Through our Lord Jesus Christ, your Son,
  who lives and reigns with you in the unity
      of the Holy Spirit,
  one God, for ever and ever.

  ● *The King of Israel, the Lord, is in your midst.* ●

A reading from
the Book of the Prophet Zephaniah   3:14-18a

SHOUT FOR JOY, O daugh-
ter Zion!/ Sing joyfully,
O Israel!/ Be glad and exult with all your heart,/
O daughter Jerusalem!/ The Lord has removed the
judgment against you,/ he has turned away your enemies;/ The King of Israel, the Lord, is in your midst,/
you have no further misfortune to fear./ On that day,
it shall be said to Jerusalem:/ Fear not, O Zion, be not
discouraged!/ The Lord, your God, is in your midst,/ a
mighty savior;/ He will rejoice over you with gladness,/
and renew you in his love,/ He will sing joyfully because
of you,/ as one sings at festivals.
The word of the Lord.
Or:

● *Contribute to the needs of the holy ones, exercise hospitality.* ●

A reading from
the Letter of Saint Paul to the Romans   12:9-16

Brothers and sisters: Let love be sincere; hate what is evil, hold on to what is good; love one another with mutual affection; anticipate one another in showing honor. Do not grow slack in zeal, be fervent in spirit, serve the Lord. Rejoice in hope, endure in affliction, persevere in prayer. Contribute to the needs of the holy ones, exercise hospitality. Bless those who persecute you, bless and do not curse them. Rejoice with those who rejoice, weep with those who weep. Have the same regard for one another; do not be haughty but associate with the lowly; do not be wise in your own estimation. The word of the Lord.

●— Responsorial Psalm (Is 12) —●

℟ (6) **Among you is the great and Holy One of Israel.**

God indeed is my savior;
  I am confident and unafraid.
My strength and my courage is the Lord,
  and he has been my savior.
With joy you will draw water
  at the fountain of salvation. ℟

Give thanks to the Lord, acclaim his name;
  among the nations make known his deeds,
  proclaim how exalted is his name. ℟

Sing praise to the Lord for his glorious achievement;
  let this be known throughout all the earth.
Shout with exultation, O city of Zion,
  for great in your midst
  is the Holy One of Israel! ℟

Alleluia, alleluia. Blessed are you, O Virgin Mary, who believed/ that what was spoken to you by the Lord would be fulfilled. Alleluia, alleluia.

● *And how does this happen to me, that the mother of my Lord should come to me?* ●

A reading from
the holy Gospel according to Luke   1:39-56

MARY SET OUT and traveled to the hill country in haste to a town of Judah, where she entered the house of Zechariah and greeted Elizabeth. When Elizabeth heard Mary's greeting, the infant leaped in her womb, and Elizabeth, filled with the Holy Spirit, cried out in a loud voice and said, "Most blessed are you among women, and blessed is the fruit of your womb. And how does this happen to me, that the mother of my Lord should come to me? For at the moment the sound of your greeting reached my ears, the infant in my womb leaped for joy. Blessed are you who believed that what was spoken to you by the Lord would be fulfilled."

And Mary said:

"My soul proclaims the greatness of the Lord;/ my spirit rejoices in God my Savior,/ for he has looked with favor on his lowly servant./ From this day all generations will call me blessed:/ the Almighty has done great things for me,/ and holy is his Name.

He has mercy on those who fear him/ in every generation./ He has shown the strength of his arm,/ he has scattered the proud in their conceit./ He has cast down the mighty from their thrones,/ and has lifted up the lowly./ He has filled the hungry with good things,/ and the rich he has sent away empty./ He has come to the help of his servant Israel/ for he has remembered his

promise of mercy,/ the promise he made to our fathers,/
to Abraham and his children for ever."

Mary remained with her about three months and
then returned to her home.
The Gospel of the Lord.

PRAYER OVER THE OFFERINGS

May our offering of this saving sacrifice
be acceptable to your majesty, O Lord,
as you were pleased to accept the charity
of the most Blessed Mother of your Only Begotten Son.
Who lives and reigns for ever and ever.

PREFACE II OF THE BLESSED VIRGIN MARY:
THE CHURCH PRAISES GOD WITH THE WORDS OF MARY

It is truly right and just, our duty and our salvation,
to praise your mighty deeds in the exaltation of all the
Saints,
and especially, as we celebrate the memory of the
Blessed Virgin Mary,
to proclaim your kindness as we echo her thankful
hymn of praise.

For truly even to earth's ends you have done
great things
and extended your abundant mercy from age to age:
when you looked on the lowliness of your handmaid,
you gave us through her the author of our salvation,
your Son, Jesus Christ, our Lord.

Through him the host of Angels adores your majesty
and rejoices in your presence for ever.
May our voices, we pray, join with theirs
in one chorus of exultant praise, as we acclaim: Holy....

COMMUNION ANTIPHON   Lk 1:48-49

All generations will call me blessed,/ for he who is mighty
has done great things for me,/ and holy is his name, alleluia.

PRAYER AFTER COMMUNION

May your Church proclaim your greatness, O God,
for you have done great things for your faithful,
and, as Saint John the Baptist leapt with joy

when he first sensed the hidden presence of Christ,
so may your Church rejoice
to receive in this Sacrament the same ever-living Lord.
Who lives and reigns for ever and ever.

SOLEMN BLESSING (optional)

May God, who through the childbearing of the Blessed
    Virgin Mary
willed in his great kindness to redeem the human race,
be pleased to enrich you with his blessing.
℟ Amen.

May you know always and everywhere the protection
    of her,
through whom you have been found worthy to receive
    the author of life.
℟ Amen.

May you, who have devoutly gathered on this day,
carry away with you the gifts of spiritual joys and
    heavenly rewards.
℟ Amen.

And may the blessing of almighty God,
the Father, and the Son, ✠ and the Holy Spirit,
come down on you and remain with you for ever.
℟ Amen.

M E D I T A T I O N   O F   T H E   D A Y

"Elizabeth, filled with the Holy Spirit, cried out"

Blessed are you among women, O maiden, and
blessed is the beloved Fruit which dwells in holiness in
your womb. Blessed is your conceiving and blessed is
the Babe of your virginity; blessed is your Babe who
removed the curse from the earth. Who grants me that
you come to me, O blessed one? You bear the Great
One who has willed to come to lowliness. Mother of
the King, with how many mouths to praise that One
who dwells in you, who has come and visited me in
my poor house! A Flame dwells in your blessed womb,

and even the Seraphim are shaken if they look at it. The living Flame and the kindler of worlds is silent in you; that Flame which purifies the thorns of false worship when it is uncovered. That Flame which kindled the world, fills your womb; the thorns which are planted in all the earth are consumed by it. A lion's whelp rises from you, O glorious one; all the wolves flee from it when they see it. You carry the Sun whose rays give light to the universe; all darkness which oppresses the world is dissipated by him.

A great light is hidden and covered by your virginity, a light which banishes all shadows from the lands. An ocean is enclosed in you, for the earth is too small to contain it; by it, sin is drowned which had overwhelmed all mankind. O Virgin full of wonder, who grants me that you come to me, because your Son is the Lord and the prime mover who cannot be dishonored. O maiden in whom the Ancient of Days willed to be carried, how can I encompass a greeting from your lips? O lady full of blessings and graces, how can I hear your voice and see your beauty and rejoice in your Son! The rock which brought forth streams cannot be compared to you, because living waters go forth from you to the whole world. Your portion is greater than the glorious chariot of the visions, because that one whom you carry, behold he grows in you, yet enriches you.

Gabriel did not reveal the mystery, but the babe who is in me is the sharer of that secret which you have borne. He shows to me that his Lord dwells in you, O blessed one.... Since I saw you, he has not ceased urging me to bless you, to do reverence, to rejoice with his Lord who has come to him. As soon as the greeting came to my ears from your lips, the babe whom I carry leaped in me with great joy. He shook in me and I trembled, and he danced in me and I marveled at you.

Jacob of Serug

Jacob of Serug († 521), called the "flute of the Holy Spirit," was a bishop born at Curtem on the Euphrates, and composed more than seven hundred Syriac poems and homilies.

Prayer for the Evening

God has come among his people:
let us give thanks and praise, alleluia!

Glory to the Father…. Alleluia!

HYMN

Meter: LM
This hymn can be sung to the tune used for
I Know that My Redeemer Lives

Enriched by Holy Spirit's gift,
Come, Mother of the hidden Christ,
And visit us as once you came
And gladdened John, who leapt for joy.

Come forward with your little Son,
That all the world may grow in faith,
And call you blessed for all time,
As lowly handmaid of the Lord.

Now greet the Church, that it may hear
Your gentle voice, so sweet and low,
That hearing, it may thrill with joy
And feel the presence of its Lord.

With you, O Virgin highly blest,
Our souls now magnify the Lord,
Who did such wondrous things in you
That men and angels praise your name.

PSALM 40

2, 4, 6-9

The King of Israel, the LORD, is in your midst. (Zep 3:15)

God's good works are not to be hidden. Just as her Son came promptly at his Father's bidding, Mary went not at leisure but in haste to share the wonder of God's gift with her cousin Elizabeth.

I waited, I waited for the Lord
and he stooped down to me;
he heard my cry.

He put a new song into my mouth,
praise of our God.
Many shall see and fear
and shall trust in the Lord.

How many, O Lord my God,
are the wonders and designs
that you have worked for us;
you have no equal.
Should I proclaim and speak of them,
they are more than I can tell!

You do not ask for sacrifice and offerings,
but an open ear.
You do not ask for holocaust and victim.
Instead, here am I.

In the scroll of the book it stands written
that I should do your will.
My God, I delight in your law
in the depth of my heart.

Glory to the Father....

Word of God
Isaiah 52:7

HOW BEAUTIFUL upon the mountains/ are the feet of him who brings glad tidings,/ Announcing peace, bearing good news,/ announcing salvation, and saying to Zion,/ "Your God is King!"

> *Say to daughter Zion,/*
> *"Behold, your king comes to you."*
> *(Mt 21:5)*

CANTICLE OF MARY
(Text, back cover A)

Sing and rejoice, O daughter Zion! See, I am coming to dwell among you, says the LORD. (Zec 2:14)

INTERCESSIONS

Let us bless our God, who ordained that all generations call blessed the Mother of his Son:

℟   Blessed are you, O Lord!

For your humble servant who accepted your Word,
– model for all those who listen: ℟

For the one who brought your Son into the world,
– Mother of the new humanity: ℟

For the one who kept watch over the childhood of Jesus,
– maternal presence in the Church: ℟

For the one who stood beneath the cross,
– strength of the sorrowing: ℟

For the one whom you filled with joy at Easter,
– hope of the living: ℟

For the one whom you assumed into heaven, to take her place with your Son,
– help of the dying: ℟

Personal intentions

Our Father....

For the kingdom, the power, and the glory are yours! Amen.

MARIAN ANTIPHON

(page 12 or 13)

❧ ❧ ❧

ACKNOWLEDGMENTS

M A G N I F I C A T ®

Publisher: **Pierre-Marie Dumont**
Vice President, Publishing: **Romain Lizé**
Editor-in-Chief: **Rev. Sebastian White**, o.p.
Senior Editor: **Very Rev. Romanus Cessario**, o.p.
Editor-at-Large: **Rev. Peter John Cameron**, o.p.
Editor for Saints: **Lisa Lickona**
Contributors: **Most Rev. Robert Barron, Rev. Anthony Giambrone**, o.p.,
**Rev. Richard Veras, Father Paul Anel,
Sonja Corbitt, Anthony Esolen, Jennifer Hubbard,
John Janaro, Heather King,** and **James Monti**
Managing Editor: **Catherine Kolpak**
Assistant to the Editor: **Alexi Sargeant**
Administrative Assistant: **Nora Macagnone**
Senior Managing Editor: **Arnaud Gancel**
Editorial Coordinator: **Julia Schmidt-Pateu**
Permissions and Editorial Coordinator: **Diaga Seck-Rauch**
Cover and Insert: **Solange Bosdevesy** (Layout)
and **Isabelle Mascaras** (Iconography)
Proofreader: **Sr. Myriam-Therese O'Hanrahan**, c.p.
Translator: **Janet Chevrier**

LETTERS TO THE EDITOR

**We want to hear from you! Email your questions and comments
about MAGNIFICAT to editorial@magnificat.com
or mail to MAGNIFICAT, PO Box 834, Yonkers, NY 10702**

Please note that MAGNIFICAT is not able to receive unsolicited manuscripts or materials.

MAGNIFICAT (ISSN 1521-5172) is published monthly with an additional Holy Week issue in the spring by MAGNIFICAT Inc., 86 Main Street, Yonkers, NY 10701. Periodicals Postage Paid at Yonkers, NY, and at additional mailing offices. Pierre-Marie Dumont: President; Axel d'Epinay: Chief Operating Officer. The annual subscription rate is US $47; single-copy price is US $5.95. Circulation records are maintained at MAGNIFICAT Inc., 86 Main Street, Yonkers NY 10701. POSTMASTER: send address changes to MAGNIFICAT, PO Box 822, Yonkers, NY 10702.

MAGNIFICAT, copyright 2019 by MAGNIFICAT Inc. With the collaboration of Martha Publishing Sprl. Printed in Germany by CPI-CLAUSEN & BOSSE.

The trademark MAGNIFICAT depicted in this publication is used under license from and is the exclusive property of Magnificat Central Service Team, Inc., A Ministry to Catholic Women, and may not be used without its written consent.

Published with the approval of the Committee on Divine Worship, United States Conference of Catholic Bishops. Published with ecclesiastical permission.

Mailing list: We occasionally make our mailing list available to other companies whose products or services might interest you. If you would prefer not to be included, please let us know at magnificat@magnificat.com or write to MAGNIFICAT, PO Box 822, Yonkers, NY 10702. Be sure to include your complete address, as shown on your magazine mailing label.

MIX
Paper
FSC FSC® C083411

CUSTOMER SERVICE
Tel.: 1-866-273-5215

Go Home to Your Family, Glorifying God for the Wonders He Does in It!

―――――――――― Pierre-Marie Dumont ――――――――――

Front Cover Artwork

While Murillo (1617–1682) was the master of Seville, Sebastián Martínez Domedel (1615–1667) was the great painter of Jaén, the gateway to Andalusia, to the south of La Mancha. Both became champions of Christian family values, finding delight in depicting scenes of the Holy Family and the Child Jesus. Through their art, they preached Christ as Savior as much in his hidden family life as in his public ministry. Christ consecrated family, social, and professional life by devoting ninety percent of his earthly existence to it! Thus, to extol properly the vocation of those disciples who accept the Lord's invitation: "Come, follow me," one must also honor the vocation of those whom the Lord calls, not to follow him, but to return to their families giving thanks for the wonders God never ceases to perform in them (Mk 5:19). Such, notably, was the case of the paralytic: Jesus sends him home to his family even though he had restored the man to the full physical and spiritual capacity to follow him on the pathways of his public life (Lk 5:24-25).

How touching is this work by Martínez. How beautifully it portrays that expression that has surprised and melted the heart of every parent the world over—that look on their little child's face that, through a smile and a glance, manages to convey both the depth of their love and the strength of their own will. "I love you with all my heart," this charming toddler seems to say to his foster father, "but I am me!" He reaches for some fruit, but Joseph prevents him. Here, the fruit basket symbolizes his mission, his Father's business which he must be about until its supreme culmination in his Passion. The red grapes symbolize divinity, the white, humanity. Between the two, the violet-red grapes allude to Christ, true God and true man. This is also the color of the Child Jesus' clothing, and that of the blood mixed with water that will flow from his pierced heart. The pomegranate with its myriad seeds represents his Body, the Church, constituted of its myriad members. The apple evokes the ransom of sinful humanity. This Child seems to say, "How I long to accomplish my Father's work to the full!" But Joseph, haloed with the light of the Father, admonishes him: "Your hour has not yet come." ∎

Eucarestia 1 (1960), William Congdon (1912–1998),
The William G. Congdon Foundation, Milan, Italy.

 HEAVEN AND EARTH, choirs of angels and men, gouged in the paint with buoyant velocity, unanimously orchestrate their praises around a soft, golden disc, slightly elevated above a bloodstained altar, radiating in all directions. *Eucarestia* was painted by the American "action painter" William Congdon in 1960, just one year after his baptism into the Catholic Faith. It is the visual *Magnificat* of a man who reached the end of a long, tiresome pilgrimage. It is as free and restless

as a jazz performance can be, and yet as reverent and still as a Holy Hour. In *Eucarestia*, Miles Davis meets van Eyck's *Mystic Lamb*!

If you have never heard the name William Congdon before, it is both sad and forgivable. Sad, because he counts among the greatest painters of the second half of the 20th century, and there was a time when he was recognized as such; forgivable, because his restlessness (one might say, his quest for the true center of his existence) drove him away, very early on, from the center of the "art world," beyond the short-range radar of critics and curators.

Born on April 15, 1912 (the day the Titanic sank, which may have been prophetic of his career, but certainly not of his art), William Congdon grew up in Providence, Rhode Island, in a Puritan family from which he inherited, besides a financial security that never failed him, a sense of hard work and restraint. The outbreak of World War II and the horror he witnessed as a volunteer ambulance driver (he was among the very first to enter the Nazi death camp of Bergen-Belsen) shattered the seemingly crystal clear morality of his upbringing. Then Congdon set out on a lifelong quest for beauty in the midst of chaos. On this journey, painting would be his instrument—his visual diary— to clarify for himself, and to communicate to others, what he was looking at.

The longing remains

Congdon's artistic and contemplative journey took off in New York City in 1948, when he joined the Betty Parsons Gallery. For a while, he was regarded as a full-blooded member of the "New York School." His works hung alongside those of Newman, Pollock, and Rothko—with whom he built a close relationship—and were reviewed by the likes of Clement Greenberg. It was also in the late 40s that the disc appeared as a recurring, almost obsessive, motif in his paintings. In an iconic 1948 canvas prophetically titled *New York City (Explosion)*, the disc took center stage, like a black hole threatening to absorb the city and its lights.

By 1951, William Congdon was a successful painter, his work attracted the attention of major museums and curators, and *Life Magazine* ran a profile of him. And yet his work during this period speaks of a deeply unsettled and tormented soul. He set off on a journey to find redeeming beauty when, there he was, acclaimed by the world for holding up a mirror to its chaos and hopelessness. He did not belong there. At the height of his worldly recognition, William Congdon left everything behind and moved to Europe. Many regarded it as, artistically speaking, a suicide. It may well have been his salvation.

The 50s was the defining decade for William Congdon. Establishing his headquarters in Venice, he periodically left the city for extended trips, mostly by himself, from France to India, and from Algeria to Guatemala. However, most paintings he made during this decade reflect his inner sense of isolation and nostalgia more than the sublime majesty of his subjects: in his paintings, Saint Mark's ordinarily buzzy square is empty and still, the Taj Mahal is oddly unsecure, and the Colosseum looks like the open mouth of a dormant volcano. Painted in 1957, his *Dying Vulture* has the poignant pathos

of an Agony in the Garden. It is—or so it seems—the swan song of a crucified artist, desperately looking for beauty.

From nostalgia to ecstasy

In 1959, William Congdon was baptized into the Catholic Faith in Assisi. The inner workings of his conversion are mostly hidden in the privacy of his heart and God's. Encounters with the founder of Pro Civitate Christiana, Father Giovanni Rossi, and later with Jacques Maritain and Thomas Merton, certainly played an important role in his decision. And so did Assisi. It was there that, for the first time, he found himself able to see in a landscape more than just the reflection of his inner landscape. "Venice was mine, while Assisi never belonged to anyone, because it was Saint Francis'…. Assisi converted me." A place that did not belong to him. A place to which he belonged.

Painted one year later, *Eucarestia* reflects the inner transformation of the artist and a kind of post-conversion euphoria. The dark orb that haunted his early works is now transfigured into a radiant halo, elevated high above the altar like a risen Christ from the tomb. The restraint of his Puritan heritage—the horizontality of his landscapes; their earthy, subdued colors; their sublime but desolate subjects—is now lifted up along a vertical axis, lines and colors bursting into an ecstatic hymn of praise.

Eucarestia was painted with febrile velocity, gushing out, as it were, from the artist's depths. A few aerial lines are enough to give life to a choir of angels dominating the scene and to a crowd of standing worshipers, stretched like arrows in the direction of the altar. The "action painting" of Jackson Pollock was a jump into the void, a high-speed, desperate ride to nowhere. William Congdon brought action painting home, allowing action to find its destination and repose in the Christ, the "still point of the turning world," as T.S. Eliot would have it, the center of our existence and of our fast evolving world.

■ *FATHER PAUL ANEL*
A priest in Brooklyn, N.Y.

To view this masterpiece in greater detail, visit
www.magnificat.com/art

For further spiritual commentaries on artistic masterpieces,
browse our art books at www.magnificat.com/artbooks

REGULAR EDITION (4.5 x 6.75 in.)

	6 MONTHS	1 YEAR	2 YEARS	4 YEARS
USA	❑ **$26** or $4.33 a month	❑ **$47** or $3.92 a month	❑ **$84** or $3.50 a month	❑ **$149** or $3.10 a month

LARGE PRINT EDITION (5 x 7.75 in.) – 30% larger

	6 MONTHS	1 YEAR	2 YEARS	4 YEARS
USA	❑ **$34.95** or $5.83 a month	❑ **$64.95** or $5.41 a month	❑ **$119** or $4.96 a month	❑ **$236** or $4.92 a month

	REGULAR EDITION	LARGE PRINT EDITION
CANADA	❑ 1 year US $54 ❑ 2 years US $99	❑ 1 year US $69.95 ❑ 2 years US $129

IN OTHER COUNTRIES (Regular size only):

Europe	❑ 1 year US $59	❑ 2 years US $104.95
Rest of the world	❑ 1 year US $64	❑ 2 years US $114.95

For our other English edition (UK, Ireland, Australia), please visit www.magnificat.com

MAGNIFICAT subscribers also have free access to our online and App editions.

A subscription to the US edition of MAGNIFICAT offers 13 issues a year (one per month and a special issue for Holy Week). This edition uses the official New American Bible Lectionary.

Please allow 4-6 weeks from receipt of order for delivery of your first issue.

Rates valid until June 30, 2019.

PLEASE RETURN THIS SUBSCRIPTION FORM TO
MAGNIFICAT
PO Box 822 – Yonkers, NY 10702
or call (866) 273-5215
or fax (914) 969-6446
or visit www.magnificat.com

MY INFORMATION

TITLE

FIRST NAME

LAST NAME

ADDRESS

ADDRESS

CITY

STATE

ZIP

COUNTRY

PHONE NUMBER

YEAR OF BIRTH

EMAIL

BA0519

METHOD OF PAYMENT

❑ CHECK ENCLOSED (CHECK PAYABLE TO MAGNIFICAT, US $ ONLY)

❑ PLEASE BILL ME (PARISHES AND INSTITUTIONS ONLY)

❑ VISA   ❑ MASTERCARD   ❑ DISCOVER   ❑ AMEX

CARD No.

EXPIRATION DATE _____ / _____   SECURITY CODE

SIGNATURE

Mailing list: We occasionally make our list available to other companies whose products or services might interest you. If you would prefer not to be included, please let us know by mail, at **magnificat@magnificat.com**, or by checking this box. ❑